...der.

...rn of items.

...by telephoning
...w.

...Due	Date Due

Urban Development

Urban Development
THEORY, FACT, AND ILLUSION

J. Vernon Henderson

New York   Oxford
OXFORD UNIVERSITY PRESS
1988

Oxford University Press

Oxford   New York   Toronto
Delhi   Bombay   Calcutta   Madras   Karachi
Petaling Jaya   Singapore   Hong Kong   Tokyo
Nairobi   Dar es Salaam   Cape Town
Melbourne   Auckland

and associated companies in
Berlin   Ibadan

Library of Congress Cataloging-in-Publication Data

Henderson, J. Vernon.
Urban development.

Bibliography: p.
Includes index.
1. Cities and towns—Growth—Mathematical models.
2. Urban policy—Mathematical models.   I. Title.
HT371.H385   1988   307.1'4   87-21955
ISBN 0-19-505157-2

2 4 6 8 9 7 5 3 1
Printed in the United States of America
on acid-free paper

Preface

This book examines the role and nature of cities, set in an economy composed of a system of cities, towns, and an agricultural sector. There are three components to this examination. The first, which is theoretical, develops a general equilibrium model of an economy composed of cities. The model allows for different sizes and types of cities, economic growth, development and technological change, international trade, and natural resource impacts. It solves the patterns of wages, prices, production and trade, investment, and residence, and how these evolve.

The second part develops a set of facts and econometric results about cities. The book focuses on production patterns and technology, the population composition of cities in terms of high skill in relation to low skill workers, the determinants of urban concentration in large versus small cities, and the process of urban decentralization.

The third component examines the impact and role of government policies. What are the impacts upon population movements and urban development of such national policies as import restrictions, minimum wage laws, price regulation, transport pricing, capital market restrictions, and subsidies to investment in urban infrastructure? What the impacts of spatial policies such as those constraining location of heavy industry, restricting city sizes and land development, and limiting infrastructure investment in particular cities? What is the appropriate role of government in a system of cities, in terms of affecting population allocation and industrial location?

This book is intended for academics, practicing professionals, and students in the fields of economic development, urban economics, regional science, and geography. Even the technical sections of the book can be read by a nontechnical audience, since they contain extensive diagrams and supplementary exposition. Large portions of the book are not technical and are policy oriented. There is a summary of the findings at the end of each chapter, as well as a chapter of conclusions drawing together the central conceptual issues in the book.

Acknowledgments

The actual writing and preparation of the manuscript and some of the research undertakings reported in Chapters 3, 5, 7, 10 and 11 were financed by Fellowships from the John Simon Guggenheim Memorial and Earhart Foundations. While parts of the book contain previously published material, there is also extensive material that is either new or not previously published. All the previously published material has been completely rewritten and often reworked, to make the book as comprehensive and consistent as possible.

The theoretical work reported in Chapters 2 to 4 and 8, the empirical and econometric work on the United States in Chapters 1, 5 and 6 and the econometric results on Brazil in Chapter 7 were supported by grants from the National Science Foundation (NSF grant numbers SOC 79-01592 and SES 8013482). The econometric and empirical work on Brazil in Chapters 1, 5, and 6 and the work on China in Chapter 11 were supported by the World Bank. The Brazil work was under the auspices of the Bank's former Urban and Regional Economics Division directed by Douglas Keare during a period of high research fertility and the China work was carried out under the auspices of the Bank's China Division. I thank these foundations and agencies for making this work possible, and contributing to the enhancement of our understanding of the nature of the world in which we live.

A project such as this involves extensive support from research assistants and fellow economists. The following research assistants worked ably on the project: B. Dillinger, J. Klerman, R. Kochhar, R. Neupert, T. Pham, H. Streeter and P. Wilson, as well as D. Brooks, J. Brown, D. Keen, K. Knapp, T. Miceli, A. Rangarajan, and J. Sheraga. Over the years strong intellectual support and inspiration for the project have been provided by Yannis Ioannides, Peter Mieszkowski, Bertrand Renaud, George Tolley, and Charles Upton. The complementary work of Oded Hochman and Yoshi Kanemoto as well as Eitan Berglas had a strong influence on my work, and they share credit for developing the foundations of an economic model of systems of cities. Other individuals providing helpful comments include Andrew Hamer, Ed Lim, Ian Porter, and Adrian Wood, all of the World Bank. Finally the encouragement and support of Douglas Keare of the World Bank and Dan Newlon of the National Science Foundation, as well as Gregory Ingram and Ed Mills are gratefully acknowledged. Also, Ed Mills and several anonymous referees read the initial version of the manuscript and made very helpful comments used in revisions.

Marion Wathey typed the entire manuscript with her (un)usual tireless efficiency and dedication.

Contents

Urban Development

Introduction

This book develops two general themes. First, basic economic forces and simple economic models can explain the key characteristics of the spatial patterns of production and population observed in a country. These models can be adapted to explain changes over time in a country or to do comparisons for a cross section of countries. For example, in developing countries, the processes of massive rural–urban migration, population explosion of large metro areas with their overcrowded industrial neighborhoods and squatter settlements, deconcentration of industries from large metro areas into specialized smaller cities, switches in production patterns of cities, draining of skilled workers from small towns, and individual city limits on growth and entry are all natural outcomes of market forces operating in particular institutional environments.

The second theme stresses the often inadvertent and misunderstood negative impacts on the urbanization processes of common government policies. The designing and construction of modern national capital regions potentially offering excellent amenities for residents, the stress on and accompanying financial inducements for development of heavy manufacturing industries, the rise of state capitalism, and even minimum wage laws all tend to increase unnecessarily the degree of urban concentration in a country. Urban concentration is a measure of the extent to which a country's population is housed in bigger relative to smaller cities. Increases in urban concentration involve further population flows from smaller traditional cities to metropolitan areas with the accompanying erosion of the country's traditional social fabric. The population flows require massive reinvestment in urban infrastructure in metropolitan areas with the accompanying financial and administrative burdens. This bias toward larger city development is enhanced by notions of hierarchy in some developing countries. Government industrial development in larger cities is viewed as being more efficient than the "uncoordinated" efforts of private producers in smaller cities, despite the clear evidence that typically the private producers who cluster in smaller cities are more efficient than the state firms located in large cities.

These two themes are developed in the book by looking at the key characteristics of cities in various countries. In particular, detailed Census Data for Brazil and the United States are utilized, as well as more general data on China, India,

3

Japan, Korea and a cross section of other countries. The key characteristics are then explained in terms of a simple general equilibrium model of a system of cities, incorporating growth, technological change, international trade, and government policies. Some of the key results and assumptions of the model are econometrically formulated and tested.

In the process of this development of the two themes a number of sets of questions are examined, as discussed next. After presenting the sets of questions, an overview of the content of different chapters is given.

1. Sets of Questions

What is it about the technology of production or consumption that induces people to agglomerate in population clusters called cities, rather than spreading out over the countryside in a completely rural existence? It is usual to presume that agglomeration in net is costly on the consumption side, producing disamenities such as congestion, pollution, crime, and so on, although there can obviously be some initial social and retailing benefits to agglomeration. Under that presumption, agglomeration must occur because of some type of scale economies in production. That raises the following questions. What is the nature of these scale economies? What is their extent? How do they vary across industries?

Given the existence of cities, what types of goods are produced for export, or traded across cities and between the urban and rural sectors? A wide range of urban goods and services are nontraded across cities, or produced and sold within the same city. In terms of traded goods, many are goods in which cities tend to specialize for production. This raises the questions of when do cities specialize and what types of goods are the ones they specialize in. When are cities highly diversified and what types of goods do diversified cities tend to produce for export?

Cities of different sizes coexist in an economy on a sustained basis. What is it about the spatial nature of national production that makes a very small city relatively just as efficient in net as a very large city? In comparing cities of different sizes how do wages, costs of living, amenities, capital intensities, and so on vary?

With population growth in an economy, do individual city sizes, city numbers, or both grow? Over the past century there has been an ongoing revolution in the nature of transport and commuting technology. What has been the impact of that on city sizes and agglomerations? How does the urban system react and adjust to a technological shock?

What is the impact of economic development on not just rural vs. urban population allocation, but also on urban concentration? Richardson (1977) suggests that many countries experience initial concentrations of resources into one or two major metro areas, followed by a period of subsequent deconcentration of resources into secondary cities. Is this explained by the nature of the development process and adaptation of existing technologies from developed countries or by changes in government policies?

In comparing different countries, how do their trade patterns affect their systems of cities? Do traditional international trade theorems extend to general equilibrium models of systems of cities with their economies of scale and implicit spatial complexities? Do countries with different endowments of natural amenities (e.g., climate) have different features to their systems of cities? Within countries dif-

ferent urban sites have different quality dimensions in terms of climate and access. How are sites allocated to different types of cities?

What are the determinants in general of the location of different industries? Which ones are resource bound to particular locations for production purposes versus footloose to pursue better amenity locations for their employees?

In some countries, there is a strong correlation between city size and skill composition of the work force, with smaller cities being drained of skilled labor. Are skilled laborers drawn to larger cities by the "bright lights"—amenities specific to their tastes? Do such amenities arise naturally in larger cities or are they the result of government policies? Are skilled laborers drawn to larger cities by relatively better job opportunities? Are skill mixes rigidly determined by the production mix reflecting the industrial base of a city, or are workers of different skills highly substitutable?

What are the determinants of urban concentration in a country, in terms of whether the urban population is primarily located in larger or smaller types of cities? How is concentration likely to vary with economic development or international trade patterns? What are the determinants of whether cities have one major business center or are multinucleated—having many major business districts? This is often the distinction between smaller cities (say under one-half million people) versus large metropolitan areas. How does multinucleation interact with urban concentration on a national level?

Finally and most centrally to the book, the role of government in influencing the development of systems of cities is questioned. Most directly is the role of the local government. Its role must be critical, since for example in the United States about 50% of urban land (Clawson, 1969) is devoted to public use. Such public use involves long-range planning and massive investment in fixed durable capital structures such as roads, water mains, sewers, public buildings, parks, and so on. How do public investment decisions affect urban growth and development? How does the degree of local autonomy impact a system of cities? Are there recognizable differences between the urban system of a federal market economy vs. the market economy in a centralized governmental system vs. a centralized planned economy?

At a national level, what are the perhaps unintended impacts of national policies such as tariff protection policies, minimum wage policies, and capital market restrictions and interventions? If there is national economic planning, it can involve restrictions on both prices and input and output allocations as in China, as well as quantity restrictions on interregional flows of goods. Alternatively it may involve mostly price interventions in the form of subsidies or taxation, plus some level of state capitalism as in the case of India. On what basis are these countries making location plans and decisions? What motivates them? What is the impact on the system of cities of different forms of control?

2. Chapter Overview

In Chapter 1, the production patterns of cities and empirical relationships between city sizes and production patterns are examined. The goods in which cities tend to specialize for traded good production are identified and sizes of different types of cities calculated. Most manufactured goods tend only to be produced in significant amounts in a small proportion of cities and for any industry most cities have no production of the good. The basic data refer to Brazil and the United States, although the data for India are also examined.

In Chapter 2, we turn to a theoretical model to explain the empirical evidence from Chapter 1. The basic model of a system of cities is presented, assuming a competitive market economy with autonomous democratic local govenments. The model yields the determinants of city sizes, wages, costs of living, and capital intensities, as well as the determinants of the size distribution of cities. Comparative static exercises are conducted to illustrate both the power and workings of the model. Finally, social and economic conflicts between different types of economic agents (e.g., capitalists vs. laborers vs. rentiers) are examined in the determination of city sizes.

In Chapter 3, the model is placed in a dynamic setting. The sources of economic development are identified and their spatial impacts analyzed. Issues include rural–urban migration and changes in urban concentration and their relationship to adaptation of new technologies and the product cycle. The impacts of population growth and of technological change in the construction of cities are assessed. For the latter the underlying issue is the impact of the successive revolutions in commuting technology over the last hundred years. Complexities in adjusting to growth and technological change such as immobility of urban infrastructure capital are considered.

In Chapter 4 the basic model is further extended to the impact of international trade on an urban system and the methodology for doing international comparisons of systems of cities. Natural resource considerations are introduced in a preliminary fashion to allow for differing natural qualities of city locations, or sites. This gives a Ricardian flavor to the model.

In Chapter 5, we turn to econometric models that test some of the basic assumptions of the model. The focus is on the nature of scale economies and their magnitude. For manufacturing in Brazil, Japan, and the United States it is shown that scale effects for an industry tend to be ones of localization (own industry) and unrelated to overall urban scale or even scale of related industries. Scale effects tend to decline as scale increases and are Hicks' neutral.

Chapter 6 introduces different skill types of laborers and estimates both their substitutability on the production side in different industries and their tastes for amenities on the consumption side. Econometric issues, such as whether skilled laborers in Brazil are drawn to large cities by the bright lights or by skill requirements of industries, are explored. Also estimated are the tastes of one skill group for the other as neighbors. The estimation issues are complex and the data for the United States on tastes and for Brazil on the technology of skill usage are excellent.

Chapter 7 and succeeding chapters raise policy issues. Three types of policies are considered: government policies with unintended spatial impacts (Chapter 7), explicit industrial location policies (Chapter 8), and city size policies (Chapter 9). In policy discussion much of the focus is on aspects of urban concentration and how resource allocation between big and small cities is affected by government policies.

Based on the theoretical model in Chapters 2 to 4, Chapter 7 examines the spatial impact of national government policies, which have no intended spatial components. Common policies of this type are trade protection policies (international tariffs or quotas), minimum wage policies, national capital region development, national subsidies to local urban infrastructure investments, and capital market restrictions. Given typical policy formulations, the general practical impact of all these policies is to increase urban concentration beyond natural developmental levels.

Chapter 8 deals with two types of explicit location policies. First is the decision in some countries to focus the location of heavy industry in very large metropolitan areas. The economic justification for this focus is explored and considered fallacious. The potential welfare costs of an improper location policy are explored with an example. Second are recent policies in some countries encouraging private industrial deconcentration from large cities. The rationale for the policies is examined. A methodology for analyzing private location decisions is developed focusing on the decisions of firms of one industry to locate in some cities and not others.

Chapter 9 examines the welfare economics of population relocation policies. Under what limited circumstances are national population policies justified? When will individual cities be induced to impose their own entry restrictions to achieve an efficient allocation of population, without national intervention. What are the bases for the urban deconcentration policies of countries determined to halt the flow of people into their largest metropolitan areas? The deconcentration policies of India are examined.

Given the focus in Chapters 7 to 9 on decentration, Chapter 10 turns to the gross empirical determinants of urban concentration in a cross section of countries. At this point it becomes essential to deal theoretically and practically with the issue of what is a city. What is New York City? Does it consist of the five boroughs, or those plus the immediately contiguous "cities"—production centers with their own residential neighborhoods? Or is it the whole population mass exceeding some critical density, ending only in the forests of Connecticut, Delaware, and New York state? A model of the clustering of "economic cities," or production centers plus their neighborhoods, into metropolitan areas is developed. Then the determinants of cross-country measures of urban concentration are analyzed. Although clustering and economic development measures play a role, the prime determinants of urban concentration are the size of the country and the system of government. Federalized countries have much lower indices of concentration, suggesting that centralization of power leads to centralization of resources and public spending.

Chapter 11 turns to the urban system of a nonfree market economy—China. The peculiarities and regularities of the Chinese urban system are presented, to the extent they are known. Then the evolution of the urban peculiarities is analyzed, to see their relationship to the special nature of the Chinese economic system in general and the tendencies inherent in a planned economy.

The last chapter summarizes the findings and conclusions, with an eye to promoting enlightened policy formulation in developing countries.

CHAPTER 1

Facts about Urban Production Patterns

This chapter examines certain key production characteristics of a system of cities. The patterns found suggest a strong link between the spatial distribution of resources in a system of cities and the composition of national output. With this link, in later chapters, government policies that affect the composition of national output can be linked to changes in the spatial distribution and concentration of resources in an economy. The empirical evidence presented is based on Brazil and the United States. However, the available evidence on China and India reviewed in this book and casual evidence on Canada, Korea, Japan, and Britain as reviewed by Richardson (1977), Renaud (1979), and others suggest the reported phenomena are widespread.

Within any city it appears that at least 50% to 60% of the labor force must be engaged in production of goods and services which are inherently nontradable across cities. Because of transport costs of shipping these outputs between cities they are locally produced and consumed. Examples are structures, landscaping, roads, services (e.g., haircuts, laundry, primary education, repairs, general retailing, warehousing, and some live entertainment) and intermediate inputs (e.g., cement, fabricated metals, and ordinary glass). Thus only a maximum of 40% to 50% of local employment is engaged in production of goods that can be traded across cities. There is an obvious difficulty in classifying production into tradable and nontradable goods. The percentages cited are based on a casual examination of employment figures for "one industry" towns, where virtually the only production for export beyond a small regional radius is all in one industry—typically iron and steel, textiles, or food processing in Brazil and the United States. It appears that maximum proportion of employment in traded good production is higher in less developed countries such as Brazil, China, and India than in the United States.

This chapter focuses on how the composition of traded good production varies across cities. Small and medium size cities, such as those with populations under 500,000, tend to specialize either in production of just one type of manufactured product or in production of traditional services for a local regional rural area. Larger cities and particularly metropolitan areas tend to have more diversified production over a range of particular manufacturing and modern service industries.

8

The numbers examined in this chapter suggest there is a link between city size and city type as defined by a city's composition of output. Then at the national level there must be a link between the composition of national output and urban concentration, or the size distribution of cities. Apart from these links, basic questions explored in later chapters are why specialization in production occurs, what products are ones in which cities specialize, and do these patterns vary with a country's level of economic development.

Section 1 of this chapter reviews evidence, partially based on Henderson (1983), describing the relationship between city size and composition of output for the United States. The results correspond to Renaud's (1979) work on Japan and Korea. Section 2 examines evidence for the United States specific to the issue of specialization, as well as location of different manufacturing activity. Section 3 repeats the examination on specialization for Brazil, and Section 4 briefly reviews evidence for India. These last two sections also examine the stability of the size distribution of cities across time in developing countries. Finally, Section 5 summarizes the implications of the results.

1. General Production Patterns

To get a general picture of the relationships between city sizes and employment in gross industrial categories, patterns of association for the United States are examined. Structural estimates and relationships are explored in later chapters; here the concern is just with associations. The association of concern is how employment in different industrial categories varies with city size and region.

To see how employment concentrations in different industries vary with city size, each industry's share of employment in each urban area is regressed on urban population (POP) and its square (POPSQ), as well as regional dummy variables and a dummy for urban areas with more than 15% of their employment in state or federal public administration. These later variables control for the exogenous influences of gross regional variations in climate and geography and location patterns of governmental activity. Data sources are detailed in Appendix A to Chapter 6; the employment figures are drawn from the Sixth Count of the 1970 Population Census. The basic sample is 242 Standard Metropolitan Statistical Areas (hereafter SMSA) in the United States. Except for the Northeast, roughly speaking, an SMSA is the area of a county or group of counties centered around one or more core cities, whose urban population exceeds 50,000. Because SMSAs are based on counties, they include rural activities and populations. In the Northeast, SMSAs are put together as collections of townships.

The gross industrial categories examined are:

1. Resource-bound manufacturing (primary metals, machinery, autos, ships, rail products, wood products, and some agricultural processing)
2. Footloose manufacturing (all manufacturing except resource-bound and high-tech)
3. High-tech manufacturing (aircraft, computers, instruments, weapons, medical equipment)
4. Professional services (health, legal, engineering, architectural, accounting, auditing, and bookkeeping and miscellaneous)
5. Wholesale services (wholesale, trucking, and warehousing and storage)

Business services (excluding repairs)
7. "FIRE" (finance, insurance, and real estate)

For each industry its share of total employment in each SMSA is hypothesized as a quadratic function of SMSA population (in thousands). The results are reported in Table 1.1, along with the mean shares for each industry.

Except for resource-bound manufacturing, the shares of activities initially rise with city size, peak, and then decline. The key numbers are the average shares and the city size at which they peak. The second to last line of Table 1.1 indicates the wide divergence in shares of the different industries, ranging from 2% to 15%. The peaks, or the city size at which each industrial activity has its greatest share in urban employment, are reported in the last line of Table 1.1. Where α_1 and α_2 are the coefficients of POP and POPSQ, respectively, the hypothetical peaks (in millions) occur where $(\alpha_1 + 2000 \, \alpha_2 \, POP) = 0$. Footloose and high-tech manufacturing and wholesaling tend to peak at SMSA sizes of around 5 million. The expanding white collar sections of the U.S. economy—business services and FIRE— peak at 8 to 9 million. Finally, the expanding professional sector appears to peak at extremely large metro areas, although the statistical relationship is weak. It should be noted that there are not sufficient data points at large enough metro areas to locate these peaks precisely; in fact, they may simply represent a flattening out of the share–city size relationship. In contrast to these industries, resource-bound manufacturing tends to decline (weakly) as SMSA size expands.

These patterns suggest two things. First, cities of different sizes do have different production patterns. Second, given this, as the United States continues its shift over the last 30 years out of resource-bound manufacturing activities into modern service and high-tech activities, urban concentration, or the proportion of the urban population in large metro areas, will increase. The fact that such a shift has been occurring, as well as several different possible reasons for the shift are noted in Chapter 3.

Table 1.1 also reports the responsiveness of employment shares to population increases in the third to last line. The elasticities of shares with respect to population (percentage change in share/percentage change in population) as evaluated at medium size cities (population = 0.5 million) are largest for high-tech manufacturing and business services, followed by FIRE and then footloose manufacturing. The shift in shares is out of resource-bound manufacturing and activities not listed in Table 1.1, such as traditional services (personal, retail, construction, etc.) and government employment. Note that the low elasticity for professional services suggests its share does not change much and its high peak may not be of great significance.

The other determinants of employment shares in Table 1.1 reflect some locational considerations. High-tech and footloose manufacturing are strongly oriented to the Northeastern United States, while resource-bound manufacturing is concentrated in the North Central region where America's coal, limestone, and iron resources traditionally have been mined. In contrast, the white collar sector plus wholesaling are oriented toward the South and West. The spatial orientation of professional services, FIRE, and business services may reflect demand on the part of these footloose workers for the locational amenities (e.g., climate) of the West and to some extent the South. While footloose manufacturing is still concentrated in the Northeast, that may be due in part to historical factors. Historically much footloose manufacturing was not so footloose. For example, textile manufacturing

Table 1.1. Employment Shares by Industrial Activity

	Resource bound manufacturing	Footloose manufacturing	High-Tech manufacturing	Professional services	Wholesale	Business services	FIRE
POP[a]	-0.127×10^{-4}	0.145×10^{-4}	0.841×10^{-5}	0.205×10^{-5}	0.571×10^{-5}	0.539×10^{-5}	0.855×10^{-5}
	(1.26)	(1.64)	(2.61)	(0.91)	(2.56)	(5.73)	(4.23)
POPSQ	0.408×10^{-8}	-0.141×10^{-8}	-0.841×10^{-9}	-0.571×10^{-10}	-0.487×10^{-9}	-0.349×10^{-9}	-0.474×10^{-9}
	(0.35)	(1.39)	(2.28)	(0.22)	(1.91)	(3.25)	(2.50)
REG NC	0.050	-0.101	-0.012	0.001	0.005	-0.002	-0.001
	(3.61)	(8.36)	(2.70)	(0.41)	(1.53)	(1.67)	(0.24)
REG S	-0.061	-0.092	-0.012	-0.003	0.014	0	0.005
	(4.58)	(7.90)	(2.72)	(1.10)	(4.92)	(0.06)	(1.91)
REG W	-0.038	-0.163	-0.006	0.004	0.009	0.004	0.006
	(2.37)	(11.64)	(1.15)	(1.22)	(2.57)	(2.93)	(1.82)
Government Dummy	-0.041	-0.037	-0.003	0.013	-0.018	0.001	-0.23×10^{-3}
	(3.15)	(3.30)	(0.77)	(4.49)	(6.14)	(0.79)	(0.09)
Constant	0.176	0.191	0.023	0.080	0.049	0.012	0.042
R^2	0.31	0.41	0.08	0.10	0.21	0.26	0.16
Percent Δ share/ percent Δ POP	-0.029	0.064	0.223	0.012	0.046	0.210	0.084
Mean share	0.15	0.10	0.02	0.08	0.06	0.02	0.05
Population for maximum share (in millions)	n.a.	5.14	5.00	(17.95)	5.87	7.7	9.02

Source: Henderson, 1983.
[a]Population is measured in thousands.

was powered by water wheels driven by accessible rivers. As textiles developed in the Northeast, a public and private capital infrastructure of transport networks, structures, and immobile equipment developed specific to that industry, and that infrastructure is still utilized today. For some other industries the proximity to the North Central region offering intermediate outputs (e.g., production equipment) used by "footloose" manufacturing is also important. Also included is a dummy for high concentrations of government employees. As expected, apart from complementary professional services, this lowers the shares of other industries.

In summary, employment shares of different industries vary by city size, peaking at different city sizes. This suggests that a relationship between the composition of national employment and the city size distribution in a country must exist.

2. Aspects of Spatial Distribution in U.S. Production

The spatial distribution of U.S. production is well documented by geographers and economists. Notable are Alexandersson's (1959) study of the location of industrial activities across cities, and Bergsman, Greenston, and Healy's (1972, 1975) classification of first cities and second economic activity by, respectively, industrial output patterns and similarity of location patterns. A key feature of the spatial distribution that is clear from these studies is that cities are relatively specialized in terms of their export base. This section adds evidence on classifying cities in the United States by production patterns and briefly explores some locational determinants. Later, Chapter 5 refers to some results on grouping industries by similar location patterns.

This section presents two sets of results on specialization and classification of cities. For both sets, using Table 1270 of the Sixth Count of the 1970 Population Census, employment of each of the 243 SMSAs is divided into 229 industries. Why Population Census data? With industrial Census or County Business Patterns data, censoring to avoid disclosure leaves big gaps in the data. Population Census data give complete coverage and are readily available. However, they suffer from two problems. First, because they are household survey data, industrial activity is self-reported by interviewees. The Census Bureau makes great effort to ensure proper interpretation of the definition and self-reporting of economic activity and, where comparable, their employment figures for different activities correspond to the industrial Census's figures. Second, location of activity is based on employee residence, not firm location. If households live in the same SMSA as they work, this is no problem, but big extra-commuting cities such as Ann Arbor, Michigan can appear to be industrial giants with 10% of their labor force in autos, for example, when in fact that 10% works elsewhere—in that case in the Detroit area.

The analysis starts with a matrix of employment in 229 industries by 243 SMSAs. Each SMSA's column of employment breakdown is divided by total SMSA employment to get for each column the shares, or fractions, of each industry in SMSA employment. The data are then "eyeballed," focusing on traded good industries and searching for unusually large fractions, representing a high concentration of an SMSA's employment in an industry. In this way about half of the 243 SMSAs can arguably be classified as being specialized in one of auto production, aircraft, shipbuilding, steel, industrial machinery, communication equipment, petrochemicals, textiles, apparel, leather products, pulp and paper, or food processing. The other half of the urban areas are either nonindustrialized state capitals, college towns, or agriculture service centers (specialized in warehousing, business, and transport services), or very large somewhat diversified metropolitan areas.

A more systematic method of classification is cluster analysis. From the 229 by 243 matrix, a 243 by 243 symmetric matrix of simple correlation coefficients between pairs of columns of employment fractions for each pair of SMSAs is formed. Thus each entry represents the closeness between two SMSA's employment patterns. SMSAs are then grouped according to similarity of employment patterns, according to the algorithm noted in Table 1.2.

The results of this grouping are presented in Table 1.2. Each group represents a cluster of SMSAs with similar employment patterns. These groups are then labeled by type of dominant activity from the original employment fraction matrix. Using a strict clustering criterion, we grouped 43% of the SMSAs into one of 15 specialized activities. The largest manufacturing groups are autos and steel, followed by textiles and apparel. Where possible the fractions of an SMSA's employment in its dominant industry or industries are indicated. They range to a high of 36% in auto employment for Flint, Michigan.

Two comments on Table 1.2 are important. First, in doing geographical definitions, the Census Bureau regularly groups into one SMSA spatially adjacent cities that historically were spatially separate and industrially independent. Thus multiname SMSAs and enormous metro areas may group together fairly independent urban areas specialized in different activities, such as apparel and steel (for Allentown–Bethlehem–Easton). Thus the degree of specialization is underrepresented in the data. Second, the casual labeling of cities by activity may obscure the fact that several industrial activities are commonly grouped with one or two dominant ones, so there is not one type of activity for that type of city, but a group of activities. For example, in aircraft cities metals and electronic support industries are also located. That gives aircraft cities similar employment patterns to, say, weapons (submarine) cities.

Another way to view specialization is to examine for each industry the employment patterns across SMSAs. Table 1.3 looks at some important three-digit manufacturing industries in the United States. From that table, the distribution of employment across SMSAs is massed close to zero. With the self-reporting of Population Census data it is not possible to distinguish accurately between zero and low employment in an SMSA, as can be done for Brazil (see Table 1.6 below). Nevertheless, the vast majority of SMSAs typically have low employment in any one industry. However, these distributions have long tails, with a significant number of SMSAs having enormous employments in a given three-digit industry. This is consistent with the notion of specialization, where a few cities have very high employments in one industry and the rest have very low.

Tables 1.2 and 1.3 focus, although not exclusively, on manufacturing activity. The situation for cities specialized in traditional service industries—higher education, state or provincial government, transport and warehousing, and personal, repair, and retail services for farmers—is similar. Table 1.2 does report clusters of state capitals, college towns, and urban service centers. For traditional services there is an enormous literature in geography detailing urban patterns of production in different countries and at different points in time, typically dealing with smaller towns, such as those under 50,000 (which are thus excluded from the U.S. sample).

This literature describes hierarchies of the smaller towns and cities in an econ-

Table 1.2. Urban Specialization in the United States of America

Auto

Bay City, MI (13%)
Cleveland, OH
Detroit, MI (17%)
Flint, MI (36%)
Jackson, MI (7%)
Kenoska, WI (16%)
Lansing, MI (15%)
Muncie, IN (13%)
Saginaw, MI (17%)
South Bend, IN (6%)
Springfield, OH (9%)
Toledo, (OH–MI) (8%)

Textiles

(excluding apparel)
Ashville, NC
Augusta, GA (10%)
Chattanooga, TE–GA (11%)
Columbus, GA
Greenville, NC (18%)
Wilmington, NC (7%)

Radio, Television, and Communication Equipment

Binghamton, NY–PA (7%)
Cedar Rapids, IA
Lawrence–Haverhill, MA–NH (7%)
Nashua, NY (8%)

Pulp and Paper

Appleton–Oshkosh, WI (13%)
Green Bay, WI (11%)
Mobile, AL
Monroe, LA
Portland, ME
Savannah, GA

Shipbuilding

Charleston, SC (7%)
New London–Groton–Norwich, CT (12%)
Newport–New Hampton, VA (17%)
Vallejo-Napa, CA (10%)

College State Capital Towns

Austin, TX
Bloomington–Normal, IL
Bryant–College Station, TX
Champaign–Urbana, IL
Columbia, MO
Columbus, OH
Durham, NC
Fargo–Moorhead, ND–MN
Gainesville, FL
Lafayette, LA
Lafayette, W. Lafayette, IN
Lexington, KY
Lincoln, NE
Lubbock, TX
Madison, WI
Raleigh, NC
Reno, NV
Santa Barbara, CA
Tallahassee, FL
Terre Haute, IN
Tucson, AZ
Tuscaloosa, AL

Service Centers

Amarillo, TX
Billings, MT
Duluth–Superior, MN
Little Rock–North Little Rock, AR
Omaha, NE
Spokane, WA
Springfield, MA

Diverse Manufacturing

Chicago, IL
Dallas, TX
Newark, NJ
Philadelphia, PA
Phoenix, AZ
Syracuse, NY

Industrial Machinery

Bristol, CT (10%)
Canton, OH (6%)
LaCrosse, WI (11%)
New Britain, CT (10%)

14

Food Processing

(excluding agricultural, fisheries, and wholesaling)
Brownsville–Harlingen–San Benito, TX
McAllen–Pharr–Edinburg, TX
Modesto, CA
Salinas–Monterey, CA
Stockton, CA (5%)

Apparel

Allentown–Bethlehem–Easton, PA–NJ (9%)
Atlantic City, NJ
El Paso, TX
Fall River, MA–RI (16%)
New Bedford, MA (13%)
Scranton, PA
Wilkes–Barre–Hazelton, PA

Steel

Birmingham, AL (8%)
Gasden, AL (11%)
Gary–Hammond–East Chicago, IN (26%)
Huntington–Ashland (W. VA, KY, OH) (7%)
Johnstown, PA (13%)
Pittsburgh, PA
Pueblo, CO (8%)
Steubenville–Weirton, OH–W. VA (29%)
Wheeling, (W. VA–OH) (7%)

Aircraft

Anaheim–Santa Ana–Garden Grove, CA (5%)
Bridgeport, CT (7%)
Fort Worth, TX (13%)
Hartford, CT (11%)
Seattle–Everett, WA (10%)
Wichita, KA (14%)

Leather Products

Brockton, MA (6%)
Lewiston–Auburn, ME
Manchester, NH

Petrochemicals

Baton Rouge, LA (10%+)
Beaumont–Port Arthur–Orange, TX (18%+)
Galveston–Texas City, TX (11%+)
Lake Charles, LA (12%+)

Source: Henderson, 1986a.

[a]To do the cluster analysis, a 229 industry × 243 SMSA matrix of the fractions of an SMSA's employment in each of 229 industries (from Table 1270 of the Sixth Count of the 1970 Population Census) for 243 SMSAs was formed. From that matrix a 243 × 243 symmetric matrix of simple correlation coefficients between pairs of columns of employment fractions for each pair of SMSAs was formed. The correlation coefficients measure the degree of similarity or dissimilarity (for negative coefficients) between employment patterns of each pair of SMSAs. The primitive cluster algorithm picks the highest correlation coefficient and combines those two SMSAs, reducing the rows and columns of the matrix by one. In terms of the correlation between the combined SMSAs and any remaining SMSA, the algorithm picks either the highest or lowest of the pair of coefficients between that remaining SMSA and the original SMSAs that were "combined." The results in Table 1.2 are based on retaining the lowest pair of coefficients. For the new 242 × 242 matrix the algorithm then repeats itself, picking the highest correlation coefficient and combining two SMSAs to be the start of a (probably) new cluster. The results in Table 1.2 are based on the clustering stopping at a correlation of .48. Most clusters have a minimum correlation coefficient for the last SMSA added to .6.

Table 1.3. Employment Concentration in U.S. Metropolitan Areas in 1970

Number of SMSAs in the Employment Interval

Employment Interval	Out of 210 SMSAs with Populations from 50,000 to 1 million				Out of 33 SMSAs over 1 million 10,000+
	<250	2000–5000	5000+	10,000+	
Blast furnaces, steel works, rolling and finishing mills	168	7	10	6	7
Cutlery, hand tools, and other hardware	164	3	1	0	0
Metal stamping	175	3	0	0	2
Engines and turbines	190	1	1	0	1
Farm machinery and equipment	185	3	2	1	0
Construction and materials handling equipment	151	9	1	0	4
Electronic computing	183	3	2	0	3
Household appliances	177	6	3	2	1
Motor vehicles and equipment	130	16	17	8	13
Aircraft and parts	143	12	9	4	11
Shipbuilding	171	4	6	2	2
Photographic equipment and supplies	206	2	1	1	0
Tobacco manufactures	193	3	3	1	0
Meat products	133	7	0	0	0
Canning and preserving	167	5	0	0	0
Knitting mills textiles	181	4	2	1	1
Yarn thread and fabric mills	145	8	6	3	1
Apparel and accessories	85	16	15	4	9
Pulp, paper, and paper board products	147	6	3	0	0
Industrial chemicals	153	4	3	0	1
Rubber products	151	12	2	1	0
Footwear	178	9	1	0	0

Source: 1970 Population Census, Sixth Count, Table 1270.

omy whose primary purpose is to provide personal, repair, and retail services to rural areas. The smallest cities in the hierarchy offer the fewest and most ubiquitous services. As the hierarchy ascends in terms of city population, the number of services offered accumulates until the largest city in the hierarchy (which in itself is quite small, e.g., under 50,000, in absolute terms) produces the whole range of traditional services. In terms of the range of services, Berry (1968) in looking at U.S. rural areas of 30 or more years ago, suggests that the smaller towns in the hierarchy will offer banking, food retailing, repair, farm machinery retailing, and physician and religious services. The next larger sets of towns will additionally offer furniture and drug retailing and then dry cleaning and legal services. The largest sets of towns will offer hospital and apparel retailing services in addition to all the others previously listed.

This section has established the notion of specialization in production by cities. A remaining question is where, or on what potential urban sites, such production centers will locate. From Table 1.1 it is clear that there are regional associations, hypothetically based on at least historical locations of natural resource deposits and on natural consumer amenities. Attempts were made to be more specific about the industrial location and geographic features associations by examining two- and three-digit manufacturing industries and specific resource deposits and amenity measures.

Two types of analysis were attempted, based on manufacturing industries that cities specialize in, as listed in Table 1.2.. One was discrete choice analysis of whether a city specializes or not and, if so, in what industry. The other was another look at SMSA employment shares, using more detailed industry data than in Table 1.1. In both cases independent variables were measures of input conditions (regional iron reserves, regional steel or textile employment, state farm population, cost of electrical power), marketing conditions (access to regional market centers), and amenities affecting production (precipitation) or consumption (coastal location, heating degree days, precipitation). The results were sufficiently disappointing to not merit presentation. First, associations with current raw material measures were weak (except for food processing). Second, amenity measures had little plausible impact, except that moisture does seem to help textiles and apparel. Only access to regional markets and cost of electrical power appeared to have plausible differential impacts across industries. In particular, access seems to be very important for transport industries and food processing compared with textiles and apparel. At the same time, the cost of electrical power has the greatest impact on textiles and aircraft. Finally, the explanatory power of the regression equations was low. This means that either much of location factors are historical or that the analysis needs much more detailed data to represent the process accurately.

3. Specialization and Cities in Brazil

This section examines production patterns of cities in a large region of Brazil, and focuses on the specialization issue. Before we look at production patterns, however, it is useful to know about the region and its system of cities.

3.1. The Brazilian System of Cities

The data on Brazil cover South and Southeastern Brazil, including the states of Espirito Santo, Minas Gerais, Parana, Rio de Janeiro, Rio Grande do Sul, Santa Caterina, and São Paulo. This region exceeds the combined sizes of France, both East and West Germany and Spain, with an urban population of around 40 million

Fig. 1.1   Brazil

in 1980. It is shown in Figure 1.1 by the area outlined by a heavy line including the south, southeast, and a small portion of the west central zone around Brasilia.

The heart of this region is the state of São Paulo, producing 60% of Brazil's national value added in manufacturing, with only 20% of the national population and having a 1980 per capita income of about $(U.S.) 4000. The state's industry is concentrated in the metropolitan area of Grande São Paulo, referred to as GSP, or along the coastal plain axis between GSP and Rio de Janeiro. Over the coastal mountains from the axis is another industrial center around Belo Horizonte, the capital of Minas Gerais. Minas Gerais is richly endowed with iron ore deposits and limestone for steel production and produces eucalyptus trees for charcoal. Much of private steel production occurs in Minas Gerais, while the dominant government sector is located in the GSP area or along the coastal axis, away from natural resources used in steel production. This locational dichotomy of steel production by type of ownership is examined in Chapter 8.

The southeast region of Brazil, both in the interior as well as on the coast, is highly developed. There is a modern infrastructure of superhighways, airports, communications, and utilities crisscrossing the whole region. In the last two decades there has been significant deconcentration of modern industry from the coast into the hinterlands to supplement the highly developed traditional textile and food processing sectors already there. While the southern region is not so highly developed, its coastal region has a strong manufacturing base coupled with high growth rates.

Overall, the south and southeastern regions of Brazil are so much more developed than the north and northeast, that it is common to think of them as almost two different countries. The developed area is industrialized and overlaid with modern infrastructure. Population movements are rapid and production factors appear mobile. With allowances for educational differences, there do not appear to be significant differences in standards of living throughout the area.

What about the system of cities? The sample consists of almost all urban areas over 20,000 in the region (a few were missed inadvertently by the World Bank in drawing the sample) and totals 126 urban areas. Urban area definitions are similar to U.S. urbanized area definitions. Geographically urban areas are composed of single or contiguous multiple "municipios," geographic units somewhat larger than typical U.S. counties. However, unlike SMSAs in the United States, the data for Brazilian urban areas only relate to the urbanized portions of the metro areas, excluding the activities of the average 10% of the areas' populations, which are rural.

The basic issue in Brazil's system of cities is whether it can be compared with that of the United States, so that one set of results can reinforce the other. Brazil is a large, developed, resource rich region in a federal governmental framework (with local democratic processes). The main relevant differences relative to the United States are as follows. Brazil is a state capitalist society, with significant government control over the capital market and production of certain heavy industrial products. The impact of this is discussed in Chapter 8. Second, Brazil has a much less well-educated population and poor schooling facilities in many towns and rural areas. The impact of this is discussed in Chapter 6. Finally, Brazil has a rapidly growing urban population, both because of higher natural population growth rates and particularly because of very rapid rural–urban migration. Migration is typically from rural villages to small towns, and then small towns to larger towns to metro areas—a staged process for a family perhaps spread over several generations (Yap, 1977).

Despite all the migratory motion and rapid urban growth rates, Brazil has a very stable size distribution of cities with fairly uniform growth rates across cities. Table 1.4a presents the distribution of population by city size category for the whole of Brazil and Table 1.4b presents the growth rates by size category for Brazil and for the southeast region. The size distribution of cities is more stable than in the United States or India (see Chapter 3 and this chapter, Section 4, respectively). Also, urban concentration is declining in Brazil, if anything, in contrast to India and the United States, although that is predominately because of the decline in Rio de Janeiro. While stability per se does not mean comparability, it does mean statements are being made about a system of cities that is not obviously in a state of great flux, in terms of comparing small cities to big cities or coastal areas to interior areas.

3.2. Production Specialization in Brazilian Cities

For Brazil it was not possible to construct a comprehensive breakdown of employment by city. In the Demographic Census data the industrial categories are

Table 1.4. Population Division and Growth Rates by City Size Category

(a) Percentage distribution of urban population: Brazil			
	1950	1960	1970	1980
Metropolitan areas	61.3	59.8	59.4	56.6
250,000–499,999	7.1	7.7	8.7	9.9
100,000–249,999	11.0	11.2	11.1	11.4
50,000–99,999	7.7	8.1	7.8	8.3
20,000–49,999	12.7	13.2	13.1	13.7

(b) Average annual growth rates: Brazil and Southeast Brazil						
	Brazil			Southeast Region		
	1950–1960	1960–1970	1970–1980	1950–1960	1960–1970	1970–1980
Metropolitan	5.0	5.2	3.9	5.3	5.2	3.8
250,000–499,999	6.4	6.7	5.8	5.6	5.6	4.9
100,000–249,999	5.7	5.3	4.8	6.1	5.3	4.9
50,000–99,999	6.2	4.9	5.0	} 5.9	} 4.6	} 4.3
20,000–49,999	6.0	5.2	4.9			
Total urban	5.6	5.4	4.4	5.5	5.5	4.1
Total population	3.0	2.9	2.5	—	—	—

Source: John F. Purdy, Jr. (1981), "The Evolution of the Brazilian Urban System Between 1950 and 1980," World Bank, mimeo. (Urban and Regional Economics Division).

too broad (only two-digit). Also, in that Census self-reporting of industry by residents results in gross errors, with metallurgy being grossly overrepresented and various categories of machinery grossly underrepresented. Thus it is necessary to rely on Industrial Census data. We had access to uncensored three-digit manufacturing data covering the spectrum of (only) important industries. Because there are holes in the manufacturing data and because the entire nonmanufacturing sector is missing, it is not possible to do cluster analysis on the data. However, considerable information about manufacturing can be derived from the data.

Using the industries for which there are data, we construct a matrix of urban area and detailed industry employment. Each column of urban area employment breakdown is divided by total urban area employment to get detailed industry shares in each city's employment. By eyeballing this share matrix looking for unusually large fractions, we can classify about half of the 126 urban areas in the sample as being primarily specialized in the production of locally exported manufactured goods. There are 22 urban areas (mostly spinning and weaving) specialized in textiles, one in apparel (shoes), six in iron and steel, ten in food processing (sugar and meat packing), five in nonmetallic metals (mostly ceramics), two in pulp and paper, two in transport equipment, one in chemicals, one in beverages, and two in nonelectrical machinery. Specialized urban areas have anywhere from 9% to 49% of their labor force in just one usually three- to four-digit industry, with a typical concentration of about 20%. In addition, there are eight large multinucleated metro areas producing a whole range of products and 10 other large urban areas that are somewhat diversified. There are over 30 other urban areas that should be classified as the agricultural service centers of a Löschian central place model. Their employment from the Demographic Census tends to be in warehousing and transportation, wholesaling, and some food processing.

Table 1.5. Employment Concentrations: Southern Brazil

Number of Cities in the Employment Intervals:

Employment Interval	Out of all 126 urban areas			Out of 26 urban areas with populations of 100,000 to 1 to 2 million	Out of 63 urban areas under 50,000 population
	0	1–150	3000+	2000+	500+
Ceramics (tile, bricks)	54	52	5	1	2
Glass and crystal	96	22	2	0	0
Iron and steel	45	49	6	4	2
Engines and turbines	82	34	1	0	1
Ventilation and refrigeration equipment	56	58	3	1	0
Machine tools and industrial equipment	58	47	2	1	0
Agricultural machinery	53	55	1	0	0
Electrical for households (e.g., toasters)	94	28	1	0	0
Communications equipment (e.g., radios, TV)	85	34	2	0	0
Accessories for auto	24	82	2	3	0
Artificial fibers	116	4	1	1	0
Spinning and weaving natural fibers	62	15	6	4	11
Spinning and weaving artificial fibers	105	8	3	1	2
Finishing of cloth: spinning	88	17	2	0	2
Sugar	84	28	1	1	1
Toys	95	29	1	0	0
Shoes	28	80	4	1	0

Source: 1970 Industrial Census of Brazil.

Finally, there are more than 10 urban areas with high concentrations of state and federal government employees including defense employees.

The results of a more systematic examination of the employment patterns for each industry across urban areas are reported in Table 1.5. The distribution is massed at zero with typically more than one half the urban areas having *absolutely no* employment in a particular industry. From zero, frequency declines rapidly with presence of long tails again. Cities with 1 to 150 employment in a particular industry are interpreted as offering repair and service activities associated with those industries (repairs are not separated out in the Census data) or very specialized subproducts for local consumption. Finally, a small number of urban areas

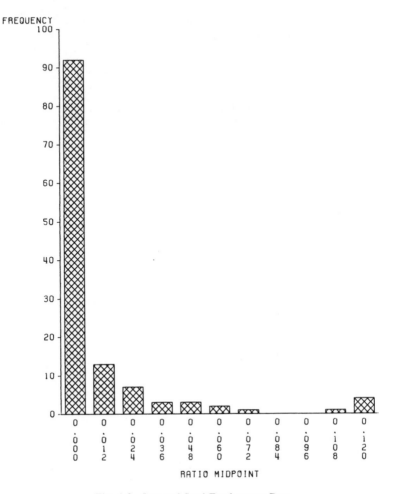

Fig. 1.2 Iron and Steel Employment Data

have very high concentrations of employment in any one industry. These appear to generally be urban areas specialized in that traded-good activity.

For Brazil, it is possible to look at employment patterns from another perspective, given the detailed data available. Five industries are picked, more or less arbitrarily. Four of the industries are ones in which cities tend to specialize: spinning and weaving, iron and steel, agricultural machinery, and ceramics. The fifth is machine tools and industrial equipment. The employment share of each industry in each city, is calculated. Then for each industry, employment shares are broken into discrete intervals, with interval size varying by industry so as to generally achieve about 10 intervals.[1] Finally, the number of cities in each interval is plotted against the midpoints of intervals, by industry. The results are reported in Figures 1.2 to 1.6.

Figures 1.2 to 1.6 corroborate Table 1.5. The distributions of employment shares are massed at zero, declining rapidly but having a long tail. However, visually

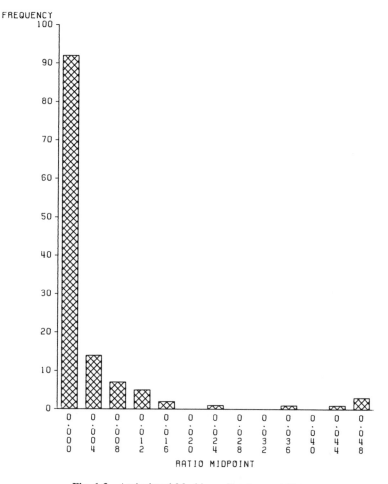

Fig. 1.3 Agricultural Machinery Employment Data

an interesting pattern appears from the plotting algorithm in all figures. The distributions appear to decline rapidly to zero or minimal frequency, travel along that frequency for several intervals, and then rise up to higher frequencies at the highest employment concentrations. Again this suggests an employment pattern where for many industries cities fall into one of three categories: absolutely no employment (most), low levels of employment in repairs or particularized production for local consumption (some), and high concentrations of employment in export production (a few). Regardless, specialization by cities in manufacturing production is a widespread phenomenon.

4. Evidence From India

In this section evidence on India is presented. In Chapter 11 China is examined. The examination of India is cursory, since the data needed to do a detailed analysis

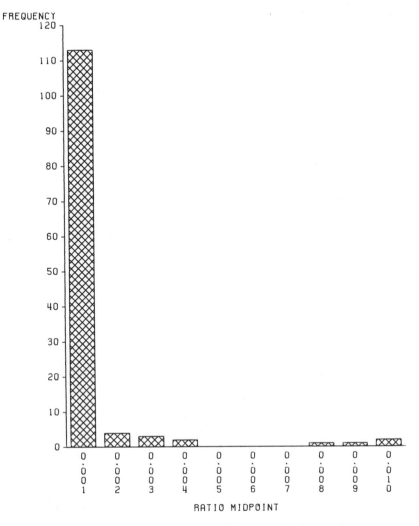

Fig. 1.4 Machine Tools and Industrial Equipment Employment Data

of urban production patterns are still unavailable. There are published volumes for each Census year giving two-digit employment data for Class I cities (towns and urban agglomerations over 100,000). These data have never been analyzed. For 1981 three-digit employment data may become available on computer for towns, but had not been released by 1986.

We will first state the most essential features of India's urban system and then turn to the issue of specialization. India is a culturally diverse federal democracy at a fairly low level of economic development—just how low is difficult to document because firms extensively underreport their outputs. India's literacy rate is low (36% in 1980 vs. 78% for Brazil or 69% for China) and the level of infrastructure development is also low relative to middle income countries such as Brazil.

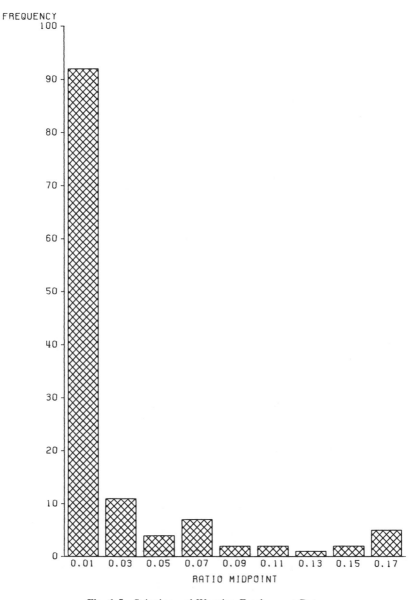

Fig. 1.5 Spinning and Weaving Employment Data

In terms of India's urban system three characteristics are noted here. First, it has a low level of urbanization, where since 1951 the percent of the population urbanized has increased from 17.6 to only 23.7 in 30 years. India has not experienced the massive rural-urban flows of so many other developing countries. Second, it has experienced a mild increase in urban concentration over the last 20 years (Table 1.6a) where Class I cities' share of urban population has increased steadily at the expense of smaller towns. Table 1.6a does not reveal, however,

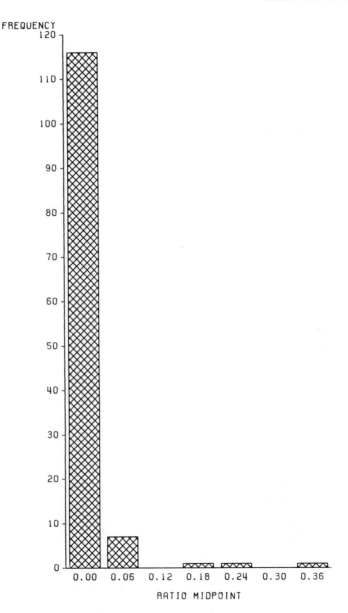

Fig. 1.6   Ceramics Employment Data

that the share of the very largest metropolitan areas is not increasing (Mills and Becker, 1986). The increase is in the middle ranks. Finally, in marked contrast to Brazil and China but similar to the United States is the complete decentralization of manufacturing noted in Table 1.6b. India's largest cities have never had a large share of manufacturing employment and that share has declined in recent years.

Table 1.6. India's Population and Manufacturing Concentration

(a) Distribution of the Urban Population by City Size Categories: India

	1961	1971	1981
Class I (100,000+)	50.8	56.2	60.4
Class II (50,000–100,000)	11.0	11.2	11.6
Class III (20,000–50,000)	17.4	16.3	14.4
Classes IV to VI (under 20,000)	20.8	16.3	13.6

(b) Percent of Manufacturing Employment in Cities with Largest Manufacturing Employment

	Largest city	Largest 5 cities	Largest 10 cities
1901	0.92	2.29	2.98
1921	1.62	2.89	3.75
1931	1.38	3.05	4.19
1951	3.61	8.87	11.20
1961	3.31	7.73	9.71
1971	2.10	4.65	5.93

Sources: Census of India 1981 and Mills and Becker (1986).

Although a detailed breakdown of industry employment by cities has never been analyzed for India it appears that specialization by cities is also the pattern. Evidence for this pattern comes from the continual reference in written work to steel towns, textile towns, and others with lists of examples, and the Report of the Task Force on *Planning and Development of Small and Medium Towns and Cities,* Volume II, Ministry of Works and Housing, 1977. This report examines the activities of 60 towns ranging in size from 5000 to 300,000 people, and notes the three major manufacturing activities of many of these towns, as well as their dominant economic activity (manufacturing or not). The wide variation in major manufacturing activities reported in Vol. II suggests a high degree of specialization. For example, in the sample with information on nine manufacturing towns, three are specialized in nonmetallic mineral production (cement, ceramics, glassware), one in cotton goods, one in petroleum, two in agricultural implements and machinery, and two in food processing.

Finally, there is Ashok Mitra's (1981) cluster analysis of employment patterns for all Indian cities, examining the proportions devoted to the primary nonagricultural activities. Out of 1466 towns and urban agglomerations analyzed in 1971, 200 had high concentrations of manufacturing employment, as opposed to service, construction, household, transport, and trade commerce. While there is no breakdown of specialization by different manufacturing activities, the specialization at just the first-digit economic activity level is pronounced.

5. Implications of the Observed Patterns

The fact that cities specialize in production, which results in different types of cities, has important implications. In theory (see Chapter 2) and in practice (see below) different types of cities have different (average) equilibrium sizes. The

Table 1.7. Average Sizes of Different Types of Cities for the U.S.A.

	Mean (millions)	Standard deviation	Sample size
Diverse manufacturing	2.600	2.416	6
Aircraft/weapons	0.771	0.457	6
Steel	0.426	0.625	9
Auto [including Detroit]	0.355 [0.660]	0.545 [1.177]	11 [12]
Service centers	0.267	0.159	7
Apparel	0.232	0.109	7
Textiles	0.213	0.103	6
College towns/state capitals	0.164	0.163	22
Pulp and paper	0.162	0.068	6
Food processing	0.158	0.046	5

composition of national output determines the composition of types of cities, and that in turn determines the size distribution of cities.

In short, national output patterns are determined by a country's overall natural resources, consumption patterns, trade relationships, and governmental policies. These production patterns then imply a system of cities, broken into different types of cities specialized in the production of different goods, where the numbers of each type depend on the level of national output of the good in which that type of city is specialized. The size distribution of cities then depends on the numbers of each type of city of differing average size required to meet overall national production patterns.

Table 1.7 presents the average sizes and standard deviations for the cities in each large cluster in Table 1.3 for the United States. Note that average sizes vary considerably, increasing sixteenfold from the smallest to largest type of city. However, within each type the standard deviations are large, indicating considerable variation within types.

In theory, given the average sizes of different types of cities in Table 1.7, we can make predictions about the impact of economic changes on the size distribution of cities. For example, when we examine developing countries, we find that as production patterns shift away from traditional industries such as natural fiber textiles, warehousing and transport for agricultural output, food processing, retail and personal services for farm communities, and ceramics toward heavy machinery and transport industries, a shift from smaller to medium size type cities would be predicted. In another example, with a shift from general manufacturing into modern services or high-tech manufacturing, another shift from medium to large size urban areas might be predicted.

Of course, predicting which particular smaller cities would grow into larger cities would be more difficult. It would depend on which locations are better endowed with amenities relevant for expanding manufacturing industries (e.g., access to natural resources for iron and steel). That is, a city's size is determined primarily by which type of industry it attracts, and that depends in part on whether its natural amenities are attractive to that type of industry. Also, in a more generalized context some cities may be more efficient at also doing investments in urban infrastructure that are attractive to particular industries. In short, the question of which particular cities end up with which particular industries is a complex one, referred to throughout the book (see especially Chapter 8).

Having suggested there is a strong link between the composition of national output in an economy and the size distribution of cities, we now suggest that making practical use of this link is very difficult. First, a large fraction of the cities in the United States and Brazil are not typed because their production patterns are too dissimilar. In particular, large metropolitan areas tend to fall outside the clusters, being both highly diversified but each having its own particular area of relative specialization: New York in apparel and publishing, Boston in high-tech, Los Angeles in aircraft and entertainment, and so on. Moreover, much heavy industrial production occurs in these large metro areas (e.g., Chicago), as well as in the typed cities. Also smaller metro areas can be highly diversified (e.g., Dallas, Syracuse). Part of this phenomenon may be historical where population has clustered around a historically resource-based core city. This possibility and the issue of large metropolitan areas are the subject of Chapter 10, where we attempt to make very gross cross-country comparisons of the size distribution of cities. However, part of the problem in classifying cities is also a lack of detailed data. Diversification and specialization undoubtedly involve complex interrelationships between specific industries indentified at a very detailed level (i.e., looking at four- or five-digit industries rather than two- or three-digit ones). The study of such data has only just started (see Bergsman et al., 1972, 1975), and such data are very limited (e.g., censored in the United States due to disclosure problems).

The second issue concerns the noise present in the city type-size relationship. In Table 1.7 the standard deviations are very large and for many clusters their average sizes cannot be shown to be significantly different from each other. Apart from the problem of typing cities in a more detailed fashion (at a four- or five-digit industrial level), Chapter 6 will show that any individual city size is strongly affected by other social, cultural, historical, and geographic factors. Among these are

Public service levels, qualities, and taxes

Quality-of-life measures, such as crime rates and pollution levels

Natural amenities, such as weather conditions affecting everything from heating costs, to health, to pollution dispersion

Geological formations affecting the city's shape and transport system.

Equilibrium city sizes are very sensitive to small changes in parameters in theory (Chapter 2) and also in practice (Chapter 6).

However, there are still important useful implications to be gotten from the observed patterns. These are listed as conclusions.

1. First and most important, we can set aside the notion that there is one universally efficient city size or the notion that larger cities are more efficient than smaller cities. It is clear that big and small size cities coexist indefinitely in market economics (see Tables 1.4 and 1.6), indicating that somehow they must have in net the same overall efficiency. The reasons why will be found in the next chapters.

2. Most smaller and medium size cities in an economy do specialize in production. This indicates, for example, that there may be benefits to a city from

tailoring its infrastructure investment to the type of industry it is best suited to attract (see Chapter 8). It also indicates that national policies, such as those prevailing in China until recently, that encourage local diversification and self-sufficiency may be inappropriate (see Chapter 11).

3. In terms of planning, equilibrium and perhaps efficient city sizes for any particular type of city are highly variable. Later we will argue that they are extremely sensitive to small changes in the specific natural and historically manmade production and consumption conditions in the city. At the present level of knowledge, it is hard to specify a rough order of magnitude for efficient size for any *particular* city, even if we know average sizes for a type.

4. In spite of (2), it may be possible to make gross intercountry comparisons and intracountry predictions about the size distribution of cities. In particular, it may be possible to asess the qualitative and rough quantitative impact on a country's size distribution of cities of changes in national output composition which are caused by government policies, economic growth, or international factors. Chapter 10 explores this possibility.

NOTE

1. This followed the internal plotting algorithm in SAS.

CHAPTER 2

Modeling the System of Cities in an Economy

This chapter presents a simple theoretical model of a system of cities in a large economy. The goal is to develop the properties of a system of cities and to argue that the complex spatial arrangement of urban populations seen in a country is to a large extent predictable and can be understood in terms of basic economic forces. Some of the model's results and assumptions are tested in Chapters 5 and 6. Chapters 3 and 4 extend the model to incorporate natural resources, growth and development, international trade, technological change, and small economies. The power of the model is its simplicity, combined with the complexity of situations about which it can make predictions.

The specification of a general equilibrium model of a system of cities is recent (Henderson, 1972, 1974, 1982a, 1982b; Hochman, 1977, 1981; Kanemoto, 1978; Upton, 1981). However, the model has important antecedents that have influenced its form and development.

The notion that economies consist of systems of cities emanates from central place theory (Chirstaller, 1966; Beckmann, 1958), which is based on a Löschian (1954) framework of retailers who have endogenously determined market areas and hence scale of production. Central place models are for traditional economies where towns exist to serve an agriculturally based population. Given that base, there is a hierarchy of cities and production patterns, in which cities export down to smaller cities and to the rural population. The models have a reduced form structure, without explicit formulation of demand and supply technology and without any consideration of the internal makeup of cities and the housing of the urban-based population. Hence, there are no prices or clearing of markets in the model (Beckmann, 1958). Nevertheless, this early literature establishes the notion of a system of cities.

The "new" urban economics literature of the 1960s moved on to try to model the modern industrial city by using full "general" equilibrium concepts. Two basic questions were posed. What are the bases for cities that have primary functions other than retailing to rural areas? How do we model the internal structure of cities? In a classic paper, Mills (1967) examined both questions. He suggested that cities form in an economy because there are scale economies in industrial production that lead workers and firms to cluster together in large agglomerations, rather than to disperse more or less evenly over the geographic area of the economy (with or without an agricultural sector). Greater scale of economic activities in cities enhances productivity through:

1. "Communications" among firms, which enhance the speed of adoption of new technological innovations and of reaction to changing national and international market conditions.
2. Labor market economies for workers and firms searching, respectively, for specific jobs and specific skill combinations.
3. Greater opportunities for specialization in firm (and worker) activities.
4. Scale economies in the provision of intermediate common inputs (docking facilities, warehousing, power, etc.)

The scale economies are dependent on workers and firms working together in close spatial proximity in, for example, a central business district (hereafter CBD) of a city. Thus workers tend to commute from residential areas surrounding the CBD to the centrally located workplaces. Finally, these scale economies apply to the production of goods that are exported from the city to other cities or economies.

At the same time, there are consumption and certain production diseconomies connected with people clustering together in urban areas, such as commuting cost increases in a monocentric city, and such disamenities as crime, pollution, and social conflict. In a monocentric city where almost all residents work in a CBD, residents on average live further and further from the city center and have to commute greater and greater distances as city size expands. The effect of these diseconomies is the eventual offset of production scale benefits as a city's size increases, limiting cities to various equilibrium sizes (Mills, 1967; Dixit, 1973).

Given that cities exist and are limited in efficient size how do they relate to each other? A basic notion (Henderson, 1972) is that there are different types of cities, and each type specializes in the production of a different traded good. It was established in Chapter 1 that smaller and medium-size cities are highly specialized in their production patterns. This fact contradicts the traditional notion that smaller and medium-size cities are part of a hierarchy as modeled in central place theory. Why do cities specialize? Henderson (1972, 1974) argues that specialization occurs if no production benefits or positive externalities can be derived by locating two different industries in the same place. If they are located together, because workers in both industries are living and commuting in the same city, this increases the spatial area of the city and the average commuting costs for a given degree of scale economy exploitation in any one industry. Separating the industries into different cities allows for a greater degree of scale economy exploitation in each industry relative to a given level of commuting costs and city spatial area.

This argument concerning scale economies is strengthened if scale economies are of localization, not urbanization. Localization economies are *internal* to each industry, where scale is measured by total employment (or output) in *that* industry in *that* urban area. Urbanization economies are external to the specific industry, and result from the level of all economic activity internal to a city, as measured, for example, by total city population. In this case, only the size of the city, not its industry composition, affects the extent of scale effects relevant to a particular industry.

If scale effects are of localization, then for a *given* city size and associated cost of living, scale effects and hence incomes are maximized by concentrating local export employment all in one industry, rather than dissipating the scale effects by spreading employment over many industries. However, if scale effects are of urbanization, then this specialization may not matter since it is the general level of economic activity rather than its industry specific concentration that enhances productivity.[1] In Chapter 5, we econometrically explore the nature of scale economies.

The extent of specialization of cities is limited. As noted in Chapter 1, there is a range of goods produced in almost all urban areas, such as general retailing, schooling, housing services, auto repairs, and dry cleaning. These services as well as some manufactured goods are nontraded simply because the transport costs of intercity trade are prohibitive. Specialization is also limited by the fact that some industries are strongly linked in production. The traditional linkages are physical input-output ones, although these may be weaker in a modern economy (Bergsman et al., 1975). There are also linkages through labor force, communications, and service input interactions among industries. Thus urban specialization in practice implies specialization in producing groups of goods, given a large nontraded good sector in each city.

In addition, Chapter 1 showed that, while the very largest metropolitan areas do exhibit some tendency toward specialization, some large part of their work force is found in a whole spectrum of industrial classifications, unlike smaller urban areas. That evidence may not be inconsistent with the notion of specialization. Given the above discussion, specialization occurs primarily at the level of a monocentric city contained in a single political jurisdiction, a description that could be given of a smaller urban area. However, a very large metropolitan area may contain several or many specialized industrial centers surrounded by the residences of their work force and governed independently in a jurisdictionally fragmented metropolitan area. In short, a large metropolitan area may contain a number of "cities" that could exist on their own, a notion that Chapter 9 develops.

Given these notions that an economy consists of a system of cities of limited efficient sizes, where different types of city specialize in different activities, a formal model of a system of cities can now be presented. Section 1 develops a formal model and illustrates some properties of internal equilibrium in a single city. Section 2 presents the primary results for a system of cities, with a diagrammatic interpretation of some basic predictions of the model. Section 3 does a comparative statics exercise to illustrate applications of the model. Finally, Section 4 solves for equilibrium city size under different assumptions about the perceptions of economic agents in the model, to indicate robustness. That section also shows that equilibrium size is Pareto efficient.

1. Model of a Representative City

In order to analyze the characteristics of a system of cities, a model of any single city in the system must be specified carefully, using a specific functional form model without explicit spatial dimensions. There are three reasons for this choice of modeling strategy. A sophisticated spatial model of a single city is too cumbersome to allow us to develop adequately the properties of a system of cities. In fact, modeling the properties of a single city if a spatial model is used is an

Table 2.1. Definitions of Variables and Parameters

$X \equiv$ traded good output	$p \equiv$ local price of housing
$N \equiv$ total local population/employment	$U \equiv$ per person utility level
$K \equiv$ total local capital stock	$k_j \equiv$ local overall capital-to-labor ratio in city
$\hat{N}_0 \equiv$ local labor employment in X production	type j
$\hat{K}_0 \equiv$ local capital employment in X production	$m_j \equiv$ number of cities of type j
$H \equiv$ housing	$\alpha \equiv$ labor distribution parameter: X production
$l \equiv$ land sites	$\beta \equiv$ labor distribution parameter: H production
$\hat{K}_1 \equiv$ capital employment in H production	$\delta \equiv$ spatial diseconomy/complexity parameter
$\hat{N}_2 \equiv$ "commuting" time in land site production	$\gamma \equiv$ public capital productivity parameter
$\hat{K}_2 \equiv$ public capital inputs in land site production	$a_i \equiv$ relative consumption share of x_i
$q \equiv$ traded good price	$b \equiv$ relative consumption share of h
$w \equiv$ wage rate	$f \equiv \Sigma a_i + b$
$r \equiv$ capital rental rate	$E_j \equiv$ constant terms
$y \equiv$ income per person	$c_j \equiv$ constant terms
$h \equiv$ local housing consumption per person	$\psi \equiv [f - b\beta(1 - \gamma)]/[\beta b(\delta - \gamma)] \equiv \psi$
$x_i \equiv$ local x_i consumption per person	$\phi \equiv$ scale economy parameter

exercise in itself (e.g., Dixit, 1973 or Wheaton, 1974). Moreover, that level of detail for a single city adds little or nothing to the analysis of the properties of a system of cities. Second, specific functional forms are used in part, because for certain propositions closed form solutions are highly desirable. However, specific functional forms are also chosen over general functional forms, because when general functional forms are used in this type of complex model with scale (dis)economies, propositions about the system can only be proved for various output elasticities (with respect to inputs) defined and treated as *global* constants (e.g., Hochman, 1977). This implicitly imposes a log linearity on functional forms; here that is made explicit.

The model of a single city consists of three components: the production sector, consumption sector, and the local government sector. We start with the production sector. The expositional strategy is to present the basic equations of the model and the final solutions in the text but to relegate all other technical details to footnotes. Table 2.1 contains a list of variables and parameters. The emphasis in writing is to communicate an intuitive understanding of the basic results.

Production. Two final outputs are produced in each city. One is the traded good the city specializes in, which is produced with capital and labor under constant returns to scale at the firm level. Firms are subject to a Hicks' neutral shift factor, where increasing industry employment results in increased industry efficiency for all firms. Since such economies of scale are external to the firm, perfect competition and exhaustion of firm revenue by factor payments prevail (Chipman, 1970). Then it is only necessary to specify production relationships at the industry (not firm) level. The traded good output is labeled X and has the production function

$$X = Ag(N)\hat{N}_0^\alpha \hat{K}_0^{1-\alpha} \tag{2.1}$$

$\hat{N}_0$ and $\hat{K}_0$ are, respectively, labor inputs and capital stock. The carets denote local employment of capital and labor within particular local activities, as subscripted. The shift factor is $g(N)$, where N is the number of city residents (who divide their time between X production and commuting). The specification of N in $g(N)$ *already presumes specialization* in X production and would not include, prior to specialization, residents employed in and commuting to other industries. Thus economies of scale are localization ones. The form of $g(N)$ will be presented below; but there are positive scale effects so $g'(N) > 0$.

The second good produced in the city is housing, a nontraded good. Housing is produced with capital and "land" sites under constant returns to scale; and the industry production function is

$$H = Bl^\beta \hat{K}_1^{1-\beta} \tag{2.2}$$

l are land sites produced with time, or labor, inputs subject to shift factors, or

$$l = (DN^{-\delta}\hat{K}_2^\gamma)\hat{N}_2 \tag{2.3}$$

$\hat{N}_2$ represents total labor resources, or time by residents, devoted to commuting in the city for a *given number of residents* (N) and public capital inputs $(\hat{K}_2)$. Thus, $\hat{N}_2$ indicates the amount of land on the flat featureless plain "claimed" through commuting by a given number of residents. $N^{-\delta}$ represents a spatial complexity factor without explicit introduction of space. If, say, both $\hat{N}_2$ and N double, land sites do not double because, in a spatial world, the new people located on the city edge must spend more time on the average getting from their home site to work and back (in a monocentric model) and hence site production is less efficient. Proceeds from site sales ("rents") are exhausted by payments to $\hat{N}_2$ (i.e., rents are distributed within the city). This "as if" model of a spatial world was introduced in Henderson (1972, 1974).

$\hat{K}_2$ represents public investment in transport facilities (roads) that reduces commuting time needed to produce sites. Note that the introduction of a public sector providing public capital is critical to the understanding of cities. Almost half the space of a city is occupied by public capital including roads, sidewalks, and public buildings (Clawson, 1969). In a growth context, a city cannot form and grow until much of its nonmalleable public capital has been laid out. In general (in)efficient operations of local governments in providing infrastructure critically affect the sizes of cities, as will be discussed in later chapters.

Finally in equation 2.3, later solutions to the model will require "overall" decreasing returns to land site production. In particular, if N, $\hat{K}_2$, and $\hat{N}_2$ all double, l less than doubles. The restriction implies

$$\gamma - \delta > 0 \tag{2.3a}$$

This represents a type of congestion effect, or diseconomy of scale in commuter-produced land sites.

To solve the production side of the model, the profit maximization behavior of firms is incorporated. This yields normal value of marginal product equals factor price equations for the production of X, H, and l, given that firms perceive input and output prices as fixed.[2] Substitution of these equations back into the production function gives the unit cost functions for X and H, which are footnoted.[3] Given perfect competition, unit cost is equated to price. Of particular interest is a rearranged form of the unit cost function for X, where the city wage rate, (w) is expressed as a function of city size and variables exogenous to a single city, of traded good prices (q), and of capital rentals (r). The equation is

$$w = c_0^{-1/\alpha} q^{1/\alpha} r^{(\alpha-1)/\alpha} g(N)^{1/\alpha} \tag{2.4}$$

Throughout the chapter, c_i refers to a footnoted parameter cluster. Note from (2.4) that when output price (q) and capital rentals (r) are held fixed, given positive

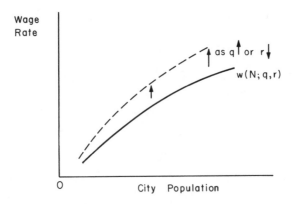

Fig. 2.1   The Partial Equilibrium Determinants of Local Wages

scale effects, wages paid rise with city size. That is, the potential benefits (greater profits for the same q and r) to firms of greater efficiency from increased industry scale are dissipated through firm competition to hire more workers in the lcoal labor market, which raises the wage rate (w). An increase in the price of the traded good increases wages while an increase in the price of the other input, capital, decreases the wages that can be paid for a given output price. The properties of equation 2.4 are illustrated in Figure 2.1.

Finally, to complete the production side of the model, there are the full employment equations for the city where

$$\hat{N}_0 + \hat{N}_2 = N \tag{2.5}$$

$$\hat{K}_0 + \hat{K}_1 + \hat{K}_2 = K \tag{2.6}$$

Consumption.   Residents have utility functions of the form $U = E' x_1^{a_1} x_2^{a_2} \ldots x_n^{a_n} h^b$ where we define $f \equiv \sum_{j=1}^{n} a_j + b$. x_j are traded goods, one of which is produced by this type of city and exported and the others imported; and h is housing consumption. Individuals derive income from wage payments and pay equal per person taxes to finance public transport expenditures. Thus

$$y = w - r\hat{K}_2/N \tag{2.7}$$

y is income, and $r\hat{K}_2/N$ are local taxes financing $\hat{K}_2$. In the presentation here of the system of cities model, we assume capital rentals are distributed to owners outside the cities or outside the country, so that they are not spent on urban housing. The algebraically more complicated case, where capital rentals are spent in cities is presented in Hochman (1977) and Henderson (1982b).

Given utility-maximizing behavior by urban residents, demand equations for x_j and h can be derived by combining first order conditions.[4] The substitution of these demand equations into the utility function yields the indirect utility function

$$U = E \left(\prod_{j=1}^{n} q_j^{-a_j} \right) y^f p^{-b}, \qquad E \equiv E' \sum_{j=1}^{n} (a_j/f)^{a_j} \tag{2.8}$$

This will be used later to solve for utility as a function of city size and prices exogenous to the city, which is then the key to deriving city size solutions.

The local government. A local government is introduced to determine the level of public investment $\hat{K}_2$. A competitive, costless, full information political process is assumed at the local level. Competing potential and incumbent governments seek to maximize the welfare of fully informed voter-residents so as to be re-elected. Alternatively, residents vote repeatedly on referenda about the level of public investment, until a dominant outcome is achieved (undominated by any other proposed investment level). In both cases, given the fixed rental price of capital in national markets, for any city population of identical individuals, the standard outcome is that the government chooses $\hat{K}_2$ to maximize utility, as analyzed below. Chapter 8 discusses what happens if the simple assumptions of perfect local autonomy in setting public investment and of a perfect political process are not met.

Solution for a single city. The model is solved by substituting marginal productivity conditions into the basic housing demand (equation (c) in note 4) equals housing supply equation 2.2. These series of substitutions after rearrangement yield equations, respectively, for the demand for labor in site production, the price of housing, and the demand for capital in housing production. These are footnoted except the one for housing price.[5]

$$p = c_2 q^{\beta/\alpha} r^{1-\beta/\alpha} N^{\delta\beta} \hat{K}_2^{-\beta\gamma} g(N)^{\beta/\alpha} \qquad (2.9)$$

Equation 2.9 indicates that the cost of housing and thus the cost of living rise monotonically with city size and shift down with increases in urban infrastructure investment, $\hat{K}_2$. To solve for urban infrastructure, the $\hat{K}_2$ is chosen that maximizes utility, allowing all endogenous variables in the city to vary with $\hat{K}_2$. The city government perceives income, the wage rate, and the price of housing to be endogenous, but the capital rental rate, r, and traded good prices, q, as exogenous. Thus into utility in (2.8) is substituted for y from (2.7), for w from (2.4) and for p from (2.9). Maximizing U with respect to $\hat{K}_2$, for any N, gives a trade-off between increased tax costs and lowered housing prices of increments in $\hat{K}_2$. Solving $(\partial U/\partial \hat{K}_2)/\hat{K}_2 = 0$ yields

$$\hat{K}_2 = (\gamma\beta b/f)yr^{-1}N \qquad (2.10)$$

This is the infrastructure level provided in a perfectly competitive, full information democratic process, with only one type of voter.

The public or private factor demand equations such as (2.9) are industry or city demand functions for factors in different uses and they display the normal income, price, and scale properties of these functions. For example, in (2.10), public investment rises with income and city population and falls with the cost of capital r. This is illustrated in Figure 2.2.

To solve for equilibrium city size, it is necessary to solve for utility as a function of city size and variables exogenous to the city. This means solving out for variables endogenous to the city. First for income y, substitute for $\hat{K}_2$ to get

$$y = f/(f + \gamma\beta b)w \qquad (2.11)$$

Then into utility in (2.8) substitute for y from (2.11), for w from (2.4), for p from (2.9), and for $\hat{K}_2$ from (2.10) to get the basic partial equilibrium (to the rest of the economy) expression for utility of any resident. This is[6]

$$U = E_0 \left(\prod_{j=1}^{n} q_j^{-a_j} \right) [c_0^{-1} qr^{-1} g(N)]^{[f-b\beta(1-\gamma)]/\alpha} r^{f-b} N^{\beta b(\gamma-\delta)} \qquad (2.12)$$

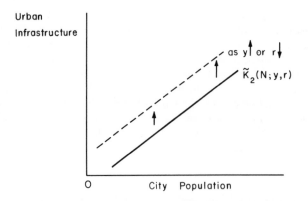

Fig. 2.2 The Local Demand for Urban Infrastructure

The usual partial equilibrium properties of $dU/dq > 0$ and $\partial U/\partial r < 0$ hold where, in evaluating $\partial U/\partial r$, $f - b\beta(1 - \gamma) - \alpha(f - b) > 0$. That is, increases in the price received by a city for its exports increases utility of residents, while increases in input prices decrease utility, all ceteris paribus. These properties are illustrated in Figure 2.3. They do not necessarily hold in the general equilibrium context of the whole economy, as will be seen in Section 3.

Of final interest are the determinants of city export production. Substituting in the production function X for $\hat{K}_0$, $\hat{N}_0$, y, and w yields[7]

$$X = c_3 g(N)^{1/\alpha}(r^{-1}q)^{(1-\alpha)/\alpha}N \tag{2.13}$$

City output rises monotonically with city size. It shifts up as output price increases and down as the cost of capital inputs increases.

Equilibrium city size. There are several equivalent ways to solve for city size. All involve setting equilibrium city size at the level where $\partial U/\partial N = 0$ for q and

Fig. 2.3 The Partial Equilibrium Determinants of Local Utility Levels

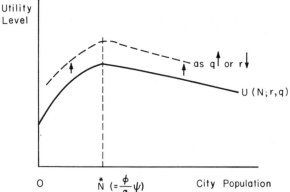

r fixed in (2.12). Holding q and r fixed is a behavioral assumption, where any one city is assumed to be one of many producing its export good and borrowing capital so its producers and consumers perceive that variations in city characteristics do not impact national or international market prices. Setting city size at the level where $\partial U/\partial N = 0$ for r and q fixed means from a partial equilibrium perspective at least that city size is efficient. That is, the welfare of city residents is maximized, given the exogenous prices they face. In deriving the city size where $\partial U/\partial N = 0$, there is an implicit trade-off between the scale economy benefits of increasing city size and the cost-of-living increases as spatial complexity, or congestion, in the city rise.

In solving for city size, first equilibrium size may be obtained through the direct actions of economic agents, such as competitive land developers. These are the entrepreneurs who set up communities or cities in a national economy. If some city sizes are not at a point where $\partial U/\partial N = 0$, developers can earn temporary profits by setting up and selling housing in cities of more efficient size—that is, they can earn a premium above the wages and capital rentals they need to pay to attract factors to their city. In particular, they can borrow at the prevailing r and pay less than marginal products to labor and still meet the prevailing U (by definition of the criterion that at an inefficient city size $\partial U/\partial N \neq 0$). Developers play an entrepreneurial role that facilitates large movements of people so that a new city can form en masse (see more on this in Section 3 of Chapter 4). Their role is identical to that of firm entrepreneurs in a usual heuristic general equilibrium model with determinant firm size, except rather than designing firms they are designing cities.

Alternatively viewed, even without developers, $\partial U/\partial N = 0$ is required. If $\partial U/\partial N \neq 0$ for the r and q's for that solution, any new cities of more efficient size (which could appear "randomly") could be sustained (attract factors), leading to an increase or decrease in the number of cities, indicating that the original solution is not a "globally" stable equilibrium. Only when all cities are of efficient sizes can new cities not be sustained. Finally, $\partial U/\partial N = 0$ can be achieved by local governments limiting city size to this utility-maximizing level, through a set of zoning ordinances (see Chapter 4). There is an extensive discussion of the mechanisms for achieving equilibrium city size along with examples in Henderson, 1977.

These same mechanisms also ensure that cities specialize in traded good production. Relative to an unspecialized city, if a specialized city is set up of, say, the same size (and hence same diseconomies in commuting), it can pay higher wages for the same other prices because of greater exploitation of scale economies in its now specialized industry. Specialization is then achieved by the entrepreneurial activities of developers.

Before solving $\partial U/\partial N = 0$ for the efficient N, we must specify the nature of the external localization economies function $g(N)$. This is done by borrowing from the econometric results in Chapter 5 and specifying that

$$g(N) = Ae^{-\phi/N} \tag{2.14}$$

Note in regard to Chapter 5 that here localization economies and specialization are assumed so there is no need to distinguish between employment in X production and total local employment. Equation 2.14 represents a declining degree, or elasticity, of scale economy formulation where

$$\frac{dg(\cdot)}{dN} \cdot \frac{N}{g(\cdot)} = \phi/N > 0$$

for ϕ defined to be positive. Apart from the fact that (2.14) will be justified from empirical work, it is critical in the overall model to break the logarithmic linearity of the system of equations so as to get unique, noninfinitesimal and noninfinite, efficient city sizes. Here this is done by causing the degree of scale economies to peter out, so that the agglomeration benefits of increasing city size die out relative to the consumption costs. It can also be done by having the degree of diseconomies in land site production escalate (i.e., increasing congestion), so that urban costs of living escalate relative to scale benefits with city size increases (Henderson, 1974), or by having city size itself be an increasing disamenity in the utility function (Henderson, 1982a, 1982b).

Substituting in (2.14) for $g(N)$ into (2.11) and solving $\partial U/\partial N = 0$, efficient city size is[8]

$$N = \frac{\phi}{\alpha} \left[\frac{f - b\beta(1 - \gamma)}{\beta b(\delta - \gamma)} \right] = \frac{\phi}{\alpha} (\psi), \qquad \psi \equiv \frac{f - b\beta(1 - \gamma)}{\beta b(\delta - \gamma)} \qquad (2.15)$$

With the specification of scale effects and equation 2.15, the determinants of utility levels in a city can be fully illustrated. In Figure 2.3 utility levels in equation 2.11 rise to a peak at $\overset{*}{N}$ where $N = (\phi/\alpha)\psi$ and then decline for capital rentals and traded good prices held fixed. Existence of positive city sizes and satisfaction of second order conditions together follow given $f - b\beta(1 - \gamma)$, $\beta b(\delta - \gamma) > 0$, or $\psi > 0$. Note $\delta - \gamma > 0$ is a restriction imposed in equation 2.3a. $[f - b\beta(1 - \gamma)]/[\beta b(\delta - \gamma)]$ is a common parameter collection throughout the book, and is redefined as ψ.

In (2.15), city size is a function both of the parameter cluster, ψ, representing the internal structure of cities and of the scale and factor usage parameters of export production. The latter parameters are analyzed fully in the next section. For now it is useful to note that as $\phi \to 0$, scale effects go to zero and hence city size goes to zero. This could be interpreted as rural production where goods produced with no scale effects are produced in "cities" of minimal size. Then in the model, farms simply become another type of "city"—ones of minimal size. However, farm production can in fact have significant economies of scale to at least firm size. Then, to get rural areas we would need to consider land intensity and introduce land as an explicit factor of production. Although farm production may have scale economies, it has sufficiently high land usage, so that spatially there are not agglomerations of people (this is explicitly modeled in Henderson, 1974).

Examining the internal structure of a city, if consumers' taste parameter for housing b/f rises, if the land intensity of housing production β rises, or if spatial complexity parameter δ rises, efficient city sizes fall. All of these factors lead to greater increases in costs of living as a city's size expands. More land is utilized by consumers, which increases commuting distances, and commuting becomes more costly. Finally, if the productivity of infrastructure investments, γ, rises, efficient city sizes rise since costs of living rise more slowly.

Basic variables have been solved for in terms of exogenous prices (r and q) facing cities. This is sufficient for partial equilibrium purposes of examining a single city and also for deriving many of the general equilibrium properties of the whole system of cities. However, for some general equilibrium properties it is necessary also to solve for economic variables in terms of a general equilibrium quantity variable, the aggregate capital-to-labor (K/N) usage in a city. Substituting into the full employment equations yields

$$r = qA(1 - \alpha) g(N) c_4^{-\alpha} k^{-\alpha} \qquad (2.16)$$

where k is the city's total capital-to-labor ratio, or usage, and

$$c_4 \equiv (1 - \alpha)(f + \gamma\beta b)/[f - b\beta(1 - \gamma) - \alpha(f - b)]$$

Note that in c_4, $f - b\beta(1 - \gamma) - \alpha(f - b) > 0$ given the definition of f. Since all other variables are functions of r, q, and N, they can be solved in terms of q, N, and k, by substituting for r. We note for later usage[9]

$$U_0 = E_1 \left(\prod_{j=1}^{n} q_j^{-a_j} \right) [qg(N)]^{f-b} (c_4 k)^{f-b\beta(1-\gamma)-\alpha(f-b)} N^{-b\beta(\delta-\gamma)} \qquad (2.17)$$

The properties of (2.17) are standard. For example, if we hold N fixed, increases in k, the capital-to-labor ratio, raise wages and utility because of basic marginal productivity effects.

2. Basic Properties of a System of Cities

2.1. General Equilibrium Properties

Using the relationships developed in Section 1, the characteristics of equilibrium in a system composed of n types of cities can be derived. We cite the equations and method of solution, but utilize also a somewhat independent intuitive interpretation of the solutions. To solve the model generally only requires imposing equilibrium in national markets. The national markets of concern are factor markets for labor and capital and output markets for the n traded goods, $X_1, \ldots, X_n$. Capital and labor are assumed for this chapter to be perfectly mobile and transport costs of trade are ignored. These assumptions are relaxed in later chapters.

At this point subscripting is introduced, where N_j, ϕ_j, α_j, w_j, q_j, etc., refer to values of parameters and variables for the jth type of city, specialized in the export production of X_j. The jth type of city is compared with the first type, where the price q_1 of the first traded good X_1 is chosen as the numeraire. That is, $q_1 = 1$. The parameters of housing and site production and all utility functions are the same across cities. Only the production sector differs. The following subsections represent the basic results.

Variations in sizes across city types. Variations in city sizes across types of cities are solved by examining the city size equation from Section 1 where city size, N_j, for the jth type of city is given by

$$N_j = \frac{\phi_i}{\alpha_j} \psi \qquad (2.15)$$

ψ in (2.15) is a parameter cluster common to all cities, and represents the non-traded good and urban infrastructure technology common to all cities. Thus comparing different types of cities, N_j is a linear function of ϕ_j/α_j, where $\partial N/\partial \phi >$

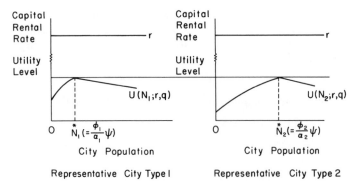

Fig. 2.4 The System in Equilibrium

0, $\partial N/\partial \alpha < 0$. ϕ_j represents the magnitude of industry level economies of scale (localization economies) for the jth traded good and hence jth type of city. City sizes increase with the degree of scale economies present, which indicates a city's ability to pay higher wages for a given capital rental. Sizes also increase with capital intensity in production where the factor share parameters $(1 - \alpha_j)$ represent capital intensity and α_j labor intensity. Increased capital intensity means that a city can support a given wage–capital rental ratio with less population and a lower cost of living. As noted in Section 1, as $\phi/\alpha \to 0$, city size becomes negligible. Goods with low levels of scale (ϕ) can be thought of as being rural or agricultural products, where the "city" becomes a family farm or small village. That is, there is nothing in the model that limits the inclusion of an agricultural sector, defined as the smallest type of "city."

Under the specification in this book, equilibrium city size for any type of city is a function of parameters and is invariant with respect to variations in capital-labor endowments or factor prices. Equilibrium city sizes only vary across types of cities as ϕ_j/α_j varies, with the largest types being those with large-scale economies and/or high-capital intensities and the smallest (farms) being those with low-scale economies and/or low-capital intensities. The size distribution of cities in an economy, as examined later in this chapter and in Chapter 3, only changes with changes in technology altering ψ, ϕ, or α, or with changes in the composition of national output altering the relative numbers of each type of city.

Note large and small types of cities coexist in equilibrium, both having the same net efficiency—offering the same capital rentals and utility levels. Although larger cities have greater scale effects in traded good production, they also have greater diseconomies in commuting and the nontraded good sector, which are offsetting.

Variations in prices across city types. To solve for the other properties of a system of cities, equilibrium in national labor, capital, and output markets is imposed. The concern is to solve for the ways wages, nontraded good prices or "costs-of-living," and capital usages vary across types and sizes of cities. As an intermediate step in solving for these relationships, labor market equilibrium gives a relationship between capital rentals and relative traded goods prices. Between any pairs of cities, laborers must be equally well off so that they do not move. Therefore, $U_j = U_1$. This is illustrated in Figure 2.4, for representative type 1

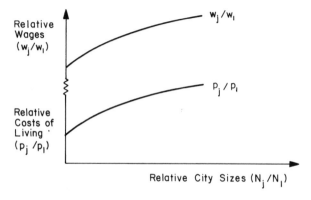

Fig. 2.5 Local Price Comparisons in General Equilibrium

and j cities. The larger type of city is arbitrarily made to be j. Given equalized utility levels and solving for q_j in (2.12) the usual general equilibrium relationship between output and capital rental prices follows

$$q_j^{1/\alpha_j}/q_1^{1/\alpha_1} \equiv q_j^{1/\alpha_j} = (Z_1/Z_j)r^{(\alpha_1-\alpha_j)/(\alpha_1\alpha_j)} \tag{2.18}$$

where

$$Z_i \equiv c_0^{-1/\alpha_i}g_i(N_i)^{1/\alpha_i}N_i^{-1/\psi}$$

Equation 2.18 states that an increase in the capital rental rate raises the relative price of the relatively capital intensive good. Thus, if X_j is more capital intensive than X_1 $(1 - \alpha_j > 1 - \alpha_1,$ or $\alpha_1 - \alpha_j > 0)$, q_j/q_1 rises as r rises. q_j/q_1 falls if capital intensities are reversed.

Equation 2.18 is then used to solve for the variations in wages and costs of living across city types. For wages, the key is the ratio of wages, w_j/w_1, in the jth to the first type of city. Forming the ratio w_j/w_1 using equation 2.4 and then substituting in (2.18) yields

$$w_j/w_1 = (N_j/N_1)^{1/\psi} \tag{2.19}$$

Similarly the key for costs of living is the ratio of housing, or nontraded good, prices, p_j/p_1, in the jth to the first type of city. Forming the ratio of p_j/p_1 from (2.9) after substituting in (2.10) for $\hat{K}_2$, and then substituting in (2.18) yields

$$p_j/p_1 = (N_j/N_1)^{1/\psi} \tag{2.20}$$

Given the exponent $\psi > 0$, equations 2.19 and 2.20 unambiguously state that in comparing different types of cities both wages and housing prices, or costs of living are *greater* as the sizes of cities rise across city types, for *equal utility levels* across cities. The point of course is intuitive and is illustrated in Figure 2.5. Wages and costs of living rise with city size because, respectively, scale economy benefits are greater and commuting distances and the corresponding housing costs are greater. To maintain equal utility across cities, in the absence of other considerations, they must each rise by the same percentage, as city size increases, so as to offset each other. The fact that wages and costs of living rise with city size is documented empirically in Chapter 6.

Variations in capital usage. Hochman (1977) pointed out that in solving for trade patterns internal and external to a country it is important to note how capital usage varies across city types. k_i is defined as K_i/N_i, or the ratio of *total* capital to total employment in a city of type i. The ratio of relative capital usage in the jth type of city (k_j) to relative capital usage in the first type of city (k_1) is examined. To solve for the way capital usage varies across types of cities, we use national capital market equilibrium conditions to solve for the ratio k_j/k_1. From national capital market equilibrium, capital rental rates are equalized across types of cities, or $r_j = r_1$, as in Figure 2.4. Equating r_j and r_1 in equation 2.16 and substituting for c_4 from (2.16) and q_j from (2.18) yields

$$\frac{k_j}{k_1} = \left[\frac{\alpha_1[f - b\beta(1 - \gamma) - \alpha_j(f - b)]}{\alpha_j[f - b\beta(1 - \gamma) - \alpha_1(f - b)]} \right] \left[\frac{N_j}{N_1} \right]^{1/\psi} \qquad (2.21)$$

From equation 2.15 relative city sizes are a function of scale and capital intensity parameters. By straight differentiation after substituting in (2.15), it can be shown that

$$\partial(k_j/k_1)/\partial\alpha_j < 0 \qquad \text{and} \qquad \partial(k_j/k_1)/\partial\phi_j > 0$$

The j type of city's capital usage increases relative to type 1 cities as its degree of scale economies and capital intensity in export production increase. That is, for $\phi_j = \phi_1[\alpha_j = \alpha_1]$, $k_j > k_1$ if $\alpha_j < \alpha_1[\phi_j > \phi_1]$. However, in equation 2.21 neither $\alpha_j < \alpha_1$ nor $N_j > N_1$ alone necessarily imply $k_j > k_1$. That is, in theory, relatively labor intensive export goods $(\alpha_j > \alpha_1)$ can be produced in high capital usage cities where $k_j > k_1$.

In this technical discussion a distinction is made between the overall capital usage of a city (including capital usage in housing and social overhead capital) and capital intensity in the production of the city's good. This distinction is critical. A labor intensive good can be produced in a high capital usage city if it has a sufficiently high degree of scale economies, so that it is produced in a very large type of city using lots of capital in urban infrastructure and housing, given congestion effects. Large types of cities have high capital usages in the nontraded good sectors so as to conserve on labor given their higher wage costs. Similarly, a capital intensive good can be produced in a high labor usage city if it is produced in a very small type of city. A sufficient condition for the type j city to have relatively high capital usage $(k_j > k_1)$ is that both X_j be relatively capital intensive $(\alpha_j < \alpha_1)$ and the jth type city be larger $(\phi_j / \alpha_j > \phi_1/\alpha_1)$.

Apart from increasing the understanding of the determinants of relative capital usages in different types of cities. this distinction between overall capital usage vs. traded good capital intensity for any type of city imposes critical restrictions on relative parameter values. In particular, in a two type of city model utilized in presenting international trade theorems, stability of equilibrium for an open economy requires that capital intensive goods be produced in high capital usage cities. That is, stability requires that $k_2 > k_1$ if $\alpha_2 < \alpha_1$. Hicksian static stability conditions also require this. These statements are proved in Chapter 4, but that result is also invoked in a comparative statics exercise in Section 3 of this chapter. Moving from a two type of city model to the more general n type, the restrictions can be loosened. However, a sufficient condition for, say, Hicksian static stability is that $k_j > k_1$ when $\alpha_j < \alpha_i$, $\forall i,j$, $i \neq j$.

In summary, while in theory labor intensive export goods can be produced in

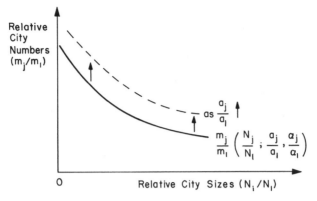

Fig. 2.6 The Determinants of the Size Distribution of Cities

high capital usage cities, in practice it will be assumed that scale and capital intensity parameters are paired such that $k_j > k_i$ if $\alpha_j < \alpha_i$. That is, relatively capital intensive goods are always produced in relatively high capital usage cities.

2.2. The Numbers and Size Distribution of Cities in a Closed Economy

This subsection solves for the ratio of numbers of each type of city. These ratios will give the size distribution of cities and the results will explain the determinants of the size distribution. Since size distributions in developing countries are increasingly a focus of national government policy, understanding their determinants is critical.

To solve for the ratio of numbers of each type of city, denoted by m_j, national demand and supply for each type of good are equated. National supply is $m_j X_j$. National demand, provided that all people have the same logarithmic linear utility functions, is $(a_j/f)Iq_j^{-1}$, where I is national income net of local taxes. Thus for any two types of cities

$$m_j X_j/(m_1 X_1) = (a_j/a_1)q_j^{-1}$$

or substituting in (2.13) for X_j and X_1 and then (2.18) for q_j

$$\frac{m_j}{m_1} = \frac{a_j \alpha_j}{a_1 \alpha_1} \left(\frac{N_j}{N_1}\right)^{-1-(1/\psi)}$$

$$= \frac{a_j \alpha_j}{a_1 \alpha_1} \left(\frac{\alpha_j/\phi_j}{\alpha_1/\phi_1}\right)^{-1-(1/\psi)} \tag{2.22}$$

The relative numbers of jth to first type cities are determined by their relative shares in consumer budgets (a_j/a_1), relative labor intensities (α_j/α_1), and relative degrees of scale economies (ϕ_j/ϕ_1). m_j/m_1 increases as a_j/a_1 (relative demand for X_j) increases. m_j/m_1 declines as N_j/N_1 increases, or from (2.15) as α_j/α_1 declines or ϕ_j/ϕ_1 increases. The later result simply indicates that, as N_j/N_1 increases, the same relative amount of X_j to X_1 would be produced in relatively fewer j type cities of larger sizes. This is illustrated in Figure 2.6.

It should be noted that the derivation of equation 2.22 and indeed (2.15) for city size assumes there is a large economy so there are no "lumpiness" problems. This means there are so many cities of each type that when the economy is divided into an *integer* number of cities of given equilibrium sizes, there is no effective problem with remainders. In particular, equation 2.26 does not constrain m_i's to be integers, but they must be to satisfy (2.15) and the treatment of N_i's as constants in all derivations. In general, $m_i = \hat{m}_i + h_i$ where $\hat{m}_i$ is an integer and $0 \leq h_i < 1$. The h_i is ignored, by taking the remainder population $h_i \times N_i$ for city type i and dividing it among the $\hat{m}_i$ cities. Then equilibrium city size equals $N_i(1 + h_i/\hat{m}_i)$. As $\hat{m}_i \to \infty$, equilibrium city size for type i approaches N_i. This is the large economy assumption. In Chapter 4, small economies are examined.

In summary, from equation 2.28 it should be clear that the sizes and numbers of each type of city reflect underlying demand and supply conditions in the economy. *Moreover, any regularities in the patterns of cities and their size of distribution imply very specific demand and supply conditions.*

Regularities in size distributions. For those versed in the traditional hierarchy models of cities it is useful to explain the implications of the results in that context. In particular, location and regional specialists often assert two empirical and quasi-theoretical regularities in the size distribution of cities. It is instructive to note these and explore their implications in one illustrative context. The point is to illustrate the direct link between demand and supply patterns in national output and spatial patterns of cities, not to champion the existence of these regularities.

The two asserted regularities are the geometric series rule and the rank size rule. For the former the different types of cities are indexed so that $N_1 > N_2 > \ldots > N_n$. Given this ranking the rule is that the numbers of cities by size and type form a geometric series where, for some parameter θ,

$$m_j = m_1(\theta)^{j-1} \qquad \theta > 1$$

The rank size rule states that if all cities in the economy are ranked so that the largest is ranked 1 and the sth largest s, and rank multiplied by population for each city, the multiple is the same number (equals the population of the largest city) for all cities in the economy. Since the rule applies to a continuum of cities, whereas a system of cities implies discrete groupings, the following interpretation is usually utilized (Beckmann, 1958) and is adapted to the present model. Suppose there are other, as yet, unspecified effects on city sizes so that cities of each type are distributed about the predicted population N_j in equation 2.15) when the predicted N_j is the population of the median city of that type, $N_{j\hat{m}}$. (Chapter 4 gives an example of such a situation.) The rank size rule, as applied to these median cities of each type, is what is considered here. The rank of city size $N_{j\hat{m}}$ is $R(N_{j\hat{m}})$, where $R(N_{j\hat{m}}) = \sum_{i=1}^{j} m_i - 1/2m_j$. The rank size rule implies that $R(N_{j\hat{m}})N_{j\hat{m}} = R(N_{i\hat{m}})N_{i\hat{m}}$ all i,j.

Suppose both rules are imposed and assume $1/\psi \to 0$ so that

$$m_j \approx m_1 \left(\frac{a_j}{a_1}\right)\left(\frac{\alpha_j}{\alpha_1}\right)^2 \frac{\phi_1}{\phi_j}$$

where $1/\psi = b\beta(\gamma - \delta)/[f - b\beta(1 - \gamma)]$ must be small (say, under 0.01 if coefficients are to take on expected values such as $b/f = 0.2$, $\beta = 0.1$ and, $(\gamma - \delta) < 0.5$. Then, combining rules yields

$$(\phi_j/\alpha_j) = (\phi_1/\alpha_1)\left[\frac{\theta - 1}{\theta^j + \theta^{j-1} - 2}\right]$$

$$a_j\alpha_j = (a_1\alpha_1)\left[\frac{1 - \theta^{-1}}{1 + \theta^{-1} - 2\theta^{-\gamma}}\right]$$

ϕ_j/α_j and $a_j\alpha_j$ are decreasing fractions of, respectively, ϕ_1/α_1 and $a_1\alpha_1$ as the hierarchy is descended.

Given these rules, econometric information on a few parameters places strong restrictions on the values of other parameters. This is illustrated by drawing from empirical work done on Saskatchewan, Canada. Schaeffer's (1977) work on Saskatchewan suggests that α_j declines rapidly moving from, say, 0.95 to 0.80 to 0.43 from the largest to the next largest to the smallest (seventh ranked) centers, reflecting perhaps increasing capital intensity as ranks move from service to manufacturing to extract centers. Suppose $\phi_1 = 100$, which is consistent with results in Chapter 5. Given these movements in α_j, given $(\phi/\alpha) = 0.105$, and given θ would equal 2 from Berry (1968) for Saskatchewan, the first equation gives the remaining values of ϕ_j's, which by the seventh rank city is very small (0.24). The second equation implies that the a_j change very little, with the ratio of a_2/a_1 being 0.59 and of a_7/a_1 being 0.55. Thus, given information only on the α_j's and ϕ_1, the empirical regularities in the size distribution of cities yield values of the remaining ϕ_j and all a_j/a_1. Note that the a_j's here are shares in the value of regional output, not local demand parameters per se, since Saskatchewan is an open economy rather than a closed one.

In summary, regardless of whether the particular parametric values are accurate or not, empirical phenomena such as the rank size rule and the geometric series rule governing the numbers of each type of city convey information about how underlying demand and supply parameters must vary across types of cities. The size distribution of cities is not an accident of nature but is directly linked to the regional composition of output and production conditions.

3. The Impact of a Shift in the Demand for Urban Exports

This section conducts an illustrative comparative statics exercise. Many more such exercises will be conducted in the chapters on international trade and on government policy. This section sets up the methodology for conducting such exercises. To simplify, assume there are only two types of cities in the economy, steel cities producing X_1 and textile cities producing X_2. Suppose there is a change in national tastes so that there is an increase in relative demand for steel products. Specifically, assume a_1 rises and a_2 falls such that $\Delta a_1 = -\Delta a_2$ and hence $f = b + \Sigma_i a_i$ and ψ are unchanged. From (2.15), then, the change in tastes has no impact on equilibrium city sizes, since in (2.15) α_j, ϕ_j, and ψ are all unchanged. However, the change will alter the composition of national output, the size distribution of cities, and relative factor returns.

To conduct the exercise it must be specified which good is capital intensive. Assume steel production is relatively capital intensive so that $\alpha_1 < \alpha_2$ or $1 - \alpha_1 > 1 - \alpha_2$. To avoid problems of unstable solutions, also assume that $\phi_1/\alpha_1 > \phi_2/\alpha_2$ or, from (2.15), that $N_1 > N_2$. Thus steel type cities are larger than textile type cities. This ensures that $k_1 > k_2$ given $\alpha_1 < \alpha_2$, or that steel type cities have

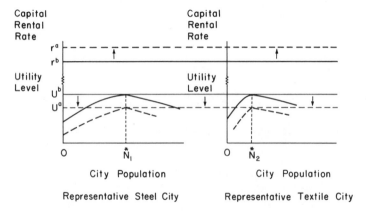

Fig. 2.7 Impact of National Demand Changes

overall a greater capital usage, as well as producing the capital intensive export good.

The starting point is an equilibrium (Figure 2.7). Figure 2.7 presents the situations in representative steel and textile type cities, each of equilibrium size N_1 and N_2. Utility levels are equalized across cities at U^b and capital rentals are equalized across cities at r^b.

The quantity side of equilibrium in national markets is not represented in Figure 2.7. First, there is full employment in national factor markets, so that labor and capital employment in all X_1 and X_2 cities sum up to national endowments, or

$$m_1 N_1 + m_2 N_2 = N$$

$$m_2 K_1 + m_2 K_2 = K$$

Combining these yields

$$\frac{m_1}{m_2} = \left(\frac{N_2}{N_1}\right)(k_2 - \hat{k})(\hat{k} - k_1)^{-1} \qquad (2.23)$$

where $\hat{k} \equiv K/N$, the national capital-to-labor ratio. Equilibrium in national output markets has already been described in equation 2.22 where for reference

$$\frac{m_1}{m_2} = \left(\frac{a_1}{a_2}\right)\left(\frac{\alpha_1}{\alpha_2}\right)\left(\frac{N_1}{N_2}\right)^{-1-(1/\psi)}$$

We can proceed now to the results. First, on the quantity side, from (2.22), if a_1/a_2 rises for (α_1/α_2) and (N_1/N_2) unchanged, m_1/m_2 must rise. This was illustrated in Figure 2.6. There is a rise in the number of steel type cities relative to textile type cities, as demand shifts toward steel type cities in a closed economy. This implies that the size distribution of cities is altered toward greater "urban concentration," or the ratio of large to smaller size cities rises. It also implies the total number of cities in the economy falls since the average city size increases. That is, some former textile cities switch to steel production and some others disappear.

Second, by differentiating (2.21), any change in national output changes urban factor usages such that

$$\frac{dk_1}{k_1} = \frac{dk_2}{k_2}$$

That is, as in any two sector general equilibrium model, factor usages rise and fall together. Then differentiating (2.23) and employing this result yields

$$\frac{d(m_1/m_2)}{m_1/m_2} = -(\hat{k} - k_2)dk_2 - (k_1 - \hat{k})dk_1$$

$$= -\left[(\hat{k} - k_2)\underset{(+)}{\left(\frac{k_2}{k_1}\right)} + (k_1 - \hat{k})\underset{(+)}{} \right]dk_1 > 0$$

(2.24)

From (2.23) the change in a_1/a_2 increases m_1/m_2 so that $d(m_1/m_2) > 0$ in (2.24). Given the assumptions about capital intensities and usages, $k_1 > \hat{k} > k_2$, or $\hat{k} - k_2$, $k_1 - \hat{k} > 0$. Then, given $d(m_1/m_2) > 0$, dk_1, $dk_2 < 0$. That is, to maintain national full employment, as the output of the capital intensive good expands by absorbing factors from the labor intensive sectors, the use of capital to labor in both sectors declines. This is a standard two sector general equilibrium result. It also tells what happens to relative factor rewards.

The usual two sector general equilibrium result is that as output of the capital intensive good expands, the return to that factor, capital, rises relative to the return to labor. This is the case here also. If we treat steel as the numeraire so that $q_1 = 1$ from equation 2.16, for capital rentals the fall in k_1 induces a rise in r. Since capital rentals are equalized across types of cities, in the new equilibrium r rises from r^b to r^a, for example, in Figure 2.7. What about utility levels?

Considering the change in tastes it is difficult to evaluate a change in utility levels per se, allowing that there has been a reordering of preferences. However, some useful statements are possible. First, there is a negative income effect on utility. Corresponding to the rise in capital rentals is a fall in wage income in both cities. For example, in equation (f) in note 9 for type 1 cities, as k_1 falls, so does w_1. Hence from (2.19) w_2 must also fall, given $dw_1/w_1 = dw_2/w_2$. In combining income and cost-of-living effects, we note that this fall in wages and rise in capital rentals also has a net negative effect on utility. This effect occurs, even though q_2 falls, because the cost of labor has fallen, which reduces the relative price of the labor intensive good. In summary, utility levels in national markets suffer in terms of income and price effects, as production shifts away from the labor intensive sector, or type of cities.[10] In Figure 2.7 utility in net is shown as falling from U^b to U^a in the national labor market to emphasize these negative income and price effects.

In conclusion, the change in tastes toward steel products increases the relative (and absolute) numbers of steel cities so as to affect the demanded increase in steel output. Although individual steel or textile cities are unchanged in size, the number of large cities in relation to small cities increases. In fact, this would not only imply that some textile cities change to steel production, but that some (presumably textile) cities disappear. That is, the increase in urban concentration implies that the economy population can be housed in a smaller number of cities overall, because of the increase in larger type cities.

Finally, given the assumptions about relative capital intensities, the shift toward

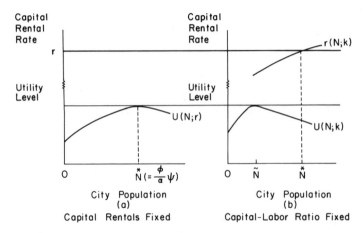

Fig. 2.8   Representation of Partial and General Equilibrium for a Representative City

capital intensive production enhances the return to capital. For labor, in terms of income and price effects, it lowers their net return, or utility.

4. City Size and the Welfare of Capital Owners and Laborers

The purpose of this section is threefold. First, it will show that capital owners and laborers have different city sizes in a general equilibrium context that are best for them. Second, it will solve again for equilibrium city size (with the same result) under different assumptions about the perceptions and information possessed by developers—the entrepreneurial agents who set up new cities. Finally, it will demonstate that equilibrium sizes are Pareto efficient. In accomplishing these purposes the solutions for city characteristics are recast in general equilibrium terms, using equations 2.16 and 2.17 where price and quantity equations for a single city are expressed in terms of capital-to-labor ratios.

For simplicity in illustrating all three points, we have assumed an economy composed of only one type of city. The extension to multiple types is in Henderson (1972, 1974).

In Section 2, in solving for city size, it is assumed that all economic agents, including developers, perceive that the price of capital is fixed to the city, and that they set city sizes to maximize the utility of laborers. Of course, in a general equilibrium context the price of capital varies with the equilibrium sizes of cities. The general equilibrium constraint is full employment. In a single type of city model where in equilibrium cities must be identical (Henderson 1972, 1974), this constraint is that each city faces a fixed capital-to-labor ratio.

Suppose competitive land developers adjust city sizes to maximize profits, seeing a fixed capital-to-labor ratio, not a fixed price of capital, as the effective constraint. Apart from the (un)desirability of this change in perceptions, resolving for city size will point out the conflict between laborers and capital owners in setting city sizes and the Pareto-efficient resolution of that conflict. Equilibrium city size from Section 2 is illustrated in Figure 2.8a, where N is set to maximize utility subject to fixed capital rentals. Suppose utility and capital rental paths are retraced so that a city's capital-labor ratio k is fixed. k with one type of city and identical cities in equilibrium is the national capital-labor ratio. From equation 2.16, capital rentals rise indefinitely with city size. From equation 2.17, utility rises, peaks at $\hat{N}$, and declines.

$$\hat{N} = \frac{\phi(f - b)}{b\beta(\delta - \gamma)} < N = \frac{\phi}{\alpha}\left[\frac{f - b\beta(1 - \gamma)}{b\beta(\delta - \gamma)}\right]$$

These new paths for any city for k held fixed are illustrated in Figure 2.8b.

With no income redistribution, clearly laborers would be better off if city sizes were less than equilibrium ones, $\overset{*}{N}$, while capital owners would prefer cities that were as large as possible. Capital owners do not have to live in the city where their capital is employed or in any city at all. They thus do not experience the rise in living costs and disamenities when city sizes increase. They only experience the rise in capital rentals. Laborers would prefer smaller cities because they must experience the disamenities of larger cities.

Given a perception that k, not r, is fixed the *competitive* solution to city sizes is as follows. If sizes extend beyond $\hat{N}$ in Figure 2.8b, laborers lose and capital owners gain. Initially the gains to capital owners exceed the losses to laborers, so that profit maximizing developers gain by increasing types beyond $\hat{N}$. That is, they can hire laborers and capital at existing factor rewards, for instance at $\hat{N}$, and have a surplus left at a size beyond $\hat{N}$. Competition dissipates the surpluses and adjusts factor rewards. At some point beyond $\hat{N}$ the marginal gain to capital owners just equals the marginal loss to laborers and then beyond that point the marginal loss exceeds the gain. Profit maximizing city size occurs where the marginal gains and losses are equalized. Let us call this size $\overset{*}{N}$.

At $\overset{*}{N}$, by this criterion

$$K\frac{\partial r(k,N)}{\partial N} = -N\frac{\partial U(k,N)/\partial N}{\partial U(y,p)/\partial y}. \tag{2.25}$$

The left-hand side of (2.25) is the change in *total* capital rentals from increasing city sizes where $\partial r/\partial N$ is the partial derivative of equation 2.16. The right-hand side is the monetized change in total laborer's welfare. $\partial U/\partial N$ is the partial derivative of equation 2.17. $\partial U/\partial y$ is the marginal utility of income from equation 2.8, or fUy^{-1}. To evaluate (2.25), substitute into $\partial U/\partial y$ for y, then w, and then r to evaluate it in terms of k and N. Solving yields

$$\overset{*}{N} = \frac{\phi}{\alpha}\left[\frac{f - b\beta(1 - \gamma)}{b\beta(\delta - \gamma)}\right]$$

That is, $\overset{*}{N}$ equals N in equation 2.15. As long as there is competition, equilibrium city sizes are the same whether or not developers perceive that r or k are fixed.

Noncompetitive elements would enter if laborers (for example, through unions) banded together to advocate national legislation resulting in smaller city sizes. On the other hand, capital owners in countries where capital ownership is highly concentrated could focus investment in only a few cities, or advocate policies restricting the number of cities. While these generally seem far-fetched possibilities and may give unwarranted sophistication to economic agents, the conflicts exist and it is useful to recognize them.

Equation 2.25 and its solution (2.15) also point out that equilibrium city sizes are Pareto-efficient ones. Equation 2.25 defines a Pareto-efficiency criterion. In the model it is uniquely met at

$$N = \frac{\phi}{\alpha}\left[\frac{f - b\beta(1 - \gamma)}{b\beta(\delta - \gamma)}\right]$$

and that size is the only Pareto-efficient size. While there are externalities in traded good and land site production, these are effectively internalized at the aggregate of the city. This point is discussed in a full welfare maximization specification of the systems of cities problem in Chapter 9. As noted there, only if the economy is not "large" are there problems of Pareto-efficient solutions diverging from equilibrium ones.

5. Conclusions

The basic results of this chapter describe equilibrium in an economy composed of a system of cities.

1. Cities specialize in traded good production in an economy, so that there are different types of cities.

2. Different types of cities generally have different equilibrium sizes. This implies cities of different sizes coexist in the same economy. Larger cities are those specialized in the production of traded goods with greater scale economies or capital intensities. In net, smaller and larger cities have the same efficiency and offer the same net factor returns. Although large cities have greater scale effects, they have correspondingly greater diseconomies in the commuting and nontraded good sectors.

3. Wages and costs-of-living rise with equilibrium city size.

4. High capital usage cities need not house relatively capital intensive traded good production. For example, labor intensive goods can be produced in high overall capital usage cities, if they have very high scale economies and are housed in larger types of cities, which require relatively high capital usage in commuting and nontraded good production. However, if labor intensive production is located in high capital usage cities, stability of equilibrium may not hold. So generally the book assumes that higher capital usage cities house higher capital intensive traded good production.

5. The size distribution of cities is determined by the national composition of output. The numbers of any type of city increase as demand for its production increases, with unchanged equilibrium size for any city of that type. If this is the demand for a good produced in a large type of city, then there will be fewer smaller cities and fewer cities in total. The reverse is the case if it is a good produced in a smaller type of city.

NOTES

1. Note specialization can occur if scale economies are only ones of urbanization, since goods with different degrees of urbanization economies have different city sizes that are most efficient for their worker-residents.

2. Note for l, this implies $w = p_l l/\hat{N}_2$.

3. Where w, r, p_l, p, and q are, respectively, the local wage rate, the national capital rental rate, the local price of sites, the local price of housing, and the national price of the traded good.

$$q = c_0 w^\alpha r^{1-\alpha} g(N)^{-1} \tag{a}$$

$$p = c_1 p_l^\beta r^{1-\beta} \tag{b}$$

where c_0 and c_1 are defined in note 3.

$$c_0 \equiv A^{-1}\alpha^{-\alpha}(1-\alpha)^{\alpha-1} \quad \text{and} \quad c_1 \equiv B^{-1}\beta^{-\beta}(1-\beta)^{\beta-1}$$

4. For housing, for example, total city demand is

$$H = \frac{b}{f}(yN)p^{-1}, \qquad f \equiv \sum_{j=1}^{n} a_j + b \tag{c}$$

5.
$$c_2 \equiv D^{-\beta}c_1 c_0^{-\beta/\alpha}$$

$$\hat{N}_2 = (\beta b/f)w^{-1}Ny \tag{d}$$

$$\hat{K}_1 = [(1-\beta)b/f]Nyr^{-1} \tag{e}$$

6.
$$E_0 \equiv E[f/(f+\gamma\beta b)]^{f+\gamma\beta b}[\beta^\beta B(1-\beta)^{1-\beta}D^\beta(\gamma\beta b/f)^{\gamma\beta}]^b$$

7.
$$c_3 \equiv c_0^{-1/\alpha}\alpha^{-1}[f - b\beta(1-\gamma)](f+\gamma\beta b)^{-1}$$

8. Note that in deriving $\partial U/\partial N = 0$, it is equivalent either to assume we are choosing the optimal N for any $\hat{K}_2$ and then substituting for $\hat{K}_2$ (if necessary) from (2.14) or first to substitute for the optimal $\hat{K}_2$ as a function of r and N, as we have done, and then optimize.

9.
$$w = [qA\alpha c_4^{1-\alpha}]g(N)k^{1-\alpha} \tag{f}$$

$$X = c_5 Nk^{1-\alpha}g(N) \tag{g}$$

$$E_1 \equiv E_0 A^{f-b}\alpha^{[f-b\beta(1-\gamma)]}(1-\alpha)^{-b+\beta b(1-\gamma)}$$

and

$$c_5 \equiv Ac_4^{(1-\alpha)}[f - b\beta(1-\gamma)]/(f+\gamma\beta b)$$

10. Formally this may be seen by differentiating utility in type 1 cities and substituting in $dq_2/q_2 = (\alpha_1 - \alpha_2)\alpha_1^{-1}dr/r = -(\alpha_1 - \alpha_2)dk_1/k_1$ from (2.18) and (2.16), respectively, to show that

$$dU/U = [-a_2\, dq_2/q_2 + f - b\beta(1-\gamma) - \alpha_1(f - b)dk_1/k_1] - \log q_2\, da_2$$

$$= \underbrace{\{b[1 - \beta(1-\gamma)] + a_1(1-\alpha_1) + a_2(1-\alpha_2)\}}_{(+)}\underbrace{\frac{dk_1}{k_1}}_{(-)} - \log q_2\, da_2$$

Thus apart from the change in tastes $(-\log q_2\, da_2)$, the impact on utility levels from income and price effects is negative given that capital usage ratios fall. The change in tastes acts to increase the cardinal index of utility, given $da_2 < 0$.

CHAPTER 3

Growth, Technological Change, and Economic Development

In this chapter, the static model in Chapter 2, describing a system of cities at a point in time, is put in a dynamic context. First, the impact of economic growth through population growth on a system of cities is considered. Second, the impact of certain types of technological change, such as commuting technology, on the system of cities is discussed. Together population growth and technological change are critical to the understanding of how a system of cities evolves over time, which can be used in at least a casual interpretation of the evolution in the United States.

Then the chapter explicitly considers the related process of economic development and its impact on a system of cities. Economic development, economic growth, and technological change involve the same processes. In examining economic development per se, we shift the focus to government policies that are enacted supposedly to spur economic growth, and to the sources of technological change. For a system of cities, the sources of technological change can be critical.

1. Economic Growth and Technological Change

This section is divided into several parts. The first deals with traditional growth models adapted to a system of cities. The other parts give the interpretation of the results specific to a system of cities. Section 1.1 models the basic results for a one-sector growth model. In a system of cities this means that all cities are of the same type. Both growth and exogenous technological change are examined in Section 1.1. Section 1.2 extends the analysis to a two-sector growth model with two types of cities.

1.1. A One-Sector Growth Model

For a one-sector growth model, there is only one type of city. Thus only one "traded" good X is produced in the economy and its price is normalized at 1. Since all cities produce the same good, there is in a one sector model no trade across cities in a closed economy. X is simply potentially tradable. In a two-sector model, trade will occur across types of cities. The second impact of there being only one type of city is that national full employment of resources then requires that the capital-to-labor ratio, k, in each city equals the national capital-to-labor ratio, since all cities will be identical in temporary equilibrium at any instant.

Growth occurs by the national population growing at a typically exogenously given rate. In particular, national population at any instant is given by

$$N(t) \equiv \bar{N} = N_0 e^{nt} \tag{3.1}$$

where N_0 is the population in a base year (time $= 0$). What happens to the national capital stock as the population grows? That depends on savings and investment behavior. Additions to the nation's capital stock are made through investment, where in physical terms, units of X may be costlessly converted into units of K. Investment equals savings. The standard neoclassical growth theory assumption is adopted, in which all and only capital income is saved. This corresponds to the assumption made in Chapter 2 that no capital rentals are spent on consumption goods in cities. Growth gives a formal outlet for capital income.

To investigate the impact of growth on the national capital stock the national capital-to-labor ratio ($k \equiv \bar{K}/\bar{N}$) is differentiated and rearranged to get

$$\dot{k} = k(\dot{K}/\bar{K} - n) \tag{3.2}$$

$\dot{k} \equiv dk/dt$ and $\dot{K} \equiv d\bar{K}/dt$, which is the growth in national capital stock for t denoting time. $n \equiv (d\bar{N}/dt)/\bar{N}$ from equation 3.1 and is the exogenous rate of national population growth (plus, if one wants, an exogenous rate of depreciation on capital). $\dot{K}$ equals gross investment by definition, which equals savings by identity. Savings in turn by assumption equals national capital income, or $r\bar{K}$. The model is solved by inserting the solution for capital rentals, r, from the systems of cities model in Chapter 2, where from equation 2.16 $r = A(1 - \alpha)g(N)c_4^{-\alpha}k^{-\alpha}$. Substituting for r yields the basic equation of motion for a growing economy

$$\frac{\dot{k}}{k} = A(1 - \alpha)g(N)c_4^{-\alpha}k^{-\alpha} - n \tag{3.3}$$

In equation 3.3, N in $g(N)$ is equilibrium size for a representative city, which from equation 2.15 is a parametric constant $[(\phi/\alpha)\psi]$ unaffected by growth. At this point we have a textbook growth situation (Burmeister and Dobell, 1970).

In growth models the first concern is the examination of steady-state solutions. In a steady state the capital-to-labor ratio does not change as the population grows. That is, the rate of population growth in equation 3.2 exactly equals the rate of capital stock growth. Thus in a steady-state $\dot{k} = 0$ and from equation 3.3

$$\overset{*}{k} = (n^{-1}A(1 - \alpha)g(N)c_4^{-\alpha})^{1/\alpha} \tag{3.4}$$

This equilibrium exists, is unique, and is "stable."[1] For the last whatever the value of k is when a steady-state does not prevail, movements are always toward the steady-state point—the value of k for which $\dot{k} = 0$. If $k < \overset{*}{k}$, $\dot{k} > 0$, so that k is growing toward $\overset{*}{k}$; while if $k > \overset{*}{k}$, $\dot{k} < 0$ so that k is shrinking toward $\overset{*}{k}$.

In a steady state what are the values of the returns to capital and labor? They are solved for by substituting into the equations for capital rentals (r) and utility in Chapter 2. Substituting in equation 3.4 for $\overset{*}{k}$ into equations 2.16 and 2.17 yields

$$r^* = n, \tag{3.5}$$

$$U^* = E_2 g(N)^{f-b\beta(1-\gamma)/\alpha} N^{-b\beta(\delta-\gamma)} \cdot n^{-[f-b\beta(1-\gamma)-\alpha(f-b)]/\alpha} \tag{3.6}$$

As always in this type of model, the steady-state return on capital equals the population growth rate n, independent of the technological parameters of the model. Increases in n raise r^* but lower U^* where from equation 2.16 the exponent of n in (3.6) must be negative. Thus a faster population growth rate from (3.4) lowers the steady-state capital-to-labor ratio. This in turn increases the return to capital and lowers the return to labor due to basic marginal productivity effects.

Results for a system of cities. Implicit in standard formulations of growth models is the notion that at a national level there are constant returns to scale. For example, in the steady state, national population and capital stock are growing at the same rate. Then output also grows at that rate, with unchanged returns to factors. In essence, the economy simply replicates itself.

Although in a system of cities there are local nonconstant returns to scale, at the aggregate level of the city there is one equilibrium size for cities. Growth then involves formation of new cities and new cities are simply replicas of old ones. That is, there are national constant returns to scale and an economy grows through new city formation. To move from this conclusion would require introducing nonconstant returns to scale, or Richardian influences, at a national level. That is done in Chapter 4.

Specifically in the systems of cities model, city size is a parameter $N = \psi(\phi/\alpha)$, which is invariant to economic growth and in which N was treated as a parameter in deriving the growth equations above. Growth then can only involve growth in the number of cities. The number of cities m is $\bar{N}/N$ where N is the individual city size and $\bar{N}$ the national population. Differentiating

$$\frac{\dot{m}}{m} = n \tag{3.7}$$

The number of cities grows at a rate $(\dot{m}/m)$ equal to the population growth rate.

This result in the one sector growth model holds in a steady-state or not. Equilibrium city size N is independent of the national capital-to-labor ratio and differentiating $m = \bar{N}/N$ involves no considerations of whether a steady state pertains. However, in some formulations of systems of cities models (Henderson, 1974, 1977, 1978) equilibrium city size also depends on the capital-to-labor ratio. Then (3.7) only holds in a steady state. Second, in a multiple sector growth model the numbers of cities of each type adjust relative to each other outside the steady-state, so (3.7) again only holds in the steady-state. This is illustrated later in this chapter. Solving equation 3.7 the number of cities at any instant t equals Ae^{nt}. Combining $m = \bar{N}/N$ and equation 1 yields the constant of integration, $A = N_0/N$, or the base year population divided by equilibrium city size. In summary,

$$m(t) = (N_0/N)e^{nt} \tag{3.8}$$

Technological change. Here we focus on technological change that directly affects equilibrium city size. Thus technological change must alter one of the parameters in $\psi(\phi/\alpha)$. The change of particular interest is technological change in the commuting, or land site production sector. This is of interest because the urban transportation revolution over the last century has altered cities dramatically. First,

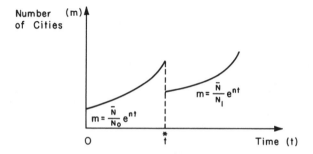

Fig. 3.1 Impact of Growth and Technological Change on the Number of Cities

the theoretical impacts of technological change on city sizes and welfare of residents are examined under different assumptions about the adjustment process. Then some casual evidence for the United States of the impacts of technological change on city sizes is presented.

Changes in the commuting sector in the model involve the "land" site sector. Recall from Chapter 2 that land sites, l, are produced with commuting time or labor inputs $\hat{N}_2$ and with public capital inputs $\hat{K}_2$, according to the production function $l = (DN^{-\delta}\hat{K}_2^{\gamma})\hat{N}_2$. Technological change in the commuting sector could be represented by an increase in γ, the exponent of public sector transport investment, or a change in the production shift factor caused by a decrease in $|-\delta|$, the exponent of city population. The shift factor $DN^{-\delta}$ represents spatial complexity where with individual city growth, people on the expanding city edge spend more and more time commuting—that is, a doubling of commuting times and population less than doubles the amount of land "claimed" by the city.

From equation 2.15, where equilibrium city size $N = (\phi/\alpha)[f - b\beta(1 - \gamma)]/[\beta b(\delta - \gamma)]$, an increase in γ or a decrease in $|-\delta|$ leads to an instantaneous increase in equilibrium city size. What is the impact of technological change in a growth context? For a change in δ or γ, there are immediate and steady-state impacts. The immediate impact of a rise in γ or a fall in δ is to increase all city sizes instantaneously and permanently. This implies in the short run that the number of cities must decline. That is, in equation 3.8 the constant term $\bar{N}/N$ experiences a discrete one time drop at, say, time $\overset{*}{t}$ of the technological change. Then growth in the number of cities resumes at the same rate n, starting from the new (lower) base at $\overset{*}{t}$. This is illustrated in Figure 3.1, where N_0 is the pretechnological change city size and N_1 is the posttechnological change size.

Technological change also impacts prices and the capital-to-labor ratio. The change in δ or γ alter r, U, and savings, starting the economy on a path toward a new steady-state equilibrium. We note that, for example, decreases in δ imply at that instant for the *current* k that r temporarily increases and $k > 0$ from the original steady state and, hence, that k^* increases. However, in the new steady state from equation 3.5 capital rentals are unchanged, but from (3.6) U has increased.[2] The steady-state beneficiaries of improvements in commuting technology are the laborers who work and live in cities—an appealing result.

It is useful to briefly comment on the adjustment to the steady state when δ changes. The adjustments from (3.3) involve Bernoulli equations of the form, for k, for example,

$$k(t) = k(\infty)\left[1 - \left(1 - \frac{N_0}{N_1}\right)e^{-n\alpha t}\right]^{1/\alpha}$$

where $k(\infty)$ is the new steady-state (higher) value of $\overset{*}{k}$ and N_0 and N_1 are, respectively, city sizes before and after technological change. Without depreciation of capital, adjustment times to cover, say, 80% of the gap between $k(0)$ and $k(\infty)$ are inordinately long. However, the introduction of depreciation as pointed out by Sato (1966) decreases adjustment times dramatically.

Adjustment to the steady state becomes more interesting when realistic complications are introduced. In particular, suppose that, unlike other capital such as machines, public capital K_2 is immobile and nonmalleable, so that it cannot be moved nor converted to other uses. Unanticipated technological change means that in the immediate process of the sizes of all remaining cities increasing and some cities "disappearing," public capital stocks will be abandoned in vacated towns. In the surviving towns that are now larger in size, the optimal public investment criterion is not met, or $\partial U / \partial \hat{K}_2 > 0$, given that private capital cannot be converted into needed increased public investment in these larger towns. In the adjustment to a new steady state, investment is initially concentrated in public transport investment, as the surviving cities adjust to an equilibrium where optimal investment and city size criteria are simultaneously satisfied, or $\partial U / \partial \hat{K}_2 = 0$ and $\partial U / \partial N = 0$. Then growth and investment are concentrated in reclaiming "ghost" towns.

There is an important contractual issue that arises with abandonment and then reclamation of public capital stocks. In vacated towns, "bankruptcy" must occur where capital owners (for example, bondholders in a financial setting) cannot collect rent on their immobile holdings of public capital. Capital owners of these abandoned towns could offer their towns at low charges for public capital to residents of occupied towns to attract residents. This competitive process would force *all* public capital rentals to zero (in the absence of quality distinctions across towns as in Chapter 4). To avoid this possibility there must be an institutional environment (Henderson and Ioannides, 1981) where (1) rents on (immobile) public capital are legislated (say, either equal to market rents or nominally fixed), (2) public capital may not be used unless rent is paid on it, and (3) rents must be restarted and paid on reclaimed public capital.

Why this focus on technological change in commuting? Over the past century, the United States has experienced significant increases in urban concentration, especially in the periods 1890–1930 and 1950–1970. This fact is noted in Table 3.1 focusing separately on the periods 1890–1930 and 1950–1970. Increases in urban concentrations are reflected by declines in the fraction of the urban population living in smaller cities and increases in the fraction living in larger cities. The pre-1940 and post-1940 figures are not comparable since they are based on different definitions of cities, the first on the political–geographic unit and the second on the urbanized area surrounding a major political unit. It is tempting to correlate these two periods of increases in urban concentration with the three major revolutions in urban commuting technology noted in Table 3.2—(a) the development of rapid transit at the turn of the century, (b) the development of the auto after World War I, and (c) the development of modern highways and higher performance autos during the 1950s. Of course, the national composition of output and the nature of production technology also changed during these periods, as

Table 3.1. U.S. Urbanization Trends

Percentage of urban population	1880	1890	1900	1930	1940	1950	1960	1970
In places 2500 to 50,000	49	47	47	37	39			
In places over 249,999	31	32	36	42	41			
In urbanized areas over 1 million						39	41	47
Places under 50,000 *outside* urbanized areas						29	24	22

Source: Historical Statistics, U.S. Bureau of the Census (1976).

noted in Chapter 1, which could account for the increase in urban concentration particularly in the more recent period. However, given the theoretical hypothesis that commuting technology strongly impacts city size, correlating Tables 3.1 and 3.2 suggests an empirical hypothesis to be tested rigorously.

1.2. A Two-Sector Growth Model

In this section a model with two types of cities is introduced to show that the basic results are unchanged. The technical exposition is briefly stated since it follows the standard literature. However, the analysis of technological change with immobile capital has an interesting twist. As before, we start with the technical statement of a standard two sector growth model and then turn to the results

Table 3.2. U.S. Changes in Urban Transportation

(a)	1890	1902	1912	1922
Electric rail passengers (millions/years)	2023	4774	9549	12667
Miles of line	5783	16645	30438	31264
(b)	1900	1910	1920	1930
Total auto registrations (thousands)	8	77	2332	8131
Auto registration per household	—	—	0.10	0.27
(c)	1950	1960	1970	
Average speed on highways	49	54	61	
Percentage of vehicles exceeding 55 mph on highways	20	37	68	

Source: Historical Statistics, U.S. Bureau of the Census (1976).

of interest here on city size distributions and numbers as they are affected by growth and technological change.

Technical exposition and assumptions. In a two-sector growth model there are two types of cities—one type specializes in the production of an export good and the other type in the production of the investment good. This adapts the traditional two-sector growth model. It is assumed the investment good is X_1, which is produced in m_1 cities of size N_1 and priced at $q_1 = 1$. The consumption good is X_2, which is produced in m_2 cities of size N_2 and priced at q_2. In examining the motion of the economy, the focus is on the national capital-to-labor ratio where $\dot{k} = k(\dot{K}/\bar{K} - n)$. $\dot{K} = m_1 X_1$ by the definition of investment goods. Second, as before, all and only capital income is saved, or savings equal $r(m_1 K_1 + m_2 K_2)$. Given these assumptions, the equation of motion after a variety of substitutions becomes[3]

$$\dot{k} = c_8 k^{1-\alpha_1} - nk \tag{3.9}$$

Therefore, in a steady state where $\dot{k} = 0$,

$$k^* = (c_8/n)^{1/\alpha_1} \tag{3.10}$$

Examining the $\dot{k}/k$ and $d^2 k/dk^2$ relationships, existence and uniqueness, as well as stability, follow immediately by standard proofs, given $1 - \alpha_1$, $\alpha_1 > 0$. By substituting into (2.16) and (2.17) for r and U, we get the new steady-state values:[4]

$$r^* = n \tag{3.11}$$
$$U^* = c_9(n)^{-(f-b\beta(1-\gamma)-a_2\alpha_2)/\alpha_1} \tag{3.12}$$

Again r^* equals the population growth rate. Increases in n raise the steady-state value of r and lower that of U. Population growth raises the return to capital at the expense of labor.

Impacts on urban patterns. As before, at any instant in temporary equilibrium, equilibrium city sizes for type 1 and 2 cities are parametric constants where $N_1 = \psi(\phi_1/\alpha_1)$ and $N_2 = \psi(\phi_2/\alpha_2)$. However, because there are now two types of cities, if k is changing (when there is not a steady state), then the ratio of X_1 and X_2 output is changing and, hence, the ratio of numbers of type 1 to type 2 cities, m_1/m_2, is changing. Thus the focus is on the steady state. In a steady state, where k is constant, the ratio of national X_1 to X_2 is constant and hence the ratio m_1/m_2 is constant—a function of parameters as defined in note 3. Then from the national full employment equation for labor

$$\dot{m}_1/m_1 = \dot{m}_2/m_2 = n \tag{3.13}$$

That is, in a steady state (only), the numbers of each type of city grow at the same rate, the rate of national population growth.

In the absence of other considerations, in the steady state, an economy again grows by replicating itself. Population growth is matched by the same corresponding increase in outputs and city numbers of all types.

Technological change. What is the impact of technological change in a multi-sector model? As before, a commuting improvement increases equilibrium sizes of all occupied cities, but in the immediate run leads to a decrease in the numbers of cities of all types. The interesting twist occurs if public capital is immobile. The likely impact is sketched out, assuming perfect immobility of public capital and perfect mobility of private capital. Suppose initially for different types of cities that $N_1^0 > N_2^0 > \ldots > N_m^0$ and $m_1^0 < m_2^0 < \ldots < m_n^0$. A favorable change in δ or γ leads to an increase in efficient city sizes that would pertain in a new steady state where still $N_1' > N_2' > \ldots > N_m'$ and an immediate decrease in city numbers of each type where $m_1' < m_2' < \ldots < m_n'$. Given immobility of public capital, the N_j' sizes would not be approached until after some period of time of additional population growth, capital accumulation, and public and private investment, if adjustment follows the one sector pattern of Section 1 with each type of city adjusting somewhat independently. There the problem is that additions to public capital are needed in all cities following technological change to satisfy the new optimal investment criterion and, hence, the initial adjustment involves focusing savings on public capital accumulation. However, with multiple sectors, it may be possible to shortcut the adjustment process and immediately approximately both satisfy $\partial U / \partial K_j = 0$ and achieve the N_j' sizes by shifting X_j production (except for X_1) to previously higher order cities with their already larger public capital stocks. For example, X_n production might shift to the previous $n - 1$ type cities with their higher public capital stock, X_{n-1} to the previous $n - 2$ type cities, and so on. Moreover, given originally $m_1^0 < m_2^0 < \ldots < m_n^0$, large-scale abandonment of cities might occur only at the lowest type of cities (n) if $m_n^0 \approx m_{n-1}'$, $m_{n-1}^0 \approx m_{n-2}'$, and so on.

The point of this scenario is twofold. First, immobility of urban infrastructure may not significantly hinder adjustment and efficient use of resources if private capital is mobile or malleable, allowing cities to alter their production patterns. Second, such immobility in itself could result in a shifting of urban production patterns over time in response to urban technological change.

2. Economic Development

Economic development and growth involve the same processes. However, in development the focus is on institutional aspects, on more detailed analysis or, at least, interpretation of the impacts of growth, and on possibilities not considered in formal growth models such as temporary disequilibrium (i.e., the possibility that at any instant, regardless of steady state or not, markets are not clearing). This section is divided into two parts. In the first, the basic developmental issues as interpreted in the growth model in Section 1 are presented. In the second, a spatial interpretation of development and its impact on a system of cities is given.

2.1. Sources of Growth and Development

Economic development is usually thought to involve a shift in production patterns away from agriculture and traditional textile and food processing industries to "modern" heavy industry such as iron, steel, and machinery. To the extent this stereotype is accurate, what causes this shift and how is it represented in a growth model?

The representation in the two-sector growth model could be a shift in output away from consumer goods X_2 toward producer–capital goods X_1. This represents increased overall investment and an increase in the economy capital-to-labor ratio, where the increased capital of course goes into the production of both consumer and producer goods. In multisector models there could also be a shift into production of new goods, not previously produced.

What can cause such a shift? Three explanations are typically given. One is disequilibrium, where labor starts off underemployed in the traditional consumer good–agricultural sector. Economic development is at least started by the "release" of this labor into the modern sector, rural-urban migration. Just why an initial disequilibrium existed, why it ends (other than by benevolent government intervention), and why it does not exist also in the modern urban sector are questions whose answers are unclear and are outside the analysis of economic growth by economists.

A second explanation is that exogenous technological change occurs that releases (saves) labor in the traditional sector, so that it flows into the modern sector, which then develops. Such technological change might occur through agricultural innovations introduced into a developing country. Alternatively, they occur through investment in human capital, gradually allowing the labor force to use more developed technologies, which already exist elsewhere in the world but need to be adopted and adapted in the developing country.

Finally, a shift can occur through governmental intervention of various forms. One form could be a forced increase in savings resulting in increased production of capital goods. Another could be tax-subsidy policies on outputs, favoring production of capital goods. A third could be regulations favoring flows of inputs into the capital good sector such as urban minimum wage policies or subsidized capital rentals on inputs into the capital-producer good sector.

2.2. Spatial Impacts of Development

Traditional analysis. Development is usually associated with an increase in urbanization and in urban concentration. For example, a government induced increase in savings and the national capital-to-labor ratio involves a shift from consumer goods to capital goods production. That hypothetically involves a shift of population from hamlets, villages and small towns producing traditional goods to larger cities producing heavy machinery. For example, where X_1 and X_2 are again, respectively, capital and consumer goods, such a shift would imply that m_1/m_2 rises. Specifically from Section 1.2 of this chapter, with such a shift, k, k_1, and k_2 all rise, which implies m_1/m_2 rises for N_1 and N_2 unchanged, assuming $N_1 > N_2$ and $\alpha_1 < \alpha_2$—capital goods are capital intensive and are produced in larger types of cities. Note N_2 is treated as being sufficiently small so that X_2 is classified as rural production. This corresponds to the suggestion in Chapter 2 that agriculture and rural manufacturing can be represented in the model as being the smallest types of cities.

As another example, technological change can involve a shift from rural to urban production. This can result from, say, an exogenous increase in efficiency of capital goods production reflected by an increase in A_1, which leads to an increase $\overset{*}{k}$ and an increase in the steady state m_1/m_2. Alternatively, a "neutral" technological change (vis-à-vis $\overset{*}{k}$ and m_1/m_2), such as an increase in both scale effects ϕ_1 and ϕ_2 by the same percent, leads to increased sizes of all cities, moving X_2 production from being defined as rural (village) to being defined as urban (town).

This type of connection between development and urbanization appears to gen-

Table 3.3. Industrial Composition and Urbanization

(a) United States of America		Percentage urbanized	No. of textile workers/ no. of iron and steel workers
	1880	27	1.30
	1960	70	0.56
(b) United States of America		Percentage urbanized	Nondurable goods workers/durable goods workers
	1940	56	1.20
	1970	73	0.73
(c) Korea		Percentage urbanized	Workers in textile and food processing/ workers in metals and machinery
	1966	35	2.7
	1978	55	1.5

erally prevail. It also is consistent in developed settings to the classification of cities by size in Chapter 1, where textile and food processing cities are smaller than heavy manufacturing cities. Note, however, that the connection is not always between urbanization and a shift to manufacturing per se. For example in 1880 the United States was 27% urbanized with 19% of its labor force in manufacturing. By 1970 it was 70% urbanized, but the percent of the labor force in manufacturing had only risen to 25% (Historical Statistics of the United States, Part 1). As suggested above, what is correlated with urbanization appears to be a shift in the composition of the manufacturing labor force from traditional manufacturing (e.g., textiles and food processing) to heavy manufacturing (e.g., metals, machinery). For example, for the United States and Korea for relevant time periods, using both general and specific industrial composition comparisons, in Table 3.3 there are dramatic drops in the ratio of workers engaged in traditional manufacturing (textiles, food processing) to workers engaged in heavy manufacturing (metals, machinery), as populations move from rural to urban areas.

Note that the shift in manufacturing composition in the United States both recently and over the last century documented in Table 3.3 also provides a competing explanation for the increase in urban concentration documented in Table 3.1—improvements in commuting technology. That is, increases in both urbanization and urban concentration might be explained by changes in output composition alone. Again, these stand as hypotheses yet to be tested empirically.

Product cycle considerations. So far, technological change has been treated as an exogenous event. For developing countries technological change typically does not mean new inventions but adaptation of existing technology from developed countries. The process of adaptation may involve product cycle notions applied to a system of cities. Let us first examine the product cycle (Vernon, 1966) as it applies to a system of cities, following Hekman (1982).

Hekman's application is to the United States and to the development of first the radio and then in particular the computer industry. The development of these industries occurred in very large metropolitan areas. Later standardized production decentralized to smaller cities (or abroad) where labor costs were lower. The presumption is that in the initial stages of product development, innovative firms experience urbanization economies. They need to be in very large urban centers where they can readily hire very particular kinds of workers in the large local labor market, where they can have access to information about the development of related activities, where they can have access to a wide variety of technical expertise, where they can have access to specialized components of the capital market that focus on investment in risky activity, and where they can easily test their product by marketing it locally in the large and perhaps sophisticated consumer market. In short, general urban scale helps provide the diversified local input and output markets necessary for effective product development. Once a product is fully developed and production is standardized, there is no need for it to remain in large metro areas with high labor and land costs. Assembly line production is decentralized to locations where land is cheap and the required semi-skilled or unskilled labor is available at a low cost. The implication is that industry scale effects switch to become effects of localization.

The application to developing countries is immediate. In the initial stages of development, when a country is adapting innovations on a wide front of activities, firms locate typically in large coastal cities so as to have access to foreign investors, to the technical expertise available in the country that agglomerates correspondingly in these cities, to sophisticated consumers (see Chapter 6), and to the ministries of the national government that are involved in financing development activities. A very large local market will be beneficial to the exchange of information, the experimentation, and the investment activity going on. Thus developing countries may experience increases in urban concentration to take advantage of the initial form that scale economies take in their developing product lines.

However, once a standardized product from a modern manufacturing activity is achieved, the plant manufacturing activities can decentralize to smaller cities with lower plant production costs. This suggests that development involves a later stage of urban decentralization. For example, this decentralization process has been noted for Japan and Korea by Renaud (1979) and Richardson (1977), and for Brazil by Townroe (1981). Korea is briefly considered here.

The example of Korea. In Korea, the dominant urban area is the Seoul national capital region in the North, which contained 45% of the national urban population in 1980 and 49% of manufacturing employment in 1978. Two phenonema mark changes in Korean industrial and population location patterns. First, the region around Busan in the South is growing faster than the Seoul region. In 1975–1980, the population of Seoul and its region both grew at 4% a year while the major southern urban areas of Ulsam, Pohang, and Busan grew at annual rates of 9.7%, 9.3%, and 5.3% for 1970–1980, respectively. Seoul's manufacturing employment growth rate for 1973–1978 averaged 5.6% per year while the rates for Busan and its province were, respectively, 12.9% and 15.6% for 1973–1978. Consequently, the urban area of Seoul's share of manufacturing employment fell from 34% in 1973 to 25% in 1978, although the national capital regon's share was unchanged.

This leads to the second phenomenon, where, within the national capital region, there is deconcentration of manufacturing from the core to outer rings. The manufacturing annual growth rate in the national capital region outside the main Seoul urban area was 23.6% for 1973–1978. More specifically, if the national capital region is divided into five rings, the Central Business District had a negative annual growth rate of −7.6% for 1973–1978. In contrast, the two rings outside the Seoul urban area but in the national capital region grew at annual rates of 22% and 34% for 1973–1978. All figures are from Kwon (1981) and Song and Choe (1982).

Part of this process of deconcentration and decentralization from Seoul is a product cycle phenomenon, where, because Korea has sufficiently developed, urbanization economies for many goods have evaporated. Then production of these goods can be expected to move from the core of the major metropolitan area into smaller cities. However, part of the process may involve the lumpy formation of new cities in a small growing economy dominated initially by one city. This aspect is reviewed in the next chapter.

In terms of the product cycle, Kwon (1981) and Song and Choe (1982) indicate that the firms most willing to move out of the main Seoul urban area are large firms in machinery and metals, producing brand name or standardized products. They are looking for cheap land and labor and want to avoid the highly congested Seoul area, given that incubator effects and urbanization economies have weakened over time for their products. If they are large firms, they can deconcentrate production, or plant operations, while retaining head offices in Seoul so as to maintain links to the central bureaucracy and for marketing purposes.

3. Conclusions

Basic economic growth as fueled by population growth involves no changes in efficient city sizes in the steady state, assuming a large economy to begin with. The national economy effectively provides constant returns to scale. Growth simply involves formation of new cities at the rate of population growth.

City sizes are altered by technological change, such as improvements in commuting technology, which reduces access costs within cities. Discrete technological improvements result in shifts up in city sizes and immediate shifts down in the number of cities, or a shift down in the growth path of numbers of cities. Adjustment to technological change is hindered if local public investment in roads, sewers, parks, water mains, etc., is immobile and nonmalleable. The initial decline in the needed number of cities results in the depopulation of some towns, perhaps to be reinhabited later.

Economic development is stereotyped as involving a shift from traditional (consumer) goods to modern (capital) goods production. Given the differences in equilibrium sizes for these types of cities noted in Chapter 1, this shift is generally associated with an increase in urban concentration. In developing countries initial increases in urban concentration are also enhanced by the process of adoption and adaptation of existing but more advanced technologies from developed countries. Such adaptation occurs most efficiently in larger cities, with their larger general input markets, consumer testing markets, and better information flows.

NOTES

1. Because $1 - \alpha$, $\alpha > 0$ as $k \to 0$, $\dot{k} > 0$. Second, as $k \to \infty$, $\dot{k} < 0$. Third, differentiating as $k \to 0$ $\partial \dot{k}/\partial k > 0$ while as $k \to \infty$ $\partial \dot{k}/\partial k < 0$. Finally, the $\dot{k}$, k relationship is strictly concave given $\partial^2 \dot{k}/\partial k^2 < 0$ for all k. In summary, in $\dot{k}$, k space the $\dot{k}$ curve in equation 3.3 is constrained to start in the positive region initially increase and then decrease

indefinitely (given strict concavity) into the negative region. Since $\dot{k}$ can thus only cross the k axis once, equilibrium is unique.

2. That is,

$$U^{-1}\frac{dU}{d\delta} = \{-[f - b\beta(1 - \gamma)]\frac{\phi}{\alpha}N^{-1} - b\beta(\delta - \gamma)\}N^{-1}\left(\frac{dN}{d\delta}\right) - b\beta \log N = -b\beta \log N$$

The expression in curly brackets disappears by substituting (2.19) for N. Thus a *decrease* in δ increases steady-state utility.

3. We substitute equations for X_1 from (2.16), for r from (2.20), and for m_2N_2 from the full employment relationship (2.23); k_1 and k_2 are solved in terms of k. The result is substituted back into (2.23) to solve for m_1 and m_2. These results are substituted into the equation of motion along with equation 2.16 for r. The equations of interest are

$$k_1 = k(c_7 + c_6 - 1)/(c_6c_7)$$

$$k_2 = k(c_7 + c_6 - 1)/c_6$$

$$m_1 = \frac{N}{N_1}c_7/(c_7 + c_6 - 1)$$

$$m_2 = \frac{N}{N_2}(c_6 - 1)/(c_7 + c_6 - 1)$$

where

$$c_6 \equiv [f - b\beta(1 - \gamma)]/[f - b\beta(1 - \gamma) - \alpha_1(f - b)]$$

$$c_7 \equiv (\alpha_1/\alpha_2)[f - b\beta(1 - \gamma) - \alpha_2(f - b)][f - b\beta(1 - \gamma) - \alpha_1(f - b)]^{-1}(N_2/N_1)^{1/\psi}$$

and

$$c_8 \equiv A_1(1 - \alpha_1)g_1(N_1)[c_4(c_6 + c_7 - 1)/c_6c_7]^{-\alpha_1}$$

4.

$$c_9 \equiv E_0F_2^{a_2}F_1^{[f-b\beta(1-\gamma)-a_2\alpha_2]/\alpha_1}$$

where

$$F_i = \alpha_i^{\alpha_i}(1 - \alpha_i)^{(1-\alpha_i)}A_ig_i(N_i)N_i^{-\alpha_i/\psi}$$

CHAPTER 4

Trade and Natural Resources

This chapter introduces a wide variety of complications that apply the model in Chapter 2 to situations facing a real-world system of cities. First, we open the closed economy of Chapter 2 to international trade, so as to assess the impact of trade on a system of cities and to start to make international comparisons of systems of cities. In Chapter 8 the impact of international trade policies, such as import restrictions on a system of cities, can then also be assessed.

Second, this chapter introduces natural resources into the model by allowing different urban sites to have different natural amenity bundles. An algorithm to solve for the allocation of cities across potential urban sites is presented. This analysis will also necessarily introduce the concept of a restricted city size, where under certain conditions it may benefit city residents on better urban sites to restrict entry into their city. This concept and solution will be referred to at various points later.

Finally, the model of Chapter 2 is applied to a "small" economy with a limited number of cities, where the lumpiness problem in solving for city sizes assumed in Chapter 2 must be dealt with. In small economies the externalities in production that are successfully internalized in large economies persist and the concept of restricted city sizes also is relevant. Finally, growth in a small economy is considered. Of particular interest is optimal planning for public infrastructure investment under realistic assumptions about the lumpiness of such investment.

1. The Systems of Cities in an Open Economy

The economy is opened to international trade by adapting traditional analyses to a system of cities. Following traditional trade theory, given only two primary factors of production, attention is restricted to an economy composed of only two types of cities. The two types of cities produce X_1 and X_2, respectively; here X_1 is the relatively capital intensive good. That is, $(1 - \alpha_1) > (1 - \alpha_2)$ or $\alpha_2 > \alpha_1$ in equation 2.1.

1.1. Relative versus Complete Specialization

The analysis starts with a closed economy, producing X_1 and X_2 in autarky, and then the economy is opened to international trade. Trade will impact the composition of national output either by increasing $\tilde{X}_2/\tilde{X}_1$ or by decreasing it. Before we assess whether $\tilde{X}_2/\tilde{X}_1$ rises or falls, the possibility that either X_2 or X_1 will cease to be produced and that the economy will completely specialize in production with the advent of trade must be considered. The basic trade theorems discussed in the book only apply under incomplete specialization. Thus the conditions under which complete versus incomplete specialization occur must be isolated.

When will an economy engaged in international trade have only one versus two types of cities? *A necessary condition for nonspecialization is that, given $\alpha_1 <$ α_2, $k_1 > k_2$. That is, the capital intensive good must be produced in the high capital usage city.* If the labor intensive good is produced in the high capital usage city, which is possible as was detailed in Chapter 2, the economy will completely specialize in trade. This condition is similar to that in Neary (1978), which states that the good which is capital intensive in value terms must be capital intensive in physical terms; it is also similar to the condition in Jones (1968), which states that for the Rybczynski and Stolper-Samuelson theorems to hold simultaneously, the good that is capital intensive at the margin must be capital intensive on average.

The capital intensity proposition may be proved in two ways. Both assume that the economy is small relative to the rest of the world and faces fixed terms of trade (TOT). A classical textbook argument is to start in autarky with the economy producing X_1 and X_2. When the economy enters the world market, "perverse" price effects must be ruled out in order for it to end up in a nonspecialization equilibrium. That is, for nonspecialization as $(\tilde{X}_2/\tilde{X}_1)^s$ rises, q_2^s must rise, or $dq_2^s/d(\tilde{X}_2/\tilde{X}_1)^s > 0$. $\tilde{X}_i^s$ is the economy supply of good i and q_i^s is the production cost of i (where $q_1^s \equiv 1$). Suppose that when the economy comes to the world market, it finds $q_2^w > q_2^s$. Producers in the economy want to expand production of the profitable X_2. If, as they start to increase $(\tilde{X}_2/\tilde{X}_1)^s$, q_2^s falls so that production of X_2 becomes more and more profitable, then the production of X_2 will expand until the country is completely specialized. Nonspecialization would require q_2^s to rise to q_2^w as $(\tilde{X}_2/\tilde{X}_1)^s$ increases. The capital intensity conditions enter because $dq_2^s/d(\tilde{X}_2/\tilde{X}_1)^s > 0$ iff $k_2 < k_1$ when $\alpha_1 < \alpha_2$. The proof of this and a technical explanation are in Appendix A along with the other method of proof.

In the discussion of trade theorems below that are applied to a nonspecialized economy, it is assumed that $k_2 < k_1$, given $\alpha_1 < \alpha_2$. In Chapter 2, it was shown that a sufficient but not necessary condition for this is $N_2 < N_1$. Finally, nonexistence of nonspecialized trade equilibria for $k_2 > k_1$ suggests there may be problems with stability in autarky. In particular, as noted earlier, Hicksian static "stability" conditions do not hold, as in Hochman (1977).

We now turn to an examination of the impact of international trade on countries that are incompletely specialized in trade. This involves adapting traditional trade theorems and interpreting their impact on a system of cities. The discussion starts with the theorems necessary for doing international comparisons of systems of cities.

1.2. International Comparisons of Systems of Cities

To do the basic comparisons two trade theorems, the Heckscher–Ohlin and Rybczynski theorems are invoked.

The Heckscher–Ohlin theorem. In comparing two countries or regions engaging in bilateral exchange of goods, the Heckscher–Ohlin theorem states that the capital abundant economy will export the capital intensive good and import the labor intensive good. For two economies, A and B, suppose $\tilde{k}_A > \tilde{k}_B$. In autarky from equations 2.16 and 2.18 as well as full employment equations, $q_2 = J_5 \tilde{k}^{\alpha_2 - \alpha_1}$. J_5 is a parametric constant, assumed to be equal in A and B, *which implies that the same types of cities are identical* across the two countries. Then $(q_2)_A > (q_2)_B$ given $\tilde{k}_A > \tilde{k}_B$. With the introduction of trade, economy A will want to buy X_2 from economy B where it is relatively cheaper, and vice versa for X_1. Thus, in a trade equilibrium characterized by incomplete specialization, following the adjustment process from autarky outlined in Section 1.1, the capital abundant economy, A, will end up exporting the capital intensive good, X_1, and importing the labor intensive good, X_2.

Rybczynski theorem. The Rybczynski theorem states that when an open economy faces fixed terms of trade (TOT), if its national capital-to-labor ratio increases, the output of its capital intensive traded good rises relative to its labor intensive good (the theorem may also be stated in terms of absolutes). On the technical side, the theorem is proved by investigating the change in the ratio of national outputs, $\tilde{X}_1/\tilde{X}_2 = (m_1 X_1)/(m_2 X_2)$, as $\tilde{k}$ increases. First, note that N_1 and N_2 are fixed from equation 2.15; and, from equations 2.16 and 2.18, if the TOT are fixed then so are r, k_1, and k_2. Therefore, from equation 2.19, city outputs X_1 and X_2 are fixed. Therefore, total national outputs, $\tilde{X}_1$ and $\tilde{X}_2$, vary only as m_1 and m_2 vary, where $d(\tilde{X}_1/\tilde{X}_2)/d(m_1/m_2) > 0$. To investigate the change in m_1 and m_2, differentiate (2.29) (given k_1 and k_2 are fixed) to get

$$d(m_1/m_2)d\tilde{k}\big|_{\tilde{q}^2} = (N_2/N_1)\frac{(k_1 - k_2)}{(\tilde{k} - k_1)^2} > 0 \qquad \text{iff} \qquad k_2 < k_1 \qquad (4.1)$$

Thus, if $\tilde{k}$ increases, if the type 1 city has relatively high capital usage, m_1/m_2 rises and, thus, the relative output of the high capital usage rises. Note, however, that the Rybcznski theorem is stated in terms of capital intensive goods, not high capital usage cities. But, for countries facing fixed TOT, nonspecialization in trade requires that high capital usage cities produce capital intensive goods.

Application to international comparisons. Combining the assumptions and results of the Heckscher–Ohlin and Rybczynski theorems, there is then a framework for doing international comparisons of systems of cities. Compare any two economies trading *freely* in the world market that have technological and consumption conditions such that the same types of cities are *identical* across the economies. Then the determinant of the relative size distribution of cities between the two economies is solely their relative factor endowments. *The relatively capital abundant economy will produce more of the capital intensive good and will have a relatively greater number of high capital usage cities.* If these are larger cities, then the relatively capital abundant economy will have a higher degree of urban concentration.

The restriction on applying these theorems is that cities of the same type must be identical across economies. This restriction means that urban technology (housing and land site production, or commuting technology), efficiency of the local public sector (setting public investment optimally), and urban demand for housing (tastes for nontraded goods) be identical across countries. This is a very strong restriction and somewhat unrealistic to assume. However, under rough similarity of the same types of cities the proposition may still hold generally.

Moreover, the Rybczynski theorem can be applied to a single economy without this restriction. If an open economy invests to expand its capital stock, it will expand its production of capital intensive goods and the numbers of cities of that type. If those are the larger type of cities, urban concentration will rise.

Other international comparisons. The other central trade theorem for international comparisons is the factor price equalization theorem, which attempts to compare factor returns across economies. There are twists to applying this theorem that have spatial implications.

The factor price equalization theorem states that if traded good prices are equalized across countries, so are factor returns. In the version applicable to an urban economy, factor returns refer to capital rentals and utility levels, not wages, since wages are not even equalized within economies. If production technology and urban characteristics are identical between any two economies, factor price equalization for r follows directly from equation 2.18, and for U follows from equation 2.12 given equalized r's.

Again in applying this theorem there is the restriction that the same types of cities be identical across cities. Analyzing this restriction becomes particularly interesting if capital rental income is introduced into cities. Throughout the book capital rental income is assumed not to be spent in cities—it is spent outside the system or reinvested in production of capital goods in a growth model. Now assume laborers get a share of capital income—which is quite realistic. The basic results derived to date hold up. However, international comparisons of cities are affected.

This situation is analyzed in Hochman (1977) and adapted here. Part of capital rental income to laborers will be spent on housing. Thus, if capital incomes increase, this will increase the demand for housing and site production—the source of diseconomies of cities. This leads to a decrease in efficient city sizes (Henderson, 1982b). That is, an increase in laborer's capital income share is like a shift in tastes increasing the demand for housing and lowering efficient sizes of cities, or the point where marginal scale benefits of increasing city size equal marginal consumption costs is shifted back. A change in efficient city size will alter all factor returns in the model.

Now compare two countries, A and B, trading two goods in the world market. The countries are identical in technology and tastes. Laborers' share in capital income is denoted by $\bar{k}$, to be distinguished from K, the general economy endowment. In A laborers have larger shares $\bar{k}$ in capital income than in B where incomes are $y = w + r\bar{k}$. That is, $\bar{k}_A > \bar{k}_B$. If $\bar{k}_A > \bar{k}_B$, for fixed terms of trade, it is possible to show that $r_A < r_B$ (Henderson, 1982b). That is, the factor price equalization theorem no longer holds.

If factor price equalization does not hold, then potentially a curious problem can arise. In particular, allow for some international mobility of factors and consider the impact of both trade and, say, international mobility of capital when factor price equalization does not hold.

Consider the case with laborers getting a share of capital rental income in comparing economies A and B, where $\bar{k}_A > \bar{k}_B$ and $r_A < r_B$. With the introduction of capital mobility, capital will flow to the high return country B. However, capital movements do not alter capital rentals because no movement of urban capital owners or change in ownership shares is implied. Thus, movement of capital will not equalize capital rentals. If q_2, $\bar{k}_A$, and $\bar{k}_B$ are unaltered, r_A and r_B will be unaltered by capital movements and hence city sizes will also be unaltered. Equalization of the r's can only occur if at least one of the countries completely specializes in the production of one of the traded goods. Then the link between q, r, and $\bar{k}$ is broken, allowing for equalization of r's even if $\bar{k}$'s differ across regions.

From the Rybczynski theorem, if the q's facing the two countries are fixed nationally or internationally, the influx of K to country B will cause country B to expand its output from high capital usage cities and reduce its output from high labor usage cities, and vice versa for country A. This inflow of capital will continue until, first, one of the countries specializes and then r's are equalized. Specialization of one of the countries occurs when either capital inflows in B cause $\hat{k}_B$ to rise to k_1 or outflows from A cause $\hat{k}_A$ to fall to k_2. In summary, the country, *where capital ownership of urban dwellers is high (low), will tend to specialize completely in the production of labor (capital) intensive goods.*

This is an intriguing possibility. It serves to point out the possibilities of what can happen if factor prices are not equalized and, say, a factor such as capital is mobile in international markets. The conditions necessary for factor price equalization are so restrictive that these types of forces surely exist. They also must exist within some large countries at the regional level, where interregional mobility of labor but not capital is restricted.

2. Amenities and City Sizes

This section considers the impact of introducing natural resources, or geographic considerations, into an economy. In this chapter urban site amenities are the natural resource. Chapter 9 examines the impact of raw material deposits. Urban site amenities could be consumer amenities such as climate, outdoor recreation alternatives, and drinking water. Producer amenities could be climate, altitude, access to water, and so on.

Potential urban sites then have different endowments of natural amenities that affect consumers and producers. Consumer amenities are represented by a vector of characteristics which, say, affect the value of the shift parameter, E, of the utility function in equation 2.8. Producer amenities affect, say, the value of the shift parameter, A, of the production function in equation 2.1. Here we focus on the impact of differences in consumer amenities for illustrative purposes.

Section 2.1 starts by analyzing the impact on a system of many cities, all of the same type. For reasons pointed out below, the analysis *is heuristic* while drawing on the formal model. We first consider the analysis of city sizes and then international comparisons. Section 2.2 analyzes the impact of restrictions on city sizes. Section 2.3 considers the impacts on a system of multiple types of cities.

2.1. Single Type of City

In a model with a single type of city, each city produces X_1 where $q_1 = 1$ is the numeraire. Therefore, from equation 2.17 utility in each city is given by

$$U_0 = E_0 \{C_0^{-[f-b(1-\gamma)]/\alpha} r^{f-b-[f-b(1-\gamma)]/\alpha}\} g(N)^{[f-b\beta(1-\gamma)]/\alpha} N^{\beta b(\gamma-\delta)} \qquad (4.2)$$

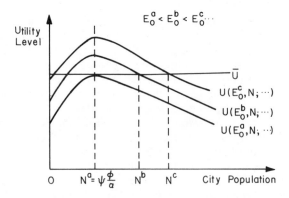

Fig. 4.1 Differences in Equilibrium City Sizes as Amenities Vary

Better amenity vectors increase the value of E_0. For example, each element of the vector e_1, e_2, e_3 representing a different amenity could enter E_0 multiplicatively so that $E_0 = e_1^{\epsilon_1} e_2^{\epsilon_2} e_3^{\epsilon_3} \dots$. For utilities to be equalized across cities, as E_0 varies so then must equilibrium size, N, vary. This occurs because the expression in braces in (4.2) is the same across cities, where the first term represents a parameter cluster and the second represents equalized capital rental prices. That only leaves N to vary with E_0.

Given that, if different cities have different site amenities and values for E_0, which means that they must have different equilibrium sizes, how are these sizes solved for? One algorithm for determining approximately (see Appendix B) how sizes vary in equilibirum is as follows. The city on the worst occupied urban site, a, is approximately set at efficient size where $\partial U/\partial N = 0$. This is shown in Figure 4.1. Setting it at efficient size will yield the highest possible realized utility for all cities in the economy under current conditions. This also gives the equilibrium utility level in the economy. In equation 4.2 this is calculated by plugging in the value of $N^a = \psi(\phi_1/\alpha_1)$ and the value of E_0 on the worst occupied site, E_0^a. Other cities on better sites have sufficiently larger sizes given $\partial U/\partial N < 0$ beyond $N = \psi(\phi_1/\alpha_1)$, so that their U is equalized to that in the city on the worst quality site, (Figure 4.1). Note that better site amenities only alter the shift term E_0 in the utility function, so the shifted up utility curves in Figure 4.1 have the same shape as the base curve for E_0^a.

Thus cities on better sites have higher equilibrium utility paths and their sizes expand until their realized utility equalizes $\bar{U}$, the level prevailing in national labor markets. From the point of view of an individual city, the benefits of having a better amenity vector are dissipated through inefficient increases in city size, driving up city costs of living. In a spatial formulation of cities, this would involve higher total and average land rents collected in cities with better site amenities as well as higher wages (given greater scale in production). That is, amenity differences are capitalized into both higher land rents on better urban sites and higher wage costs.

Finally, it is important to note that only the highest quality sites in an economy are occupied. If there exists a higher quality site than a current occupied one, a developer could set up a city on this site, paying competitive capital rentals and utility levels, and earn a temporary profit (by paying wages below marginal prod-

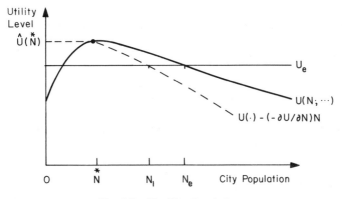

Fig. 4.2 City Size Restrictions

ucts) relative to a city on an inferior quality site. Following the mechanisms of Chapter 2, this would displace this inferior city.

International comparisons and growth. Does it pay an economy to have a better set of urban sites? Suppose that there is only one site amenity whose cardinal measure varies continuously. Each economy gets a drawing of urban sites with this amenity that is one equal length unbroken segment from a uniform continuous distribution of possible sites. So, if the possible cardinal measures of site amenities lie on the real line between 0 and 1, each economy gets an equal length segment of the line of length $b - a > 0$, where $a \geq 0$ and $b \leq 1$ with at least one strict inequality holding. The segment $b - a$ is randomly drawn for each economy. Then compare two countries, 1 and 2, of approximately equal population so that the occupied proportions of their equal length segments will be similar. However, one country, assume 1, has a better segment, or $b^1 > b^2$ (where $b^1 - b^2 = a^1 - a^2$ by assumption of equal length segments). Then in that country the base utility level in the worst occupied site should be higher and laborers in that economy should be better off (assuming essentially the same capital rental and output prices across countries).

This, of course, is a Richardian formulation of resources in an economy, similar to that in Dornbusch, Fisher, and Samuelson (1970). As any economy grows it proceeds down its distribution of urban sites to lower quality sites, lowering the base utility in the economy as dictated by the lowest quality occupied site. The method of solving for this is outlined in Appendix B.

2.2. City Size Restrictions

Amenity differences across cities is a situation ripe for city size restrictions. Consider one city in the economy on a better site than the base city. Its situation is shown in Figure 4.2 where with free entry its size is N_e, given U_e prevailing in the economy. Do the residents of this city have an incentive to restrict size? In part, that answer depends on how city size is restricted.

Assume as a benchmark that entry to the city can be regulated costlessly and that effective lump-sum residence fees can be charged. The residence or entry fees arise because if, for example, city size is restricted to N^*, excluded residents would be willing to pay a premium equal to the monetized value of $\hat{U}(N^*) - U_e$ to live in this city. In a spatial model, entry could be regulated through zoning ordinances restricting the number of dwelling units. The premium would then be on the key to entry—obtaining a dwelling unit—and this premium could be a lump-sum rent surcharge above opportunity costs. That is, the benefits of living in the city would be capitalized into land prices, rather than dissipated by city expansion. In a nonspatial model the premium could equivalently be viewed as a direct residence fee imposed by the owner(s) of the site upon which the city is situated (i.e., the owners of the land-development corporation). In a single-period model, these owners in theory should be (absentee) rentiers. It is also possible to develop heuristically a situation where the owners are some group of "original" residents of the city who collectively (equal shares) own the site or control entry (see later). In either case, the solutions are basically equivalent. Note that, if residents are renters, they can only lose from city size restrictions since any potential surplus above U_e is reflected in higher prices they pay.

If entry is controlled by rentiers, who are unrestricted by the local political process in choosing city size and residence fees, the rentiers seek to maximize FN, where F is the per person (per period) residence fee. Profits are maximized subject to the constraint that realized utility $\hat{U}$ is equal to or greater than U_e, with income now defined as $y - F$. As city size moves beyond $\overset{*}{N}$, the rentiers are trading off a lower per person fee given declining potential utility where $\partial U/\partial N < 0$ beyond $\overset{*}{N}$ against increased numbers of fee payers. Maximizing profits with respect to F and N and solving yields

$$F = [(-\partial U/\partial N)/\gamma]N \qquad (4.3)$$

where γ is the marginal utility of income, F is the benefit from increasing city size and $(-\partial U/\partial N/\gamma)N$ is the cost, which is the decline in fees of existing residents (the marginal evaluation of the negative impacts on U of an increase in N multiplied by the number of residents).

Charging the F of the profit-maximizing solution results in an N that will lie between $\overset{*}{N}$ and N_e at, say, N_1 in Figure 4.2. In essence, there is a curve marginal to U approximated by $U - (-\partial U/\partial N)N$ (given $F\lambda \approx U - U_e$), that intersects U_e where (4.3) is satisfied and city size is N_1. At the intersection point the postfee realized utility, $\hat{U}$, by solution equals U_e. The discussion has been deliberately phrased in general terms because the exact way in which the fee is imposed affects the precise solution, and the forms of precise solutions are not simple (Henderson, 1982a).

The solution in (4.3) is essentially the same if some group of "original" residents own the right to entry. Although "ownership" is not relevant in a single period model, the model can heuristically be extended to multiperiods. Doing so, however, requires careful specification of expectations and initial ownership and entry conditions to arrive at a specific distribution of wealth. Consider a rather arbitrary and simplistic method for the purposes of illustration. Assume there are initially atomistic holders of farm land. A city is established and migrants enter sequentially, naively assuming utility will remain at the level at the time of their entry. The atomistic holders sell to entrants at the competitive price of the fixed opportunity cost of land in agriculture. Once entrants accumulate to a level of $\overset{*}{N}$, current utility starts to decline with further entry. The accumulated or "original" residents suddenly wake up to this fact and collectively vote to impose entry restrictions. If this "waking up" (to the shape of U) occurred at a size less than $\overset{*}{N}$, then that size would define the group of "original" residents. We have simply assumed that the shock of U starting to decline is what wakes up residents. Given this waking up, how are entry restrictions chosen?

Ultimately these original $\overset{*}{N}$ residents would want to restrict entry so as to maximize their utility U^* for income defined as $y - F(N - N^*)/N^*$ where fees are charged to new entrants $(N - N^*)$ only and redistributed among original residents (N^*) only. These original residents maximize their $U^*(\cdot)$ subject to the constraint that the utility of incoming residents, $U(N, -F; \ldots)$ equals or exceeds U_e. The result is (4.3) if income effects (between original and new residents) are ignored. Note that if resident-owners cannot charge residence fees, they will simply set city size at $\overset{*}{N}$ where their potential (equals actual in this case) utility is maximized. In a multiperiod model these benefits to original resident owners would be capitalized into their land values (or value of shares in their land-development cooperative), if they sell and move to another city.

In practice, it is difficult to restrict city size in the manner implicit in this benchmark solution. It was assumed that all local markets continue to operate efficiently (without distortions), that entry fees are explicit, and that entry restrictions can be direct (although imposition of a direct fee in the benchmark is sufficient to limit city size to the desired level). In practice, entry restrictions and the imposition of fees are indirect. Rather than imposing a direct fee and limiting city size through the fee, in familiar legal-political environments the procedure is to limit city size through inhibiting land development, to create a scarcity on entry, and to collect rents on the scarce good that provides entry—typically the purchase or rent of a lot. This indirect collection of fees presents problems. For example, although the city can stop further land development within its boundaries, it is hard to prohibit more residents from crowding into existing developments or from setting up residence outside the city limits to get costly access to city employment and services. These activities represent inefficiencies in land markets and the political process, lowering the utility available to any resident at any city size. This problem is discussed at length later.

In summary, the existence of amenity differentials across cities introduces new complications into the analysis of city sizes. Other sources of differences among cities of the same type appear in later chapters. They are important to the understanding of systems of cities. However, like almost all complications they limit the power to make precise predictions. For technical reasons outlined in Appendix B, it is difficult to specify determinant solutions to the model.

2.3. Multiple Types of Cities

If there are multiple types of cities, the problem of solving for equilibrium becomes even more difficult. Amenity differences have the same type of impact on city sizes. The question is which types of cities occupy the better quality sites. It is hypothesized that the larger types of cities would occupy better quality sites.

Order cities so that the largest type (largest ϕ_j/α_j) is indexed 1, the next largest 2, and so on. Then, it is hypothesized that the m_1 cities of type 1 occupy the best m_1 sites, type 2 cities the next best m_2 sites, and so on. Why is this reasonable? In the problem, the factors affecting the E's are like public goods. Larger cities

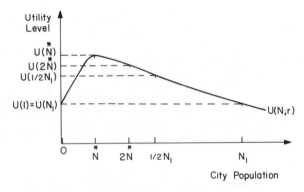

Fig. 4.3   City Sizes in a Small Growing Economy

have more people to enjoy the public good benefits and thus are willing to pay more in total for amenities through, say, land rents in an explicit spatial model. In competition they thus can pay more for sites of better quality and can bid them away from smaller types of cities.

3. Small Economies

The analysis of small economies is covered in some detail by Henderson (1972, 1974) and Upton (1981) for equilibrium properties, by Henderson and Ioannides (1981) in a growth context, and by Flatters, Henderson, and Mieszkowski (1974) and Henderson (1977b) for welfare properties. This section summarizes this work to illustrate the main difficulties presented by small economies. They arise from the lumpiness problem, described in Chapter 2, of dividing the population into an integer number of cities of discrete size. Also, the analysis of small economies is critical to understanding the urban development of countries such as Korea, for example.

Consider the simplest case, which is an economy composed of only one type of city, facing a fixed rental rate on capital (rather than fixed capital stock). An example would be a small open economy borrowing in international markets that specializes in (urban) export production. The analysis starts off with the economy so small that it can support only one city. The situation facing that city is shown in Figure 4.3, where $U(N;r \ldots)$ plots the utility for the economy as a function of economy (= city) population.

Initially, as the economy population grows, utility rises, peaks at $\overset{*}{N}$, and then declines. Once past $\overset{*}{N}$ in Figure 4.3, at some point the economy will split into two cities. The question of when can be posed either as a growth question or as an international comparison question. For the later, the issue is at what size of economy is there a move from one to two cities in international comparisons.

The atomistic solution is for the first city to grow to size $N_1 + 1$ where $U(1) = U(N_1)$, so one person defecting to form their own city (of size 1) is better off than people in the single large city. That is, a second city only forms when utility falls in the first city all the way to the no city level. With one defection, more follow until there are two cities each of size $\frac{1}{2} N_1$ offering utility $U(\frac{1}{2} N_1)$. This occurs because the curves are drawn to avoid stability problems (see Henderson, 1986c), ensuring that utility rises faster in the initially smaller city as it gains population than in the larger city as it loses population.

In Chapter 2, the atomistic solution was implicitly rejected. Once the population of the initial city reaches $2\overset{*}{N}$, competitive developers ensure the formation of a second city, given that they can *guarantee* utility levels in the new city as high as $U(\overset{*}{N})$, where $U(\overset{*}{N}) > U(2\overset{*}{N})$ and, hence, they can attract people away from the old city. The role of competitive developers then is to facilitate large scale movements of people by guaranteeing the high utility levels resulting from mass population movements, which are unavailable with atomistic movements. Thus a second city under nonatomistic behavior forms well before utility levels fall to $U(N = 1)$. Note that a second city cannot form before the first city reaches size $2\overset{*}{N}$. Two identical cities of size less than $\overset{*}{N}$ are unstable with respect to random factor movements (i.e., utility in the gaining [losing] city rises [falls]). Two non-identical cities on different sides of $\overset{*}{N}$ offering equal utility have populations exceeding $2\overset{*}{N}$, if the utility path is restricted to be steeper (at each U) to the left of $\overset{*}{N}$ than to the right (see above).

Assuming new cities form in this nonatomistic fashion a third city forms when the first two cities each have population $\frac{3}{2}\overset{*}{N}$ and an mth city forms when the existing $m - 1$ cities each have population $(m/m - 1)\overset{*}{N}$. As $m \to \infty$, the large economy case in Chapter 2 emerges where $(m/m - 1)\overset{*}{N} \to \overset{*}{N}$.

Although market mechanisms do exist to eliminate the inferior atomistic solution, a nonatomistic solution presumes an institutional environment with free-wheeling land developers, able to undertake large-scale developments. That requires a land market with clear titles and private ownership (or least unrestricted leasing of public land) and a flourishing capital market where developers can borrow against future earnings. In many developing countries these presumptions are unreasonable, and this problem is discussed later in Chapter 9 when analyzing urbanization policies. It is also useful in evaluating situations such as in Korea discussed in Chapter 3, Section 2.2. Although the extremes of the atomistic solution may not result, a second city may not form until the first is well beyond $2\overset{*}{N}$. However, that problem is complicated by the possibility of city size restrictions where the initial city once past $\overset{*}{N}$ may try to limit immigration, forcing new population into an inferior size city.

In a small growing economy, the application of small economy analysis can become quite complex if more realistic assumptions are imposed. Of particular concern is the notion that public (or private) capital may be immobile and non-malleable. The solutions in Figure 4.3 involve large-scale displacements of population, with the initial city getting as large as $2\overset{*}{N}$, shrinking to $\overset{*}{N}$, rising to $\frac{3}{2}\overset{*}{N}$, shrinking to $\overset{*}{N}$, rising to $\frac{4}{3}\overset{*}{N}$, and so on as a stable $\overset{*}{N}$ is approached. If free capital mobility is presumed, the capital stock would also follow this increasing, shrinking, increasing process until it approaches a stable $\overset{*}{K}$. Suppose some capital, however, cannot shrink—for example, the roads and water mains of public investment. In particular, to highlight the issues, assume all public infrastructure investments must be done at once so that additional investments (at least in the intermediate run) are not feasible. This could be because of technical consider-

ations (adding new water mains to old ones) or because of efficiency considerations based on scale economy arguments. Assume further that depreciation is zero or negligible. Then there is an extremely complex optimal investment problem (Henderson and Ioannides, 1981), where the result is some permanent level of public investment larger than that which is optimal at $\overset{*}{N}$ with free capital mobility, and smaller than that which is optimal at $2\overset{*}{N}$ with free capital mobility. Its magnitude depends on the growth rate of population—slower rates indicating a long horizon of large city sizes and hence greater investment. It also depends on the discount rate—high rates discounting future smaller city sizes and resulting in greater investment.
sizes and hence greater investment. It also depends on the discount rate—high rates discounting future smaller city sizes and resulting in greater investment.

Finally, there is the issue of externalities. Given that all laborers are constrained to have equal utility levels with only one type of city, there is no problem. Since for equal utilities these cities are always identical, any marginal externalities (population scale economies and diseconomies in traded good and lot size production, respectively) of "over" or "under" population are equalized across cities, indicating an optimal solution.

However, with multiple types of cities with one of each kind, then net marginal externalities will generally be unequal across cities, indicating an inefficient solution. Chapter 9 reviews this problem.

4. Conclusions

1. Comparing economies with similar technologies, tastes for nontraded goods, and institutions, relatively capital abundant economies will tend to specialize relatively and to export capital intensive goods internationally. If these goods are produced in relatively larger types of cities, then capital abundant economies will have higher degrees of urban concentration.

2. If economies are dissimilar so that cities of the same type have different equilibrium sizes and characteristics, the traditional international trade theorems do not hold. A sufficient dissimilarity is the average capital income of laborers. For the example with international capital mobility as well as trade, ceteris paribus, economies with high capital ownership of laborers will tend to completely specialize in the production of labor intensive goods.

3. If Ricardian aspects are introduced into the model as a spectrum of urban sites upon which cities of differing qualities form, the equilibrium sizes of cities will vary within the same type. Existing cities will occupy the best available sites. Only the city on the worst of these occupied sites will approach "efficient" size, or be at the height of its utility path. The rest will have sizes in excess of this. The best quality sites will be occupied by the largest types of cities.

4. If cities of the same type offer different potential utility levels at the same sizes, such as when they face different amenity endowments, restricted as opposed to free entry city sizes must be considered. Generally, restrictions on city size only benefit landowners.

5. In small economies, lumpiness problems in solving for city size result where, ceteris paribus, the sizes of a city fluctuate as the economy grows from small to

large. The efficient timing of the formation of new cities requires at least freely efficiently functioning national land and capital markets.

Appendix A. Conditions for Non-Specialization in Trade

The technical explanation for the classical model of when nonspecialization in trade occurs is as follows. For nonspecialization in trade to occur from autarky where $q_2^w > q_2^s$, as output of X_2 increases with the introduction of trade, q_2^s must rise (to q_2^w in a nonspecialization equilibrium). As $\tilde{X}_2/\tilde{X}_1$ rises, q_2 will rise only if the relative price of the factor which X_2 uses intensively rises. w/r and, hence, q_2 will only rise if k_2 rises (and, hence, $k_{02} = \hat{K}_0/\hat{N}_0$ in X_2 production rises). If $k_2 < k_1$, as $(\tilde{X}_2/\tilde{X}_1)^s$ increases by shifting production from type 1 to type 2 cities, k_2 and k_1 must necessarily rise to maintain full employment (in standard trade models this is illustrated in an Edgeworth box diagram). Hence, $dq_2^s(d\tilde{X}_2/\tilde{X}_1)^s > 0$ if $k_1 > k_2$. However, if $k_1 < k_2$, as $(\tilde{X}_2/\tilde{X}_1)^s$ rises, k_2 and k_1 must fall; hence, w/r will fall, and thus q_2^s will fall. Note, if $k_1 < k_2$ at any $(\tilde{X}_1/\tilde{X}_2)^s$, then $k_1 < k_2$ and $dq_2^s/d(\tilde{X}_2/\tilde{X}_1)^s < 0$ for all feasible $(\tilde{X}_1/\tilde{X}_2)^s$, because k_1/k_2 equals a parametric constant in equation 2.27.

To prove $dq_2^s/d(\tilde{X}_2/\tilde{X}_1)^s > 0$ iff $k_2 < k_1$ when $\alpha_1 < \alpha_2$, we note $dq_2^s/d(\tilde{X}_2/\tilde{X}_1)^s$ has the opposite sign to $d(\tilde{X}_1/\tilde{X}_2)^s/dq_2^s$. We evaluate the latter expression. To do so, we combine the economy full employment equations to get $m_1/m_2 = (N_2/N_1)(k_2 - \tilde{k})(\tilde{k} - k_1)^{-1}$. We substitute this into $(\tilde{X}_1/\tilde{X}_2)^s = (m_1/m_2)(\tilde{X}_1/\tilde{X}_2)^s$, as well as equation 2.20 for $(\tilde{X}_1/\tilde{X}_2)^s$ and equations 2.20 and 2.24 for q_2 to get $(\tilde{X}_1/\tilde{X}_2)^s = J_3(k_2^{1-\alpha_2-\alpha_1} - \tilde{k}k_2^{2-\alpha_1})(\tilde{k} - k_1)^{-1}$; J_3 is a constant. We differentiate this, substituting in $dk_1 = (k_1/k_2)dk_2$ to get

$$d(\tilde{X}_1/\tilde{X}_2)^s/dq_2^s = [d(\tilde{X}_1/\tilde{X}_2)/dk_2](dk_2/dq_2^s)$$
$$= J_4(\tilde{k} - k_1)^{-2}k_2^{\alpha_2-\alpha_1-1}[\tilde{k}(k_2 - k_1)$$
$$- (\alpha_1 - \alpha_2)(k_1 - \tilde{k})(\tilde{k} + k_2)](dk_2/dq_2^s)$$

By substituting into (2.20) for r from (2.24) in terms of k_2 and differentiating, we know $dk_2/dq_2 > 0$ given $\alpha_1 - \alpha_2 < 0$. Thus, given $k_1 > \tilde{k} > k_2$, $d(\tilde{X}_1/\tilde{X}_2)^s/dq_2^s < 0$ and $dq_2^s/d(\tilde{X}_2/\tilde{X}_1)^s > 0$ iff $k_2 < k_1$.

This classical adjustment process and in particular its rigorous version for local stability has been criticized as being bizarre (Neary 1978, footnote 11) because it assumes factor markets adjust completely to each potential price (q_2^s), even though the final price q_2^w is a parameter. More recent treatments of stability examine local stability in an entirely different adjustment model, where capital and labor do not move instantaneously among sectors. However, the result is the same. Neary's analysis of stability follows for interested readers.

Within each city, competitive factor markets always clear to ensure local full employment of factors, which in turn ensures national full employment. Within these local markets, firms' competition for factors ensures that unit production costs always rise to meet the world price level; competition for factors always eliminates profits. The stability question is whether from any initial trade equilibrium we will return to that equilibrium when the allocation of factors *between* types of cities is shocked so that $U_1 \neq U_2$ and $r_1 \neq r_2$. After the shock, capital and labor move among types of cities in response to factor return differentials.

Assuming that resources are always fully employed, the adjustment equations are $d(N_1m_1)/dt = d_1(U_1 - U_2)$ and $d(K_1m_1)/dt = d_2(r_1 - r_2)$. Differentiating and substituting in the economy full employment equations and doing a Taylor series expansion of U_i and r_i about the initial equilibrium values of K_1^* and N_1^* (where potentially $U_1 = U_2$, $r_1 = r_2$), we end up with the equations $\dot{\pi} = A\pi$, where $\pi_k = K_1 - K_1^*$. Stability or convergence over time to the solution K_1^*, N_1^* requires the matrix A to have a dominant negative diagonal (McKenzie, 1960). In our model, this requires $k_2 < k_1$ when $\alpha_1 < \alpha_2$, which is the condition for stability stated above.

Appendix B. Equilibrium when Cities of the Same Type Have Different Sizes

The presentation of the impacts of amenity differentials on city sizes is nonrigorous, because a precise presentation is very difficult (see Upton, 1981, for an attempt in a related setting). What is the problem in attaining closed form solutions in the model? We focus on the free entry solution in Figure 4.1. The restricted entry case is even more difficult. We outline the algorithm to attain a solution for the free entry case to reveal the difficulties. First, assume a (experimental) number for the number of cities occupied. Then solve for $\overset{*}{N}$ in the worst quality site and hence the base utility level $\bar{U}$ in the economy. Solve for remaining city sizes by solving for the N_i that equates U^i with $\bar{U}$ given the higher values of E_0 in other cities. Finally, we equate r's in equation 2.16 where

$$r = [A(1 - \alpha)c_4^{-\alpha}]g(N)k^{-\alpha}$$

Given the different N's for each city, there is a corresponding set of k's that equalizes r's. The absolute values of K's are set to exhaust the national supply of capital $\bar{K}$. Given the value of k will vary across the very large number of cities, the economy full employment equations are messy to utilize and expressing the solutions in closed form is impossible. Note that the number of cities must be very large, as before, to avoid lumpiness problems in solution and in particular to assume the city on the worst quality site approaches $\overset{*}{N}$. This problem is also discussed in Chapter 10.

This whole solution is then repeated for different possible numbers of cities. Then one outcome is chosen amongst the different solutions for different possible total numbers of cities. It is tempting simply to pick the solution yielding the highest utility level, $\bar{U}$. However, there are two factors of production involved. If we follow Section 4 of Chapter 2 we find that a total income comparison is required, and we must pick the equilibrium number of cities that maximizes the sum of total capital rentals plus monetized utility levels. This is the allocation of sites that would be realized by profit-maximizing entrepreneurs.

CHAPTER 5

Evidence on the Nature
of Agglomeration Effects

From Chapter 2, the key to the existence of cities, or of large agglomerations of a population into small spatial areas, is scale economies in production. Chapter 1 showed that cities tend to specialize in production, due at least in part to the nature of these scale economies. The nature of scale economies thus has implications for industrial location. It also helps in understanding issues such as why big cities per se are not inherently more efficient than small.

This chapter econometrically explores the nature of scale economies external to the firm. In an urbanization context these are agglomeration economies. The issue is whether these economies are ones of localization or urbanization. Do they derive from own industry scale or also from the scale of interconnected industries with perhaps similar production patterns? What is the magnitude of measured scale effects? Do they persist over all city sizes or do they tend to peter out as scale rises? Are they Hicks' neutral or do they affect one factor relative to others?

In examining these questions the work of Henderson (1986a) on the United States and on Brazil is reported. This work is related to earlier work by Sveikauskas (1978) on the United States. Also reported is the corroborative work of Nakamura (1985) on Japan. Chapter 6 contains additional work on scale economies in Brazil, although the focus of Chapter 6 is on other aspects of production technology.

This chapter is intended to give technical support to the critical assumptions made in Chapter 2 concerning the nature of scale economies, as well as support to the reasoning used in Chapter 1 in explaining observed production patterns across cities. However, the nature of scale economies is a controversial issue in the literature, which has raised important conceptual questions. These are now reviewed to indicate what the econometric work has to say about them.

Urban external economies of scale arise from placing relevant resources in close spatial proximity such as in the same urban area, which improves the productive environment of local firms. The nature of these scale economies determines what external environment is relevant to a firm's productivity. For example, if external economies of scale are ones of localization, then the scale factor affecting a firm would be measured by total employment (or output) in that firm's industry in that

urban area. Such economies could reflect (1) economies of intraindustry specialization where greater industry size would permit greater specialization among firms
in their detailed functions, (2) labor market economies where industry size reduces
search costs for firms looking for workers with specific training relevant to that
industry, (3) scale of "communication" among firms affecting the speed of, say,
adoption of new innovations, and (4) scale in providing (unmeasured) public intermediate inputs tailored to the technical needs of a *particular* industry.

On the other hand, if scale economies are based on urbanization, they are external to any industry, and result from the general level of economic activity internal to an urban area, as might be measured by total city population or employment. These economies would then reflect benefits of operating in a larger
urban environment where there is a large overall labor market, a larger service
sector interacting with all manufacturing, and so on. While different industries
might experience different degrees of urbanization economies, only the size of
the urban area, not its industry composition, affects the extent or level of scale
effects relevant to firms in each industry.

What are the implications of whether scale economies are primarily ones of
localization or of urbanization? First, there is the issue raised by Moomaw (1981),
Segal (1976), and Sveikauskas (1975) of whether production resources are more
efficient in larger versus smaller cities. At a gross level, there is no question that
resources are in some sense more productive in larger cities—otherwise larger
cities with their higher costs of living could not pay the higher wages necessary
to attract residents. Why does this occur? One answer is that generally economies
of scale are ones of urbanization, implying that all types of resource employment
are more efficient in larger cities per se. This notion, however, raises the question
of how small cities then manage to exist, attract resources, and thrive. An alternative answer is that larger cities are, in gross, "more productive" because their
industrial compositions are different from those of small cities. Small cities contain types of industries with low localization economies while larger cities contain
ones with higher localization economies. However, in net, as in Chapter 2, once
consumption conditions are introduced, both types of cities are equally efficient.
Industries with high localizaltion economies simply require larger cities to exploit
their potential.

Note that these notions imply that it is critical to estimate the nature of scale
economies industry by industry, rather than to specify an aggregate production
function for the city (where an aggregate function also involves mixing different
technologies, which makes it difficult to interpret any estimates). An aggregate
production function by definition can have only urbanization economies represented in it. There is then no way of determining whether the resulting urbanization measures only capture industrial composition effects, in which industry
composition is shifted toward industries with greater localization economies, as
the city size distribution ascends. The empirical results suggest this is exactly what
happens and contrast with the results of Tobin and Nordhaus (1972), Kelly (1977),
Mera (1975), Segal (1976), and Moomaw (1981).

The nature of scale economies has related detailed implications for industrial
location. As suggested in Chapter 1, if scale economies arise primarily from localization benefits, then monocentric cities of the urban literature will tend to
specialize completely in production of goods that are traded across cities.[1] In that
case, the relevant question is not whether resources are more productive in larger
versus smaller cities, but what types of industries are best off (and likely to be

found) in what sizes of cities. The empirical work will point out a strong correlation between those industries that exhibit localization economies and those industries in which cities tend to specialize.

1. Methodology for Measuring the Nature and Extent of External Economies of Scale

1.1. Sources and Magnitudes of Scale Effects

To estimate the nature and extent of external scale effects, two general approaches are used. For Brazil, versions of both approaches are employed to check that they yield the same results. For the United States, there are only the data for the second type of approach.

Approaches to specifying technology. The first approach is to estimate a production function relationship where

$$X = g(\mathbf{S})\,\hat{X}(\mathbf{K}) \tag{5.1}$$

$\hat{X}(\mathbf{K})$ is the firm's own constant returns to scale (CRS) technology for $\mathbf{K}$ a vector of inputs. $g(\mathbf{S})$ is a Hicks' neutral external shift factor whose arguments are scale and technology measures specific to an industry in an urban area. Since $\hat{X}(\cdot)$ is CRS, firms can be aggregated to use industry-urban area observations, which is the only way Census data appears. In practice strict constant returns to scale need not obtain. CRS could prevail for firms above some critical minimum size or over some interval of sizes (i.e., there could be a flat bottom to a U-shaped firm cost function). It is important to note that the assumptions of Hicks' neutrality and CRS are *tested empirically* in this chapter and found to be warranted.

Equation 5.1 may be rewritten as $X/N_0 = g(\mathbf{S})\,X(\mathbf{k})$ where N_0 is labor inputs and k is the vector of ratios of remaining factors to N_0. Taking logarithms, defining $\log[X(\mathbf{k})] = f(\log \mathbf{k})$ and doing a second order Taylor series expansion of $f(\cdot)$ about all $k_i = 1$, yields a trans-log type of specification for the estimating equation

$$\log (X/N_0) = C_0 + \log g(\mathbf{S}) + \sum_i \alpha_i \ln k_i$$
$$+ 1/2 \sum_i \sum_j \gamma_{ij}\, [\log (k_i)][(\log k_j)] \tag{5.2}$$

In Chapters 2 to 4, we assume a first order Taylor series expansion, or a Cobb-Douglas technology, in order to achieve tractable theoretical solutions. The estimations in this chapter and Chapter 6 attempt to achieve a greater degree of precision with some limited success.

To infer scale effects, this chapter only estimates equation 5.2 rather than a traditional multi-equation model with a primary production function (equation 5.1) plus factor share equations. The factor share equations provide no direct information about $g(\mathbf{S})$ and estimates of the primary production equation are subject to an *incredible* degree of multicollinearity, which equation 5.2 avoids.[2] Since the focus is on scale effects and not on elasticities of substitution, equation 5.2 is chosen as the approach. Chapter 6, using a cost function, experiments with more sophisticated specifications of technology for Brazil. Scale economy estimates will result as a byproduct of the analysis. They corroborate the results here.

The second approach employed in this chapter is to define the unit cost function consistent with (5.1), the Hicks' neutrality, and CRS assumptions. Then unit costs, c, are

$$c = [g(\mathbf{S})]^{-1} c(\mathbf{p}) \tag{5.3}$$

for $\mathbf{p}$ a vector of input prices and $c(\cdot)$ the dual representation of the firm's CRS technology. The $g(\cdot)$ function is the same as that in equations 5.1 and 5.2. From Shephard's lemma $\partial c / \partial w = N_0 / X$ where N_0 is the labor input and w its price.

Taking the reciprocal and then logs yields

$$\log (X/N_0) = \log g(\mathbf{S}) + \log [(\partial c / \partial w)^{-1}] \tag{5.4}$$

We call equation 5.4 the dual factor usage equation. Again in the spirit of the translog approach, the second term on the RHS of (5.4) is defined to be a function ϕ (log p_i). It is approximated by a first order Taylor series expansion about $p_i = 1$. Given that equation 5.4 is already a differentiated function, second order terms are not necessary to represent a sophisticated technology (see also note 4). Thus

$$\log (X/N_0) = C_1 + \log g(\mathbf{S}) + \sum_i a_i \log p_i \tag{5.5}$$

The use of (5.5) and its interpretation contrasts with some approaches in the literature, as will be noted below.

Specification of scale effects. The scale measures in equations 5.1 to 5.5 relate to measures of localization and urbanization economies. The former are measured by own industry employment in an urban area and the latter by either urban area population or total local employment (the results are identical). Both samples experimented with various specifications for scale effects. In both cases, the experiments described later strongly indicate that generally the best specification is

$$g(\cdot) = e^{-\phi/N_0} N^{\epsilon_N} \tag{5.6}$$

where

$$\epsilon_0 = d (\log X)/d (\log N_0) = \phi/N_0$$

N_0 is own industry employment in an urban area and N is population of the urban area. The interpretation of the ϵ_0 and ϵ_N elasticities is that a 1% increase in, respectively, N_0 or N leads to a ϵ_0 percent or ϵ_N percent increase in the output of any firm in the industry in the urban area, *holding the firm's own inputs fixed*. The specification of a declining ϵ_0 is strongly supported by evidence presented later. It also has the advantage of reducing collinearity between the scale measures. Note the negative sign in front of ϕ in (5.6) is done, assuming positive localization effects, so that ϕ will generally be positive in the estimations.

In the estimation, for the United States and Brazil, the unit of observation is an urban area. For smaller and medium size urban areas, that observation is consistent with the monocentric city assumed in Chapters 2 to 4. For large metro areas many communities and production centers are included in the unit of observation. More theoretical work dealing with the specific nature of metro areas appears in Chapter 10. Econometrically, at present, it means local employment measures for an industry can cover an enormous area and several production centers for the industry. Thus for localization economies it is not possible to distinguish between whether economies depend only on own industry employment in nearby firms or on own industry employment scattered throughout the metropolitan area. Fortunately, only about 10% of the observations present this kind of problem. Second, for Japan in Section 2.8, it is possible geographically to basically distinguish between production centers and the overall urban area. For Japan, using scale measures defined at the overall level of the urban area versus communities within the urban area does not usually make a significant difference.

Control for other effects. Usable technology for an industry, in the sense of the specific production innovations that firms adopt, may vary across urban areas as the education and experience of the industry labor force varies. To control for this and other impacts of labor force quality, measures of age and educational attainment *specific to an industry in an urban area* [as arguments of $g(S)$] are inserted.

Finally, in equation 5.1, $\hat{X}(\cdot)$ may not be homogeneous of degree one. To allow for degrees of homogeneity different from one, we control for the average firm size for each industry in each urban area. Although this is a direct test of the degree of homogeneity, it is not a direct test of the assumption that $\hat{X}(\cdot)$ is homogeneous to some degree, an assumption that allows aggregation across firms. Although a significant coefficient for average firm size under these assumptions measures a degree of homogeneity different from degree one, it would also raise a suspicion of general nonhomogeneity. Finally, scale effects may not be Hicks' neutral. The tests of Hicks' neutrality and the results confirming neutrality are discussed later.

1.2. Empirical Implementation

Statistical problems. A basic problem in estimating equations 5.2 and 5.5 is that many right-hand side variables are endogenous, so that ordinary least squares estimates will be biased and inconsistent. There is the traditional problem that factor ratios and the measures of own industry scale are endogeneous firm and industry choice variables. However, the problems are potentially much worse than that. For many of the industries, in some urban areas the industry is the dominant export industry of the city. In any theoretical model (e.g., Mills, 1967) this means own industry employment, local wage rates, taxes and city population are jointly determined. Thus factor prices and city populations may also be viewed as endogenous variables.

The remedy for the problem is to use Two Stage Least Squares (2SLS), given a proper set of instruments. For Brazil, there was simply not enough other information on cities to provide a list of suitable instruments to test for proper specification or to do 2SLS work. For the United States in estimating equation 5.5 there is the same problem of endogenous RHS variables such as wages, labor force quality, and scale measures. However, for the United States it was possible to gather a long list of possible instruments. Hausman (1978) specification tests were used to test for orthogonality of explanatory variables to the error term, and relevant 2SLS results for the United States are reported.

Data. For the United States the primary data source is the 1972 Census of Manufacturers. Labor force quality measures and demographic information were obtained by utilizing tables from the Sixth Count of the 1970 Population Census, accounting for major changes in Standard Metropolitan Statistical Area (SMSA) definitions between 1970 and 1972. The basic sample covers 238 SMSAs. Details of variable definitions and other data sources are given in Appendix A to the chapter.

For Brazil, the primary data source is the 1970 Industrial Census. The data provided are remarkable. Included are data on different taxes, wage supplements and fringes, and current market value of equipment and structures. Industry specific labor force quality measures were obtained from the 1970 Demographic Census. Details of the sample and data are given in Appendix B; the geographic coverage of the sample is discussed in Chapter 1.

Specifics of estimating equations. For the United States, the dual factor usage equation 5.5 is estimated where output is measured by the value of production, which is the now preferred alternative to value added (Fuss and McFadden, 1978). The corresponding relevant input prices on the right-hand side of equation 5.5 are wages w, capital costs, and materials costs. For the last two prices there is no specific data. The location theory literature is predicated on the presumption that certainly gross materials prices vary across space in a consistent fashion with distance from regional market centers. Moreover, the notion of transport cost delineated market areas is consistent with empirical evidence (Weiss, 1972). Therefore, materials price are assumed to vary by distance u from regional market centers, so that price is $p_0 (1 + bu)$ for p_0, the price in regional market centers. The sign of b is not restricted.[3] In estimation log $[p_0 (1 + bu)]$ is approximated by log $p_0 + bu$. Second, three regional dummy variables (RD_i) are inserted to allow for regional market center price (p_0) differences relative to the northeast. The regional dummies also may capture regional differences in the cost of capital. Thus, equation 5.5 is revised to become

$$\log (X/N_0) = \log G(\mathbf{S}) + A_0 + \beta_1 \ln w + \beta_2 u + \sum_{i=1}^{3} \delta_i RD_i \qquad (5.5a)$$

The flexible function form approach inherent (5.5a) allows direct estimation of the characteristics of $G(\mathbf{S})$, without having to interpret them under the restriction that technology is precisely represented by one particular specific functional form.[4]

For Brazil, in estimating equations 5.2 and 5.5a, output is measured by value added because there is not a good measure of value of production.[5] For value added, inputs are capital and labor. In estimating equation 5.2, inclusion of both the log k and $(\log k)^2$ terms results with one exception in insignificant $(\log k)^2$ terms, and thus $(\log k)^2$ is generally dropped. In essence, in Brazil with the smaller sample sizes, the data only permit approximation of technology by a first order Taylor series expansion—a Cobb-Douglas function. In equations 5.2 and 5.5a for Brazil, despite the absence of materials the distance terms are left in. In the Brazilian institutional context, in equation 5.5 the distance terms allow for capital market imperfections where the price of capital rises with distance from major market centers, in the absence of other information on overall capital costs. Second, inclusion of the distance terms in the context of a less developed country to control for possible variations in net output prices seems reasonable.

2. Empirical Results

In presenting the empirical results, we start by reporting the results on the external economies of scale. The primary ordinary least squares (hereafter OLS) results for two-digit industries are presented first for Brazil and then for the United States. Then 2SLS results for the United States and results from experimenting with the functional form specification of scale effects are discussed. Finally, other possible sources of external economies of scale are examined. Having completed the examination of scale effects, we give results on other variables in the basic OLS versions of equations 5.2 and 5.5 for two-digit industries for the United States and Brazil. The section concludes with an examination of whether scale effects are Hicks' neutral.

2.1. External Economy of Scale Estimates

Brazil is presented first to demonstrate the consistency of results obtained from the production (equation 2.2) and dual factor usage (equation 2.5) equations. Then results for the dual factor usage equation for the United States are given.

Brazil. Table 5.1 presents the results for Brazil of equations 5.2 and 5.5 for the component $\log g(S) = -\phi/N_0 + \epsilon_N \log N$. Note that for positive localization economies $\phi > 0$ and

$$\epsilon_0 = \phi/N_0$$

On the left-hand side of the table are the production function (equation 5.2) results and on the right-hand side the factor usage (equation 5.5) results. The right-hand side results were obtained early in the project for (only) the sample of industries shown; since the production function became the primary equation only, it covers all industries. All two-digit industries, for which there was sufficient sample size, are represented by the production function.[6]

Examining the estimates of ϵ_N on the left side, for the production function, there is almost no evidence of urbanization economies except in printing and publishing and some weak evidence for nonmetallic minerals and furniture. For the other industries, sign patterns are mixed and coefficients hover near zero.

In contrast, there is the strong evidence of localization economies. Except for printing, all ϕ coefficients are positive and hence all scale elasticities positive. Given the multicollinearity between N_0, $\log N$, and firm size, most of the coefficients of $1/N_0$ are significant at a reasonable level. We also reestimated the production equations, dropping the $\log (N)$ term where it had a trivial impact (arbitrarily defined as both a coefficient under 0.03 and t-statistic under 0.75). These results are reported in square brackets in Table 5.1, beside the first column of figures. Dropping $\log (N)$ has little impact on the ϕ coefficients; however, in all but one case t-statistics are raised.

While there is evidence of localization economies in most industries and little evidence of urbanization economies, the evidence is considerably stronger for heavy industry than for light industry. This pattern also will reappear for Japan below. Whether this is fact, or represents estimation problems specific to certain light industries (for U.S. results see below) or problems in geographically specifying localization effects (for Japan results see below) is unclear.

The localization effects are large in Table 5.1. Median employment across urban areas for most industries in the sample is 350 to 500 employees, although for iron and steel and textiles it is nearer 900. Evaluating the elasticities at 500 employees yields the figures in the second main column. The numbers are typically over 0.1, meaning that at 500 own industry workers in a city, a 10% increase in own industry employment in the city will cause a firm's output to rise by 1%, without the firm's increasing its own inputs. Put in a different light, a 10% increase in industry employment will allow the industry (for the same cost of capital) to raise wages by $1/\alpha\%$ where α is labor's share in a Cobb–Douglas production function.

Finally for Brazil, from the right-hand side of Table 5.1, the estimates of external economies of scale based on the dual factor usage equation are very close to those for the production function. This was most encouraging because for the United States there is only the dual factor usage equation. We turn to the U.S. results now.

Table 5.1. External Scale Effects for Brazil: Two-Digit Industries

	Production Function Equation[a]					Factor Usage Equation[b]	
	ϕ	ϵ_0 $(=\phi/500)$	ϵ_N	N		ϕ	ϵ_N
Iron and steel	101.233 (1.79)	93.721 (1.94)	0.20	−0.021 (0.26)	36	109.49 (2.30)	−0.036 (0.57)
Nonelectrical machinery	36.100 (1.85)	43.749 (2.71)	0.07	0.027 (0.71)	57	28.00 (1.39)	0.015 (0.34)
Transport equipment	69.885 (2.43)	65.616 (1.97)	0.14	0.009 (0.20)	26	69.80 (2.04)	−0.003 (0.05)
Chemicals (including petrochemicals)	103.657 (2.59)		0.21	0.084 (1.28)	28	128.26 (2.10)	0.017 (0.15)
Textiles	60.273 (1.54)	57.812 (1.57)	0.12	−0.010 (0.20)	58	64.88 (1.93)	0.004 (0.09)
Apparel	15.992 (0.49)	22.797 (0.92)	0.03	0.018 (0.23)	42		
Pulp and paper	65.958 (1.32)	65.259 (1.51)	0.13	0.005 (0.06)	21		
Food processing	21.586 (0.78)		0.04	−0.038 (0.76)	107	36.136 (1.53)	−0.060 (1.31)
Nonmetallic minerals	27.941 (1.00)		0.06	0.080 (1.33)	75	36.852 (1.86)	0.066 (0.14)
Furniture	24.066 (1.13)		0.05	0.049 (1.15)	53	37.406 (1.67)	0.020 (0.42)
Printing and publishing	−9.461 (0.36)			0.177 (3.56)	32	25.302 (1.16)	0.180 (2.88)

Source: Henderson, 1986a.

Note: t-statistics are in parentheses.
[a]The basic estimating equation is (definitions of variables are given in Appendix B) $\ln (X/N_0) = f(1/N_0, \ln (N),$ $\ln$ (average f.s), u, $\ln (k)$, average age, percent l.f. illiterate).
For industries with less than 35 observations, average age, percent l.f. illiterate and u are dropped.
[b]The estimating equation is equation 5.5a without regional dummies (given only one region in the Brazilian sample).

Table 5.2. External Scale Effects for the United States: Two-Digit Industries

	OLS				2SLS		
	ϕ	ϵ_N	$\epsilon_0(=\phi/5)$	$\epsilon_0(=\phi/20)$	ϕ	ϵ_N	N
Primary metals	1.201	0.073	0.24	0.06			98
	(2.12)	(1.96)					
Electrical machinery	1.087	0.022	0.20	0.05			110
	(2.84)	(1.07)					
Machinery	0.673	0.033	0.13	0.03			168
	(2.56)	(0.20)					
Petroleum	2.226	−0.302	0.45	0.11			36
	(2.50)	(3.26)					
Apparel	0.665	0.055	0.13	0.03	2.226	0.050	70
	(0.97)	(1.58)			(2.23)	(0.88)	
Textiles	−0.042	−0.036	—	—	1.648	−0.070	64
	(0.07)	(1.06)			(1.25)	(1.36)	
Leather products	0.695	−0.016	0.14	0.03			37
	(1.47)	(0.58)					
Wood products	0.542	−0.025	0.11	0.03			128
	(1.93)	(1.21)					
Pulp and Paper	.460	−0.021	0.09	0.02			105
	(2.15)	(2.27)					
Food products	1.007	−0.013	0.20	0.05	2.063	−0.047	211
	(2.78)	(0.56)			(2.11)	(1.09)	
Printing and publishing	0.120	−0.013					210
	(0.65)	(0.73)					
Furniture	−0.441	0.022					95
	(1.89)	(1.05)					
Fabricated metals	−0.179	−0.028					185
	(0.71)	(1.58)					
Nonmetallic minerals	−0.859	0.074					164
	(4.50)	(4.00)					
Rubber	−0.293	0.004					97
	(0.89)	(0.17)					
Chemicals	−0.739	0.022					125
	(2.29)	(0.72)					

Source: Henderson, 1986a.

United States. The left-hand side of Table 5.2 contains the OLS results on external economies of scale for the United States.[7] For the United States only nonmetallic minerals has significant positive urbanization effects. For the remaining industries there is an almost equal division between positive and negative urbanization effects.

In contrast, except for textiles, for the top panel of industries localization economies are consistent, strong, and generally significant. The localization elasticities are also somewhat larger than the Brazilian numbers as evaluated at the same point (500 employees). However, median U.S. employment in any industry across the sample of SMSAs is typically near 2500 employees, so that elasticities evaluated near the median are much smaller.

Allowing for differences in industry definitions and coverage, similar industries do or do not exhibit strong localizaltion effects in the United States and Brazil. Similar patterns of strong localization effects hold for the heavy manufacturing industries in the first three or four rows of Tables 5.1 and 5.2. (In Brazil the chemical industry includes petrochemicals that have strong localization effects in the United States.) The lighter manufacturing industries in which urban areas do specialize (leather products, wood products, pulp and paper, food products) also demonstrate localization effects. This is truer of the United States (apart from textiles in OLS estimates) than Brazil.

The right-hand side of Table 5.2 presents relevant 2SLS results. 2SLS estimates would treat wages, population, industry employment, and labor force quality measures as endogenous for all industries, utilizing a long list of instruments (see Appendix A). Before doing 2SLS, we used the simple specification tests in Hausman (1978) to test for orthogonality of the explanatory variables to the error term for industries where this would potentially present a problem (industries in which cities specialize, such as food products, textiles, apparel, leather products, wood products, pulp and paper, primary metals, machinery, and electrical machinery). Significant evidence of nonorthogonality for *any* variables (including $1/N_0$) exists *only* in food products, textiles, and apparel. Evidence of nonorthogonality in other industries was weak although at times the power of the tests appeared also weak (see Henderson, 1986a). However, only for food products, textiles, and apparel is there good a priori evidence that the 2SLS estimates will be an improvement over OLS.

Table 5.2 presents the results for food products, textiles, and apparel. From Henderson (1986a), with one exception, these industries also experience the biggest impact of switching to 2SLS. They go from displaying moderate or negligible localization economies to very strong effects. Note that these three industries are light ones, indicating that the problem of simultaneity (caused by, say, a higher degree and frequency of specialization by towns in these industries) may be more relevant for light industries. If 2SLS were possible for light industries in Brazil, perhaps localization effects in these industries would be strengthened.

An alternative for Brazil in investigating the impacts of simultaneity biases is to use three-digit data to look at more microindustries that (a) represent more precisely defined technologies, and (b) may be less subject to simultaneity biases since they are a smaller portion of urban employment than their two-digit counterparts. This cannot be done for the United States, because disclosure problems too severely censor three-digit data. The Brazilian three-digit data is uncensored. Table 5.3 examines spinning and weaving (textiles), shoes (apparel), ceramics

Table 5.3. Scale Effects: Brazilian Three-Digit Industries

	ϕ		ϵ_0 $(=\phi/500)$	ϵ_N	N
Spinning and weaving of natural fibers	118.234 (3.71)		0.24	.059 (1.58)	51
Shoes	35.580 (1.41)	[40.139 (2.24)]	0.07	.013 (0.26)	21
Ceramics	48.060 (2.02)		0.10	0.054 (1.36)	27
Auto accessories	49.701 (1.50)	[69.590 (2.70)]	0.10	0.030 (0.59)	21
Agricultural machinery	94.907 (1.75)		0.19	−0.110 (1.46)	21

(nonmetallic minerals), auto accessories (transport equipment), and agricultural machinery (nonelectrical machinery). For other three-digit industries the sample size is small or the product is not defined more precisely at the three-digit level. In Table 5.3 the estimates in square brackets are for localization elasticities when urbanization effects are omitted in cases where they are unimportant. In Table 5.3, relative to Table 5.2, the improvement for light industries is quite dramatic, suggesting localization economies are just as strong there. This also corresponds to the results in Chapter 6, on sophisticated technology specifications for Brazilian three-digit industries.

2.2. Localization Economies and Specialization

In both the United States and Brazil there is a strong general relationship between industries in which cities specialize and industries having localization economies. For the United States, the top panel of industries in Table 5.2 are all ones in which SMSAs specialize. They roughly correspond to 9 of the 13 manufacturing clusters in Table 1.1 of Chapter 1 where three of the others deal with transportation and are omitted from the sample (because of censored data). In contrast, in the bottom panel of Table 5.2 the more ubiquitous consumer industries (printing, nonmetallic minerals) or ones found in many cities that often mostly service local manufacturers with intermediate inputs (fabricated metals) exhibit either no localization effects or even negative ones.

For Brazil the specialized types of cities were identified in Chapter 1 as iron and steel, nonelectrical equipment, transport equipment, chemicals, textiles, apparel, pulp and paper, food processing, nonmetallic minerals, and beverages. There are not production function estimates for the last type. The other types of cities correspond to the first nine industries listed in Table 5.1—an almost perfect overlap. Again printing and publishing and other more ubiquitous industries such as furniture and nonmetallic minerals show weaker localization economies.

2.3. Specification of Localization Economies

In Tables 5.1 and 5.2 elasticities of localization are specified to be declining. This specification was chosen for two reasons. First, relative to a constant elasticity, it generally yields a noticeably lower standard error of estimate (60–70% of the time for both the United States and Brazil) and rarely a noticeably higher one. The only dramatic change is for printing and publishing in the United States, which shows a switch to significant positive localization economies. Second and most critically, the declining elasticity form in both samples is strongly supported by a quadratic specification of the form

$$\log g(S) = \alpha \log N_0 + \beta (\log N_0)^2 + \epsilon_N \log N.$$

Results for the United States are presented in Table 5.4 for the upper panel of industries in Table 5.2 except textiles which showed no localization effects. Despite high multi-collinearity the results are indicative of a nonconstant elasticity. The simpler declining elasticity form is preferred to the quadratic because of its global properties and attractiveness for use in theoretical modeling or simulation, as well as the reduction in multi-collinearity. In general, the elasticities from the quadratic form are larger at median employment, but in industries where both

Table 5.4. Functional Form: United States Quadratic [$\alpha \log N_0 + \beta (\log N_0)^2$]

	α	β	Median N_0 (in 100s)	ϵ_0 Quadratic (median employment) ($\alpha + 2\beta \log N_0$)	ϵ_0 Declining (Table 5.2, Column 1) (median employment) (ϕ/N_0)
Primary	0.281 (2.14)	−0.030 (1.72)	30	0.077	0.043
Electrical machinery	0.190 (2.34)	−0.020 (2.01)	41	0.041	0.024
Machinery	0.094 (1.61)	−0.006 (0.80)	33	0.052	0.021
Petroleum	1.228 (3.00)	−0.181 (2.60)	12	0.327	0.221
Apparel	0.155 (1.67)	−0.008 (1.16)	20	0.107	—
Leather products	0.334 (2.15)	−0.044 (1.89)	18	0.079	0.074
Wood products	0.173 (1.46)	−0.023 (1.09)	10	0.067	0.056
Pulp and paper	0.067 (0.97)	−0.002 (0.22)	18	0.055	0.031
Food products	0.161 (1.76)	−0.014 (1.03)	20	0.077	0.048

Source: Henderson, 1986a.

terms of the quadratic are statistically strong, by mean employment, they are similar or even lower for the quadratic.

2.4. Other Sources of Scale Effects

There remains a question not asked previously of whether scale economies for an industry, rather than resulting from only either own industry scale or general urban scale, might come from the scale of related industries. To determine which are related industries, one could use cluster analysis to determine which industries tend to locate together and then see if productivity in an industry is affected by the scale of related industries (other industries in the cluster). However, it is critical to note that similar location patterns may in no way be connected with scale effects, but may simply be connected with, for instance, transport cost considerations. For example, steel production generally occurs only where there are limestone deposits. However, the scale of employment in local limestone extraction and processing may not enhance *productivity* in steel production, even if close proximity enhances profitability.

A drawback of the cluster procedure is that, when estimating productivity equations, measures of own scale of related industries are by definition highly collinear, given the basis for selecting the latter. Thus, in any estimation, one must have serious doubts about whether the effects of scale of related industries have been separated out from the fact of close proximity per se.

For the United States using Population Census data (to avoid holes in the data created by censorship of Manufacturing Census data), cluster analysis on 229 industries (defined over all economic activity) clustered together industries with very similar location patterns.[8] The results focus on related activities that are an input to the base industry whose productivity is being examined.

For the two-digit industries in Table 5.2, printing and publishing, leather products, nonmetallic minerals and iron and steel products, are not in clusters from which they receive inputs, so they have no related industries in the current frame of reference. Second, more than half of the industries that are part of clusters derive nonpositive scale benefits from the related industries. These industries with their related activities in parentheses are textiles (synthetic fibers), rubber (petroleum refining), fabricated metals (primary metals), furniture (lumber and mill products), machinery (fabricated metals), and electrical machinery (rubber). Five of the industries appear as though they might receive some scale benefits from related industries. These with their related activities in parentheses are petroleum (petroleum extraction), apparel (textiles excluding floor coverings), pulp and paper (forest products), food products (agricultural products), and chemicals (petroleum refining). In deciding if the results really indicate productivity benefits, there is a severe multicollinearity problem, although localization effects are only dramatically altered for apparel. Given the overall impact of including related industries, including the six with negative effects, it seems that inclusion of related industries only creates spurious relationships, if any at all.

The results for Brazil are no more encouraging. Cluster analysis for Brazil was not possible because the data were unavailable (see Chapter 1). However, a priori related industries can be specified, for example, as other three-digit industries in two-digit categories. Taking the three-digit industries in Table 5.3, for each of them in each urban area, employment in the other three-digit industries of the corresponding two-digit industrial grouping was calculated. On average for the industries, over 30% of the urban areas had employment in none of the other corresponding three-digit industries. For the industries, only in spinning and weaving did the scale of the other three-digit industries in the same two-digit category play *any* role. In the case of spinning and weaving, the scale of other textile industries did enhance productivity significantly. For the $1/N_0$ variable, the coefficient (absolute value) dropped to 54.9 ($t = 1.52$) and the coefficient of the log of employment in other textile subindustries was 0.092 ($t = 2.46$). A significant effect in only one out of six industries, however, again suggests that the impact of the scale of related industries can usually be ignored, or worse, is spurious.

2.5. Nonexternal-Economy Variables

The estimating equations contain variables relating to input prices, capital-to-labor ratios (Brazil), labor force quality, and firm size. The results are not all reported here, since they are not generally relevant. However, there are some comments. In equation 5.5a, the wage terms are generally positive and significant, indicating expected negative own gross substitution effects. The other price type coefficients have no ready traditional interpretation. In equation 5.2, the capital-to-labor ratio is generally significant with expected magnitudes, ranging from 0.144 for furniture to 0.430 for iron and steel (Henderson, 1987a).

In the work great attention was paid to labor force quality measures with disappointing results. Productivity seems weakly related to age. For the United States the percent of the labor force 29 years or younger in an industry, representing inexperience, produced a negative sign in 15 of the 16 industries with half of the coefficients being significant. However, controlling for educational attainment seems irrelevant to productivity. In Brazil the percent of the labor force with three or less years of schooling (effective illiteracy) produced an "incorrect" sign 50% of the time. Similarly in the United States the percent of the labor force with eight or less years of education also produced an incorrect sign 50% of the time. Experimenting with different threshold attainment levels produced equally dismal results. This result contrasts with results obtained from estimating wage equations (e.g., Brown and Medoff (1978), as well as wage equations for these data). It also contrasts with the results in Chapter 6. However, the results in Chapter 6 suggest that high and low skill labor are not really substitutable, so that there is little scope for variation in effective educational attainment. Nonetheless the results are puzzling and indicate a need for more work on the subject.

In terms of other variables, inclusion of firm size tests the assumption that firm production functions are homogeneous of degree one. For both Brazil and the United States, average firm size had no consistent impact on productivity across industries and often no robust effect across specifications within an industry. Moreover, in Brazil, any positive firm size effects seem to reflect industry composition differences (e.g., for furniture) across cities between factory standardized products and small-scale special order products (which are quite different products to the consumer).

2.6. Hicks' Neutrality

The discussion of external economies presumes Hicks' neutrality. Here, that assumption is directly tested for Brazil. Taking marginal productivity conditions for capital and labor based on equation 5.2 and combining yields the general result

$$k = k(w, r, \mathbf{S}) \tag{5.7}$$

where k is the capital-to-labor ratio, w and r the factor prices of labor and capital, and $\mathbf{S}$ the vector of scale and technology measures. If the impact of these later measures on production is Hicks' neutral, then the impact of $\mathbf{S}$ on k should be zero. A significant positive or negative impact indicates that scale or technology improvements are respectively capital or labor using. Thus, estimating equation 5.7 constitutes a direct test of Hicks' neutrality.

In estimating, it is assumed the pretax cost of capital is either the same everywhere or increases with distance from major financial centers. The posttax cost of capital varies with the effective local property tax rate (pt) on capital, specific to industry and urban area. Based on variable definitions in Appendix B, the estimating equation is

$$\ln (k) = \alpha_0 + \beta_1 \log (w) + \beta_2 u + \beta_3 pt + \beta_4 \% \text{ illiterate} \tag{5.7a}$$
$$+ \beta_5 \text{ average age} + \beta_6 \ln (fs) + \beta_7 \ln (N_0)$$

The results for β_7 are in Table 5.5. Other results are in Henderson (1985). It should be noted that equation 5.7a is well behaved. For example, the price variables (w and pt) have expected signs and consistent magnitudes, where either raising w or lowering the cost of capital by 1 percent should have the same percentage impact on k (so as to imply the same elasticity of substitution).[9]

In terms of scale effects, across industries the sign patterns are completely mixed and the variable is never significant at the 0.05 level. The hypothesis of nonneutrality of scale effects is rejected, and we conclude that external economies are

Table 5.5.   Hicks' Neutral of Scale Effects for Major Industries in Brazil

	Scale [ln (N_0)]	Adjusted R^2
Textiles	0.051	0.24
	(0.81)	
Iron and steel	−0.025	0.40
	(0.21)	
Chemicals	0.209	0.42
	(1.60)	
Transport equipment	0.005	0.57
	(0.04)	
Nonelectric machinery	0.017	0.40
	(0.29)	
Nonmetallic minerals	0.073	0.43
	(1.07)	
Apparel	−0.093	0.24
	(1.83)	
Pulp and paper	0.090	0.50
	(0.55)	
Food processing	0.054	0.18
	(0.83)	
Furniture	0.036	0.22
	(.50)	
Printing	−0.011	0.38
	(0.16)	

Hicks' neutral in their impacts on capital and labor. Addition of an urbanization economy measure ($\log N$) produces the same neutrality conclusion.

2.7. Results for Japan

Nakamura (1985) has conducted the same type of investigation for Japan, as there is here for Brazil and the United States. His approach differs in four respects. First, he uses the sophisticated type of production specification such as in Chapter 6, focusing upon a primary production function plus factor share equations. Second, he assumes a constant elasticity of localization economies. Third, he uses 3SLS methods, although his instruments are variables such as city population, city employment, and city manufacturing capital stock. These could be considered to also generally be endogenous variables, especially for industries in which cities tend to specialize.

Finally, his geographic area is generally the political unit of a city, although he has measures of prefecture level employment (Japan is divided into 47 municipally independent regions). Being able to use the political unit is an intriguing aspect of the work. In the United States large metro areas contain several historical cities that are still politically independent. Chapter 9 suggests that they may also be somewhat independent in terms of production structure, each specializing in their own activity. That is, metro areas to some extent may be clusters of different types of "cities." Being able to separate out some of the elements of the cluster is a distinct advantage in helping to understand more of the workings of urban economies.

Nakamura's results on localization and urbanization economies are presented

Table 5.6.   Urbanization vs. Localization Economies in Japan

	ϵ_{pop}	ϵ_0 (political city)	ϵ_0 (prefecture)
Iron and steel	−0.034	0.062	
	(1.68)	(2.40)	
Nonferrous metal	−0.008	0.064	0.053
	(0.43)	(2.94)	(1.04)
Nonelectrical machinery	0.028	0.082	
	(1.99)	(6.31)	
Electric machinery	0.015	0.075	
	(0.65)	(3.03)	
Transport equipment	0.022	0.042	0.095
	(1.26)	(2.12)	(2.31)
Precision machinery	0.027	0.038	0.049
	(1.21)	(1.69)	(2.34)
Textile products	0.067	0.035	0.087
	(3.31)	(1.66)	(3.98)
Apparel	0.032	0.064	0.078
	(1.70)	(3.73)	(1.15)
Pulp and paper products	0.013	0.014	0.056
	(0.50)	(0.43)	(2.44)
Leather products	0.054	0.033	
	(1.73)	(1.14)	
Food products	0.045	0.030	−0.135
	(2.10)	(0.71)	(1.94)
Lumber products	0.057	−0.010	
	(2.22)	(0.29)	
Nonmetallic minerals	0.010	0.039	0.001
	(0.52)	(1.86)	(.03)
Metal products	0.012	0.032	
	(0.88)	(2.32)	
Rubber and plastics	−0.008	0.065	
	(0.31)	(2.24)	
Chemicals	−0.004	0.030	0.051
	(0.12)	(0.58)	(2.42)
Furniture	0.069	−0.004	
	(2.68)	(0.18)	
Printing and publishing	0.078	0.039	
	(2.83)	(1.97)	

Source: Based on Tables 2 and 3 in Nakamura (1985).

in Table 5.6. They are very supportive of the work here. Table 5.6 is broken into three panels. The top contains heavy industries that display predominantly localization economies in Brazil and the United States. The middle panel contains light industries. The bottom panel contains heavy industries that do not generally display localization economies in Brazil and the United States. For heavy industries that exhibit localization economies in the United States (top panel), external economies of scale in Japan are also ones of localization. For these industries urbanization economies for heavy industry are mixed in sign and of much smaller magnitude. Moreover, even heavy industries (lowest panel) that exhibit indefinite localization economies in the United States and Brazil may have significant localization economies in Japan, dominating urbanization effects. This may occur because Nakamura is able to use the political city rather than metro area as the unit of observation.

However, for light industries, when the measure of localization is employment in the political city (Nakamura's preferred measure) while localization effects exist for some corresponding U.S. industries, they are dominated by urbanization economies. The exception is apparel, which has dominant localization economies. Earlier in the chapter based on U.S. results and Brazilian implications, it was suggested that weak localization effects for light industries can be strengthened dramatically if simultaneity problems can be dealt with statistically (something Nakamura's instruments may not do).

Table 5.6 also indicates for which industries the relevant localization measure is own employment in the political city or own employment plus some industry employment in the contiguous areas making up a prefecture. In half the cases (not shown) both measures yield similar results. For nonferrous metals, apparel, food products, and nonmetallic minerals, the political city employment produces the strongest localization effects. For transport equipment, precision machinery, textiles, pulp and paper, and chemicals overall local regional employment in the same industry seems to be a more important measure than just the immediate employment in the political city. For this later set of industries, it would appear that having several production centers clustered into the same metropolitan region is beneficial.

3. Conclusions

1. Economies of scale in manufacturing are generally ones of localization, not urbanization, indicating that agglomeration benefits derive from local own industry employment, not overall urban size. Localization economies appear to be stronger for heavy than for light industry, although if one can correct for simultaneity problems in estimation, localization economies may be as strong for light industry.

2. Industries with significant localization economies are ones in which cities tend to specialization. The issue then is not whether bigger cities are more productive than smaller—in net they are equally efficient. The issue is what types of industries are better off in smaller cities vs. bigger cities.

3. Localization economies appear to have declining elasticities, or to peter out as scale increases.

4. Employment in industries related by similar locational patterns or SIC coding appear to have no consistent positive impact on own industry productivity, per se. Their similar locational patterns would appear to occur, for example, to reduce transport costs of interindustry trade.

5. Localization economies are Hicks' neutral in their impact.

NOTES

1. With urbanization economies, specialization may also occur if the degree of urbanization economies varies across industries. However, in this case the forces for special-

ization are much weaker than with localization economies, once intercity transport costs are introduced.

2. For example, for Brazilian machinery, iron and steel, and electrical machinery and for United States fabricated metals and machinery (where capital stocks for 55 to 60 SMSAs were laboriously calculated from investment series), the simple correlation coefficients between *any* pair of output, labor, and capital stock were *over* 0.95 in every case.

3. That is, some raw materials may be more expensive in market centers than near their hinterland source.

4. If the terms in equation 5.5a beyond ln *w* are dropped, this truncated form of (5.5a) happens to be the same as a factor productivity equation based on a CES production function. Like Sveikauskas (1975, 1978) or Hansen (1983) we also do not interpret the results in the context of a CES function, but utilize the direct flexible functional form interpretation of (5.5a), or even any truncated form of (5.5a). There are three reasons for doing so. The extensive econometric work of the last decade on production technology has decisively rejected most traditional specific functional forms such as, in particular, the conventional CES (see Fuss and McFadden, 1979, for a review). Second, the statistical work supports this rejection and indicates that the terms beyond ln *w* in equation 5.5a are generally significant (and so can be additional second order terms) (see Henderson, 1986a). Finally and perhaps most critically, in the Brazil work where both equations 5.2 and 5.5 can be estimated, the two sets of results (production function and dual factor usage equation) for the form of the log $G(S)$ function are almost identical under the flexible functional form interpretation of equation 5.5a, but radically different under, say, a CES interpretation of a truncated equation 5.5a, where a CES is "unstable" for elasticities of substitution near 1. In a CES the estimates of scale effects are obtained by combining the estimates of $G(S)$, with the coefficient of log *w*, in which, as the coefficient of log *w* (the elasticity of substitution) approaches 1, the equation exhibits "instability" and there is a sign switch in the interpretation of scale effects. For example, a coefficient of 0.1 on ln *N* is interpreted as a positive scale elasticity of 10 if the point estimate of the coefficient of ln *w* is 0.99, and a negative scale elasticity of -10 if the point estimate of the coefficient of ln *w* is 1.01. We interpret the elasticity directly, stating that a 1% increase in *N* will raise productivity by 0.1%.

5. There was a problem both with the materials data and with inclusion of home production.

6. For Brazil there is a problem that the repair and other servicing activities associated with a two-digit industry are put in the manufacturing sector, not the service sector. To avoid having observations where there was only a service component in the urban area, we excluded observations where employment fell below 100 in the urban area from the beginning. (Also two-digit but not three-digit industries were censored.) Note that in the United States data observations where employment is only 100 almost never appear—they are automatically censored out. All observations are included in Chapter 6, which focuses on elasticities of substitution using a translog equation system for detailed three-digit industry data where activities are more homogeneous. The localization versus urbanization results are just as strong.

7. The transport industry is omitted because censoring removes almost all important data points. Two-digit industries 38 and 39 are omitted on the basis that they are simply groupings of miscellaneous activities. Tobacco is omitted because the sample size is only four.

8. In the original 229 industry × 243 SMSA matrix of employment fractions mentioned in Chapter 1, pairs of rows of employment fractions for each pair of industries are correlated to form a 229 × 229 symmetric matrix of correlation coefficients between industries representing similarity of location patterns. Primitive cluster analysis (see Table 1.1 in Chapter 1) was then performed on this matrix. The correlation coefficient for the *last* industry added to any cluster was 0.42. Most clusters had much higher minimums.

9. A 1% increase in *w* typically raises *k* by 0.8%. A 1% increase in the cost of capital

(interest and depreciation of 0.13 plus a typical property tax rate of 0.02) leads typically to a 1.0% decrease in k (for a pt coefficient of -7, the elasticity is -7×0.15).

Appendix A. U.S. Data

Primary data sources are the 1972 Census of Manufacturers and the 1970 Census of Population. In moving between 1970 and 1972 we accounted for the grouping of eight 1970 SMSAs into four 1972 SMSAs, and the 1970 urban population measure is based on 1972 SMSA definitions. Key variable definitions are below. Instruments used in Table 5.2 estimation are driving time to regional market, regional dummies, annual precipitation, heating degree days, coastal dummy, labor force participation females, percentage of males commuting to CBD, percent of families with children, percent of public administrative employees over 60, percent of population with a college degree, percent of manufacturing employees who are black, ratio of state to federal employees, percent of state labor force unionized, farm population of state, percent of housing built before 1950, multiple name SMSA, percent of females in manufacturing, driving time to national market, federal and state percent of total SMSA revenues, percent of families housed in one unit structures, and cost of electrical power. These are taken from *1972 City and County Data Book, Climatological Data* (National Oceanic and Atmospheric Administration) 1976, *1972 Statistical Abstract, Waterborne Commerce of the U.S.A.* (U.S. Corps of Engineers), *1972 Census of Governments, Uniform Crime Report,* 1970 and 1971 (FBI), *Typical Electric Bills* (U.S. Federal Power Commission) 1970, and 1970 Population Census.

Variable Definitions and Sources

Variable	Definition
X	Value of production from Manufacturing Census.
N_0	Annual hours of work for production workers plus 2000 hours/year times number of nonproduction workers.
w	Total wages and salaries divided by N_0.
Percent < 8 years schooling	Percentage of two-digit industry specific labor with eight or less years of schooling as calculated from the Sixth Count of 1970 Population Census, by combining Table 124D's matrix of education by 27 manufacturing occupations in each SMSA with Table 1250's matrix of 27 occupations by 20 manufacturing industries to get SMSA specific matrices of education by industry.
Percentage > 55 years of age	Percentage of two-digit specific labor force that is 55 years of age or older from Table 1290 of Sixth Count of 1970 Population Census.
u	Distance to nearest regional market center. These are the 27 National Business Centers, as defined by Rand McNally (based on volume of financial activity and wholesale and retail trade). Distance is in hours of driving time based on Rand McNally estimates (with gaps filled in based upon likely routes and speeds of travel). We also calculated driving times to the nearest of six national market centers (New York, Chicago, Los Angeles, San Francisco, Atlanta, and Dallas).

Appendix B. Variable Definitions for Brazil

Variable	
X	Value-added: value of production less total materials costs less-production taxes. Production tax rates vary spatially and their differences may not be passed onto consumers. Including production taxes in value added has a minimal impact on the results.
N_0	Average monthly number of employees less owners and directors (a trivial number). Hours of work information is not collected.
w	Total salaries less payments to owners and directors *plus* firm contributions to social security, private insurance, and pension programs, all divided by N_0.
K	Market value of capital stock.[a] The census question asks what firms could sell their equipment, structures, and land for today (other questions ask book value and depreciated book value).
fs	Average firm size: N_0 divided by number of firms.
pt	Property tax rate: Industry property tax payments divided by K. This varies by industry and urban area according to exemptions granted.
Percentage illiterate	Percentage of labor force by two-digit industries with three or less years of schooling. Calculated directly from 25% "long-form" sample of 1970 Demographic Census.
Age	Average age of labor force by two-digit industry, from 1970 Demographic Census.
u	Distance in kilometers to nearest coastal port. For all six ports the urban area is a major metropolitan area. There is only one major interior metropolitan area in the sample, Belo Horizonte. São Paulo is counted as a "port" although it is 75 km from the sea and the actual port is Santos.

[a]Is this a good measure of physical units? If capital is perfectly malleable, since a depreciated *quantity* of capital has the same *value* as the same quantity of new capital (where value equals cost of producing new units of capital in perfect competition), the quantity of capital is directly proportional to the value of capital regardless of age distribution. Value is also approximately *proportional* to quantity regardless of age distribution if capital is non-malleable but "infinitely" lived and decaying exponentially.

CHAPTER 6

Population Composition of Cities: Bright Lights or Productivity?

Wages rise with city size
[We are] probing all the whys
Is there seduction by bright lights
Or production growing with insights?

Douglas Keare,
an early 1980s doodle

This chapter investigates the determinants of the population composition of cities, based on results for the United States of America and Brazil. Population composition refers to the allocation of population between different skill or education groups, typically utilizing a twofold division as between skilled vs. unskilled, literate vs. illiterate, higher education vs. not, and so on. While population composition is not explicitly incorporated into the theoretical model of Chapters 2 to 4 for reasons discussed in Appendix C, the econometric model developed in this chapter is in the spirit of the theoretical model.

Differences in skill composition across cities have a variety of important implications in both developed and less developed countries. Disparities between large and small cities or between regions mean that some areas have well-educated voting populations influencing the quality of local public decision making and the local quality of life and that other areas do not. Some areas can attract industries with advanced technology; other cannot. Some areas can offer a sophisticated service infrastructure for producers and consumers; others cannot.

In most developing countries, there is a strong positive correlation between the ratio of high to low skill population and city size. For example, in Brazil for measures defined in Appendix B this correlation is 0.69 (Table B.3) across all cities and virtually the same even amongst nonmetropolitan areas. In the United States for corresponding measures the correlation is zero. Why is this so? Are there market forces in developing countries that disproportionately draw skilled people out of rural areas and smaller towns, so that the loss of an educated labor force and local voting population is a natural consequence, for example of the process of economic development? Or are there government policies in developing countries that are inappropriately biased toward attracting disproportionate numbers of skilled people to larger cities?

The discussion starts with an overview of the determinants of population composition in cities and the issues that arise from modeling population composition differences. Then Section 1 gives the exposition of an econometric model and Section 2 presents the results for the United States and Brazil.

The skill composition of any city is determined by the interaction of demand and supply forces. First, there is the demand for different skill groups by the city's industries, reflecting both each individual industry's own demand and the industrial mix of the city. A crucial element for any industry is the degree of substitutability between high and low skill workers in production technology. A high degree of substitutability means that skill composition for an industry is very flexible and will respond readily to supply conditions, so that in some sense the production side does not strongly influence urban skill composition. In contrast, a low degree of substitutability means that fairly rigid skill mixes are needed in production, so that in some sense "skill requirements" become an operational concept. Then a city's population composition will be influenced by its industrial mix, or the mix of skill requirements of different industries. Thus cities with industries with low skill requirements will have a largely unskilled labor force.

That begs the question of what determines a city's industrial mix. There, of course, is an interaction between demand and the supply side yet to be discussed. It may be that supply conditions will determine population composition, which will then attract the appropriate skill usage industries. However, it may be that production amenities such as access to certain raw materials or cetain types of markets will determine industrial mix, which may then determine population composition.

Whichever is the case, the focus of this chapter in terms of the demand side is twofold. First, are skill requirements an operational concept, so that industrial mix strongly influences population composition? Second, is there an interaction between population composition and city size? This question raises a second element of skill demand by an industry. Scale economies in production analyzed in the previous chapter may be biased, favoring the use of high relative to low skill workers in larger cities. For example, large cities with their more developed communications "networks" in labor or output markets may favor more highly educated workers who both better utilize and constitute this network. This question is investigated.

On the supply side it is assumed that both high and low skill workers are effectively perfectly mobile (see note 2). Thus, relative differences in mobility and initial endowments are not the issue. Amenity differences mean that different urban sites offer different natural or exogenous amenities such as climate, access to recreational settings (e.g., beaches, forests, and mountains), quality of drinking water, soil fertility for cash crop fruits and vegetables, etc. If different skilled people value these amenities differently and hence have different appropriately defined willingness-to-pay for these amenities (see below), there should be Tiebout type stratification of the population on the supply side. Those skill groups valuing some amenities more than other groups should be concentrated on sites where those amenities are abundant. In the absence of production amenity considerations, industries intensive in those skill groups will then go to those sites. The extent of stratification is limited by any requirements that some workers from all skill groups may be required in production of most goods. On the other hand, it is enhanced by specialization of cities in production, so only industries intensive in skill groups valuing local amenities need locate there. All this, of course, holds constant production amenities, which will also affect location decisions of firms and industries.

The first basic issue then on the supply side is whether different skill groups value amenities differently (defined rigorously later as differential percentage impacts on willingness-to-pay as reflected through wage rates). If they do not, then differentials in natural amenities do not impact population composition. If they do, then Tiebout type stratification forces should affect population compositions.

The second issue also concerns amenities exogenous to the city but endogenous to the economy, such as local public services set by state or national governments. For example, school teachers may be appointed at the state or national rather than local level. A national government may favor some cities or regions with better teachers and pupil–teacher ratios, drawing families who most value those amenities to those cities and regions.

The supply side, however, does not simply involve examining exogenous amenities to the city. There are also locally endogenous amenities. In particular, city size and population composition themselves may be direct amenities or may indirectly affect crime rates, peer group effects in schooling, local public decision making, and so on. Moreover, city size and composition may interact, with different skill groups having different evaluations of size and relative numbers of more educated people. A major focus of this chapter is exploring this interaction in Brazil and the United States.

Having stated the determinants of population composition and the issues to be explored in this chapter, the question of why Brazil has such a strong positive correlation between city size and greater skill composition of the population, while the United States does not, can be reexamined. One hypothesis involves skill requirements. In Brazil, in contrast to the United States, either because of natural technological conditions or because of government industrial location policies, industries requiring high skill intensity are found in larger cities. An alternative hypothesis is a bright lights one. High skill people are disproportionately drawn to larger cities either because of the amenities naturally found or produced by market forces there or because of government policies biased toward larger cities, which results in the disproportionate production of public services valued by high skill people.

A general model of the demand and supply of population composition that can be implemented econometrically is presented next. For reasons to be analyzed, the two sides are treated differently—one at a macro level and the other at a micro level. Joint estimation of both sides is not possible with currently available data sets. However, demand and supply interaction can be accounted for and integrated into the estimation procedure. The results of the estimation will help answer the questions raised in the above discussion.

1. An Econometric Model of the Demand and Supply of Population and Population Composition for a City

The supply side, which also provides an overview of the model, is examined first. A division of the population into two skill groups based on educational differences is assumed, so there are skilled vs. unskilled workers and families. The division of skilled vs. unskilled will differ for Brazil and the United States given the different levels of economic development. The division into only two as opposed to many skill groups, presents the usual implicit aggregation assumptions. The defense is that a start must be made somewhere in differentiating the population, and the first step is to attempt a two group division. That is one step ahead of the bulk of analysis, which assumes completely homogeneous populations.

1.1. The Supply Side

In examining the supply side, consider first low skill people. These people operate in a national, or at least regional, labor market so that the supply curve of low skill people to any urban area is infinitely elastic at the going regional or national utility level. The assumption is *not* critical,[1] is in part tested econometrically (see note 4), and is consistent with recent empirical evidence.[2] The indirect utility of any low skill worker actually in the city is given by

$$U_L = U_L(w_L, p_L(N, \ldots), \hat{A})$$

where w_L is the wage paid to a low skill worker, $\hat{A}$ is a vector of amenities, taxes, and quality characteristics of local public services, and $p_L(N \ldots)$ is the cost of housing to low skill people in the urban area. In the absence of cost-of-living data the Alonso–Muth–Mills rent gradient model is employed to specify that the cost of living varies across cities primarily as housing costs vary (apart from the taxes in $\hat{A}$), and that the cost of housing is primarily a function of city population, N, as well as being influenced by, say, urban infrastructure measures and the mix of high and low income people in the city. That mix is defined by N_H/N_L, where $N_H + N_L = N$. These latter items determining $p_L(\cdot)$ may also appear in the $\hat{A}$ vector. Breaking N_H/N_L and N out of the $p_L(\cdot)$ function and amenity vector yields the implicit function:

$$\bar{U}_L - U_L(w_L, N, \frac{N_H}{N_L}, \mathbf{A}) = 0 \tag{6.1}$$

where U_L is the going utility level in national (or regional) labor markets for the infinitely elastic supply of low skill people to any city. A is now a vector of nonpopulation amenities. By the same reasoning, for high skill people we have the corresponding implicit function:

$$\bar{U}_H - U_H(w_H, N, \frac{N_H}{N_L}, \mathbf{A}) = 0 \tag{6.2}$$

What econometric specifications arise from (6.1) and (6.2)? There are several endogenous variables and several specifications, including asymmetric vs. symmetric and price vs. quantity ones. All of these variables in theory yield the same information, in terms of marginal evaluations and impacts on city sizes of amenities. An asymmetric quantity specification is chosen because it is econometrically robust and reduces multicollinearity relative to a symmetric specification. Second, it presents results directly in terms of the variables of interest: city size and population composition. In Henderson (1985) symmetric quantity results based on estimating inverted forms of (6.1) and (6.2) are also presented, and in Henderson (1982c) symmetric price results are presented on a different U.S. data set. The

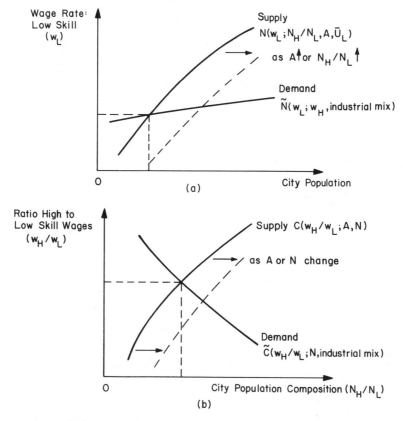

Fig. 6.1   (a) Demand and Supply Determinants of City Sizes (b) Demand and Supply Determinants
of Population Composition

results are all reasonably similar; but the asymmetric ones presented here are the
preferred ones for both the United States and Brazil.

For the asymmetric specification, (6.1) we invert to get a city size equation and
the ratio of (6.1) to (6.2) is formed to get a composition equation. Each of these
is examined in turn.

City size equation. Inverting (6.1) yields the city size equation

$$N = N(w_L, \frac{N_H}{N_L}, \mathbf{A}; \bar{U}_L) \qquad (6.3)$$

where

$$\frac{\partial N}{\partial Z} = \frac{\partial U_L (\cdot)/\partial Z}{-\partial U_L/\partial N} \qquad (6.3a)$$

for Z any argument of (6.3).

The city size equation in (6.3) can be viewed as a population supply function
to the city in N, w_L space, with the following types of properties and interpretations. These are illustrated in Figure 6.1. To evaluate whether supply shifters

shift the supply curve up or down (and to evaluate what shifters are (dis)amenities), the impact of wages on supply must first be determined. It is hypothesized and *empirically shown* that the supply curve in N, w_L space is upward sloping, where that means $\partial N/\partial w_L = (\partial U_L/\partial w_L)/(-\partial U_L/\partial N) > 0$. On the right-hand side of this equation, theory requires $\partial U_L/\partial w_L > 0$; thus, the empirical result that $\partial N/\partial w_L > 0$ implies $-\partial U_L/\partial N > 0$. Therefore, we note for later reference that in evaluating the other derivatives of equation 6.2, $\partial N/\partial Z = (\partial U_L/\partial Z)/(-\partial U_L/\partial N)$, the denominator is always positive.

$(-\partial U_L/\partial N) > 0$ is consistent with stability of equilibrium or the upward sloping supply curve in Figure 6.1 is consistent with stability in a demand and supply curve framework. It is also consistent with theoretical models of city size, where controlling for scale effects in production (i.e., controlling for wages), increases in N cause utility losses through, for example, cost-of-living increases or disamenity increases (Mills, 1967; Dixit, 1973).

The other arguments of equation 6.3 are supply shifters. For example, an increase in a positive amenity shifts out the supply curve in Figure 6.1 and leads to an increase in city size, or $dN/dA = (\partial U_L/\partial A)/(-\partial U_L/\partial N) > 0$ if $\partial U_L/\partial A > 0$. An intuitive explanation of why an increase in a positive amenity increases N is as follows. As A increases, the potential utility of low skill people in the city rises. However, given the going utility level U_L in national markets, the potential ("temporary") rise in utility causes immigration of low skill people to the city. This increase in city size raises cost of living and continues until the benefit of the increase in the amenity is completely offset by increased costs of living. Of course, the shift in the city's supply curve in w_L, N space interacts with the demand curve in Figure 6.1, affecting the equilibrium values of all endogenous variables such as w_L. For an upward (downward) sloping demand curve generally, w_L will rise (fall) as the amenity increases.

There are two final comments on equation 6.3. First, it has the same form as a hedonic wage equation for low skill people, except that two endogenous variables, N and w_L, are switched between the left and right-hand sides. To obtain the hedonic wage coefficients for low skill people, equation 6.2 is differentiated setting $dN = 0$ (i.e., controlling for N), yielding for any amenity $dw_L/dA = -(\partial N/\partial A)/(\partial N/\partial w_L)$.

Second, in equation 6.3 it is hypothesized a priori that the ratio of high-to-low skill adults is viewed as an amenity by low skill people. This was mentioned earlier. First, it may be an amenity in itself. Second, an increase in N_H/N_L may lead to better public decision making and, perhaps, more favors from the state and federal government. Third, the ratio may be a strong determinant of better quality quasi-public services, such as health care and education, for which there are not useful measures (see later).

Population composition equation. To get the population composition equation, from (6.1) and (6.2) we form the ratio $\bar{U}_H/\bar{U}_L - U_H(\cdot)/U_L(\cdot) = 0$ and invert it to get a composition equation with one simplification[3]:

$$(N_H/N_L = C\left(\frac{w_H}{w_L}, N, \mathbf{A}; \frac{\bar{U}_H}{\bar{U}_L}\right)$$

(6.4)

In (6.4), for any argument Z

$$\frac{\partial(N_H/N_L)}{\partial Z} = \frac{\partial(U_H/U_L)/\partial Z}{-\partial(U_H/U_L)/\partial(N_H/N_L)} \qquad (6.4a)$$

Equation 6.4 is interpreted as a supply curve of population composition in N_H/N_L, w_H/w_L space, as illustrated in Figure 6.1. It is hypothesized and empirically shown that this curve is upward sloping, or that

$$\frac{\partial(N_H/N_L)}{\partial(w_H/w_L)} = \frac{\partial(U_H/U_L)/\partial(w_H/w_L)}{-\partial(U_H/U_L)/\partial(N_H/N_L)} > 0$$

Given that the numerator must be positive, an upward sloping supply curve implies that the denominator is also positive, which is consistent with stability in the model. The strong empirical result that $\partial(N_H/N_L)/\partial(w_H/w_L) > 0$ and its implication that $\partial(U_H/U_L)/\partial(N_H/N_L) < 0$ in equation 6.4a also means that increases in N_H/N_L benefit low skill people more (defined by percent changes in utility) than high skill people. Thus, for example, while increases in N_H/N_L may raise within limits the public quality of life in a city (e.g., crime rates, public recreation, public schooling, health care) for low skill people, the greater income of high skill people ensures high levels of many of these quality of life items through personal consumption patterns alone. This result held in estimations of all specifications, symmetric or not.

The other arguments of equation 6.4 are supply shifters in Figure 6.1 and tell which amenities and public services high skill people value more than low skill people. That is, in the numerator of equation 6.4a if $\partial(U_H/U_L)/\partial A > 0$, high skill people have a greater percent increase in utility from an increase in A than low skill people. (We operate here under the implicit assumption in estimating that in any city high and low skill people consume the same level of the "citywide" amenities.) Since equation 6.3 tells how much low skill people value an amenity and equation 6.4 tells how much high skill relative to low skill people value an amenity, combining the two equations yields high skill people's absolute evaluation. These calculations are illustrated below when interpreting the empirical results. Second, in equation 6.4 and N_H/N_L, w_H/w_L space, if $\partial(N_H/N_L)/\partial A > 0$ for a positive amenity, this means that when A increases in a city there is the following effect. As an amenity more highly valued by high skill people increases, to maintain $\bar{U}_H/\bar{U}_L$, ceteris paribus, N_H/N_L must also increase so as to have a negative offsetting impact on U_H/U_L (given N_H/N_L is more highly valued by low skill people). Of course, the shift in the supply curve in N_H/N_L, w_H/w_L space will impact all endogenous variables (which must be accounted for to estimate consistently the parameters of equation 6.4).

1.2. The Demand Side

A city's "demand" for population is directly related to labor force demand functions through labor force participation coefficients or functions. Given these functions, the industrial demand for labor comes from two components. One is the nontraded good component (housing, retail, and personal services), which is similar in every city. The other is the export good component, which varies across cities as industrial composition varies with urban specialization. Thus a city's industrial composition determines its total demand for labor and its skill composition demand.

The total demand for labor in the export sector of the city and, hence, the demand curve for the whole city may generally be upward sloping, as illustrated in Figure 6.1a. Given fixed prices in national markets for output, capital, and materials, as scale increases in a city the wages it will pay given intracity competition will generally increase, as can be seen from equation 2.4. The demand for labor varies across cities as the degree of scale economies of the city's export goods change with changes in specialization and industrial composition.

The demand for high skill in relation to low skill workers depends on industrial composition in the city. The *extent* of composition demand depends on the high relative to low skill "intensity" of the export good(s) a city produces. The *elasticity* of skill composition demand with respect to changes in the relative prices of high and low skill labor depends on the degree of substitutability between high and low skill labor for the export good(s) the city produces. Figure 6.1b illustrates a downward sloping composition curve as predicated by theory. The extent of composition demand may also depend on the nature and extent of scale economies, where scale economies may be Hicks' neutral, or high relative to low skill using. This is reflected by shifts in the composition demand equations.

The econometric specification of the demand side focuses on estimating the skill intensity, elasticity, and bias parameters for different manufacturing industries in Brazil and the United States. Thus compared to the supply side, which focuses on the determinants of aggregate urban measures, the demand side necessarily focuses at a more micro level, estimating the technology of individual industries and the parameters affecting their demands for high skill in relation to low skill workers. Although obviously it would be desirable to integrate the two sides and estimate them simultaneously, data availability prohibits this, not to mention complexity (where an integrated model could easily involve 15 to 20 equations). In particular, to integrate the demand and supply side, production relationships for *each* of the major export industries of each city (see Section 3) must be included. However, because U.S. Manufacturing Census data are censored for disclosure reasons, for most cities data on one of their major export industries are completely missing. For Brazil two-digit data are censored and three-digit coverage is incomplete.

The estimation of technology on the demand side is sufficient to establish the general properties of demand curves in Figures 6.1. We will learn whether scale economies mean the demand curve is upward sloping in Figure 6.1a, whether the slope of demand in Figure 6.1b is elastic (labor inputs are highly substitutable) or inelastic (skill requirements) and whether the height (skill usages) varies across industries. As noted earlier, the determinants of industrial composition per se, which depend on urban site amenities and government policies, are not estimated. The impact of site amenities is discussed in Chapters 1 and 7 and the impact of government policies in Chapters 8 and 9.

2. Econometric Results: Supply Side

As noted earlier, a first focus on the supply side is on discovering whether different skill groups evaluate various amenities differently. If so, for exogenous amenities, that becomes a basis for population stratification. A second focus is on the examination of endogenous amenities such as population composition and city size and determining their interaction. It will turn out that population amenities are critical to understanding the allocation of population. A third focus will be on determining which amenities are valued by either high or low skill people and which amenities are not valued at all. An empirical measure of an amenity may be recorded as having no evaluation if the amenity it measures is indeed not valued, if it does not properly measure the quality of the amenity, or if the amenity it measures is not a citywide amenity, but is entirely a neighborhood phenomenon with little or no correlation in quality levels across the neighborhoods of a city.

The results support related work, Smith (1978), Getz and Huang (1978) and Henderson (1982c), indicating that some amenities are evaluated differently by different skill groups. However, the work reported here is unique in terms of its sample size, its handling of simultaneity bias, its rich data base for the United States on different amenities, its incorporation of population amenities, and its examination of a developing country.

The supply side focuses on results for the United States, because of the far richer data base for supply side estimation for the United States than Brazil. The reverse will be the case on the demand side. In terms of supply, for Brazil there is an incomplete set of amenity measures and a limited list of instrumental variables for Three Stage Least Squares (3SLS). However, the Brazil results are interesting and support the more comprehensive United States results. First, there is a general discussion of econometric implementation of the supply side model. Then, the U.S. results and next the Brazil results are presented.

2.1. Econometric Implementation

The price and quantity variables in equations 6.3 and 6.4 are specified in log form and other variables in linear form:

$$\log N = \alpha_0 + b_w \log w_L + b_c \log (N_W/N_L) + \mathbf{Ab} + \epsilon_N \qquad (6.5a)$$
$$\log (N_w/N_L) = \alpha_1 + \beta_w \log w_H/w_L + \beta_N \log N + \mathbf{A\beta} + \epsilon_C \qquad (6.5b)$$

The drawings for each error term are assumed to be identically and independently distributed, but are contemporaneously related, reflecting the communality of the stochastic processes affecting N and N_H/N_L within a city.

In estimating equations 6.5 the right-hand side of both equations contain variables that are clearly endogenous to any city. From Chapter 2 and Appendix C to this chapter, $w_L, w_H/w_L, N$, and N_H/N_L are obviously endogenous variables. However, some local public service variables are also endogenous, being influenced in the local political and economic environment by population and income variables and hence the stochastic elements ϵ_N and ϵ_C. For example in the United States local public service variables include property taxes on the cost side, direct output variables such as urban infrastructure measures, and variables such as crime rates and pollution levels that reflect in part local public sector decisions and are strongly influenced by population size and composition. To efficiently account for endogeneity of right-hand side variables and contemporaneous covariance, equations 6.5 are estimated by three-stage least squares (3SLS) to obtain consistent estimates. For the United States, exogenous variables and instruments include a very extensive list (see Table 6.1) of geographic and weather variables pertaining to the locality and region, variables determined by socioeconomic forces beyond the city (e.g., cost of electrical power) and variables pertaining to historically determined development and sociological environment (housing stock, racial,

Table 6.1. City Size and Population Composition (Absolute t-statistics in Parentheses)

	Size ln (N)	Composition ln (N_H/N_L)
	3SLS[a]	3SLS[a]
ln (w_L)	2.005	—
	(2.71)	
ln (w_H/w_L)	—	1.450
		(3.05)
ln (N_H/N_L)	0.485	—
	(1.98)	
ln (N)	—	0.116
		(2.36)
Precipitation	-0.679×10^{-2}	-0.314×10^{-2}
	(1.39)	(2.03)
Heating (°) days	-0.108×10^{-3}	-0.948×10^{-5}
	(2.59)	(0.78)
Coastal dummy	-0.321	-0.834×10^{-2}
	(2.55)	(0.18)
Tons particulates per square mile	-0.227	-0.017
	(2.35)	(0.56)
Murder rate	0.042	-0.033
	(2.30)	(4.73)
Buses per square mile	1.302	-0.188
	(5.66)	(2.28)
Driving time to regional market	-0.049	0.011
	(2.06)	(1.51)
Property tax ($M) per capita (thousand)	-0.532	-0.003
	(0.62)	(0.01)
Median years of schooling for females	—	0.450
		(11.56)
Constant	-11.473	-5.618
N	207	207

Source: Henderson, 1985.

[a]Instruments are precipitation, heating degree days, coastal dummy, driving time to regional market, driving time to national market, state farm population, state forest land, state iron reserves, state oil reserves, regional (16) textile employment, regional dummies (3), percent of houses built prior to 1950, ratio of female to male family heads, ratio of blacks to whites, ratio of one to multiple family housing units, ratio of children to adults, percentage of state labor force unionized, cost of power, and federal–state revenue subsidy rate. Endogenous variables are ln (w_L), ln (w_H/w_L), ln (N), ln (N_H/N_L), tons of particulates per square mile, murder rate, buses per square mile, property tax per capita, and median years of schooling for females.

and age compositions). For Brazil, the list of instruments (see Table 6.4) is more limited but plausible.

2.2. U.S. Results

In the estimation, high and low skill are classified by educational attainment on the basis of whether they have at least completed high school or not. Variable definitions and sources are given in Appendix A. The sample is the 207 Standard Metropolitan Statistical Areas (SMSAs) for 1970 for which there are complete data; most variable measures fall in the period 1969–1971.

The results for equations 6.5 are in Table 6.1. These are 3SLS results. In Henderson (1985), OLS results are also presented for comparison to confirm the expected impact of controlling for endogeneity. The impact of amenities on city size and composition are presented in elasticity form in Table 6.2. The willingness-to-pay for amenities is analyzed in Table 6.3 and defined below. All the results are discussed by blocks of variables, as marked off by the panels in Table 6.1. Size and composition results are discussed together for each block of variables, since a proper evaluation of amenity preferences of low skill versus high skill people requires joint consideration.

Wage variables. The wage variables in both sets of equations in Table 6.1 have positive coefficients, indicating that the supply curves in N, w_L, and N_H/N_L, w_H/w_L space are both upward sloping. Both coefficients are highly significant and confirm the assumptions in equations 6.3a and 6.4a that $\partial U_L/\partial N < 0$ and $\partial (U_H/U_L)/\partial(N_H/N_L) < 0$, respectively.

The estimation of equations 6.5 yields reasonably large wage coefficients, as expected. As w_L in a city rises, for $\bar{U}_L$ to remain constant, city size must increase along the supply curve sufficiently so as to just offset the benefits on $U_L(\cdot)$ of the wage increase. The offsetting occurs because as city size increases the cost of living increases, as in a Muth–Alonso rent model. Thus, controlling for other arguments in $U_L(\cdot)$, Table 6.1 states that, along the supply curve a 1% increase in wages across cities is associated with a corresponding 2% increase in urban area population and that 2% is the response that indirectly (through cost-of-living increases) maintains $\bar{U}_L$ along the supply curve. Similarly, in the earlier discussion of equation 6.4, the coefficient of w_H/w_L measures the response in N_H/N_L that offsets the impact on U_H/U_L of the relative wage change so as to maintain $\bar{U}_H/\bar{U}_L$.[4]

A final comment on the wage results is that generally in estimating equation 6.5a, it is important to control for (endogenous) median years of schooling of females, given that the wage, but not population, variables are based on males.

Population amenities. Based on Section 1, a positive coefficient of N_H/N_L in the city size equation indicates that the ratio of high-to-low skill people is an amenity to low skill people, while the positive coefficient for N in the composition equation indicates that city size is less of a disamenity for high skill than for low skill people. This latter result held under all specifications and could represent greater availability and lower price (scale in markets) in larger cities of certain goods and services consumed more by high relative to low skill workers.

Combining equations 6.5a and 6.5b gives the actual willingness-to-pay for population amenities of both high and low skill people. For low skill people, differentiating equation 6.5a, respectively, holding N_H/N_L and N constant, yields

$$d \log w_L/d \log N = b_w^{-1}$$
$$d \log w_L/d \log (N_H/N_L) = -b_c/b_w \qquad (6.6)$$

For high skill people we differentiate (6.5b) holding N_H/N_L and then N constant and substitute in the above expressions for $d \log w_L$ to get:

$$d \log w_H/d \log N = -\beta_N/\beta_w + b_w^{-1}$$
$$d \log w_H/d \log (N_H/N_L) = \beta_w^{-1} - b_c/b_w \qquad (6.7)$$

These results are presented in Table 6.3. They are all in elasticity form and are

Table 6.2. City Size and Composition Elasticities of Amenities (Evaluated at Mean Amenity Levels)

	Precipitation	Heat (°) days	Coast dummy	Pollution	Buses/ square mile	Drive time: Reg markets	Property tax	Murder rate
Size	−0.25	−0.49	0.32	−0.16	0.53	−0.17	−0.10	0.31
Composition	−0.11	−0.05	0	−0.01	−0.08	0.04	0	−0.24

Source: Henderson, 1985.

Table 6.3. Willingness-to-pay Elasticities for Amenities ($-d \log w/d \log A$)

	Size (N)	Composition	Precipitation	Heat (°) days	Coast dummy	Pollution	Buses/ square mile	Driving time to regional market center	Property tax
Low skill	−0.50	0.24	−0.12	−0.24	0.16	−0.08	0.26	−0.09	−0.05
High skill	−0.43	−0.44	−0.20	−0.27	0.16	−0.09	0.21	−0.04	−0.05

Source: Henderson, 1985.

defined as the negative of (6.6) and (6.7) to reflect, for example, the positive willingness to pay for an amenity through wage reductions.

As noted in the wage section, the rise in wages necessary to compensate low skill people for a 1% increase in city size is 0.50%. For high skill people the compensation required is less at 0.43%, reflecting their greater preference (less aversion) for larger cities. In terms of composition, low skill people are willing to give up 0.24% of their wages for a 1% increase in N_H/N_L. For high skill people this is not the case.

The surprising result in Table 6.3 is that high skill people appear to view population composition as a negative amenity. Although the magnitude of this affect was sensitive to specification, it was always negative. This could to some extent reflect differential cost-of-living impacts for high and low skill people of increases in N_H/N_L when we hold N fixed.

Interpreting the results jointly, they suggest that while low skill people may want to live next to high skill people, high skill people have a stronger preference to live in large cities. Thus, ignoring all other factors, this could suggest a situation where low skill workers "follow" high skill workers into large cities, helping to make large cities large, although still relatively high skill. In the United States, however, there is a zero correlation between SMSA size and population composition. Either other endogenous disamenities associated with large SMSA sizes drive high skill people out (see later), or the industries of large SMSAs are not high skill intensive (see Section 2.2) and thus the demand side of the model does not generally support an overall positive correlation between city size and relatively high skill composition.

General amenities: Low skill preferences. The city size equation reflects the preferences of low skill workers. Table 6.2 shows the impact of amenities on city size per se. These elasticities are simply the coefficients in Table 6.1 multiplied by the mean level of amenities. Table 6.3 presents the willingness-to-pay for amenities by low skill people through wage changes. These elasticities are for any variable

$$\frac{-d \log w_L}{d \log A} = \frac{b_A}{b_w} \cdot \bar{A} \tag{6.8}$$

where $\bar{A}$ is the average amenity level. Averages and standard deviations for different $\bar{A}$ are given in Appendix A, Table A1. The choice of amenity variables reflects the (dis)amenities found to be important in other work—climate, pollution, crime, and recreation potential. New measures representing the quality of local public services were also experimented with.

In terms of the variables, it is hypothesized that consumers prefer warm, sunny climates. The two climate variables are annual precipitation, which is a proxy for the extent of sunshine (a variable with too many missing values) and heating degree days. The latter variable, besides being a disamenity, also affects the cost of living in a city. Both these variables have very strong effects on city sizes and wage levels (Tables 6.2 and 6.3). To emphasize this, note that a one standard deviation increase in heating degree days leads to a 23% decline in city size, holding wages constant, or an 11% increase in wages, holding city size constant.

Outdoor recreation potential is represented by the city being on the coast of a major body of water. That advantage increases city size by 32%, ceteris paribus (including controlling for access to regional market centers). More detailed state and data on miles of beaches and square miles of parks in one state produced nonrobust results. Air quality is represented by particulates per square mile (see Appendix A) and is a strong disamenity. Pollution measures on sulphur oxides did not enter robustly.

The crime situation is represented by the reported murder rate (the crime variable that has by far the best accuracy in terms of victim reporting). In the city size equation, murder has the wrong sign. This may indicate that treating the murder rate as an SMSA-wide, rather than strictly neighborhood variable, is inappropriate.

Urban infrastructure is measured by buses per square mile (see Appendix A). This is an inordinately strong public service variable. It appears that at a minimum the variable is an indicator of some overall impact of general local public transport inputs on costs of housing and retail goods in a city. This variable had a robust coefficient over all specifications and its inclusion versus exclusion in the estimating equations did not have strong impacts on the other results. Thus, while there may be some hesitation in interpreting its impact, it is included in the results.

The final results on amenity evaluations of low skill workers are not in the existing literature, nor are they reported in Table 6.1. A very rich data base, in part from the Sixth Count of the 1970 Population Census, was constructed to try to capture aspects of the quality of local public services in the urban area not usually represented—education and public administration of the city. Represented were the percent of students in public versus private schools and the ratio of teachers to administrators in public schools, as well as measures of the age, sex, race and education composition of public employees broken down by administrators and production versus nonproduction workers, plus measures of total public employees per capita. None of these had any consistent impact on the city size equations. Either they are not appropriate measures, or they measure amenities at a metropolitan areawide level which are, in fact, only neighborhood amenities.

General amenities: High versus low skill preferences. Let us turn to the results for the composition equation. From the discussion of Section 1.1 a positive (negative) coefficient on an amenity variable in equation 6.4 indicates that it is more (less) highly valued by high skill people. Amenities thus have a direct effect on population composition, if they enter equation 6.5b with a significant coefficient. These composition elasticities, which equal $\beta_A \bar{A}$, are reported in Table 6.2. The composition equation results combined with the city size equation also identify the preferences of high skill people. The willingness-to-pay for amenities by high skill people through wage reductions, holding city size and composition fixed, is:

$$\frac{-d \log w_H}{d \log A} = \left(\frac{\beta_A}{\beta_w} + \frac{b_A}{b_w}\right) \bar{A} \qquad (6.9)$$

These results are reported in Table 6.3. Note that if β_A is not significantly different from zero, high and low skill people have the same marginal evaluation of amenities, as measured by the *percentage* impact on wages.

When we look at the basic results, the differences in the United States in willingness-to-pay between high skill and low skill people are generally rather modest. Note that the differences in *absolute* evaluations, rather than elasticities, are even smaller. For low skill people this is calculated by multiplying the elasticity in Table 6.3 by average low skill wages, ($\bar{w}_L = 9806$), whereas for high skill people it is calculated by multiplying by $\bar{w}_H = 11,596$), and in both cases dividing by A. High skill people have significantly different elasticities for infrastructure (buses per square mile) and sunny climates. They also have strongly different estimated valuations of murder (see Table 6.1) to the extent that this is a properly measured amenity. The results that high skill people value better climate and lower crime rates more than low skill people appear elsewhere in the literature (Getz and Huang, 1977 and Henderson, 1982c). The difference in evaluations is not as strong or pervasive as expected, perhaps because of the implicit assumption in estimation that both groups in a city consume the same levels of these amenities within each city.

Cost of living. The fourth panel of variables are those which might affect urban costs of living, over and above the impacts of city size, urban infrastructure, and heating degree days. An increase in driving time to regional markets is hypothesized to raise the cost of importing retail goods to a city and appears to do so, with a lower impact on high skill people. The property tax variable is weak, although it appears to have the expected negative impact. Again there is a problem of to what extent this is effectively a neighborhood and legislatively a community rather than SMSA-wide variable.

Summary. In summary, Tables 6.1, 6.2, and 6.3 show the following. First, high skill people have a preference for larger SMSAs. Note that in the United States this result cannot represent a spurious correlation, since that correlation would be zero. Second, population composition appears to be an amenity for low skill people, where low skill people prefer living in a community of relatively high skill people. This phenomenon of low skill people wanting to live next to high skill people, of course, encourages heterogeneity. Finally, in general, high skill people seem modestly more impacted by amenity differentials, indicating that they should tend to gravitate toward (bid the most for) urban sites offering better amenity bundles.[4]

2.3. Brazil Results

For Brazil, the definition of high and low skill is also based on educational attainment. The two class division is between those with more than primary school education (six or more years in Brazil) and those with primary school or less. This is usually about a one-fourth/three-fourths division. The sample is 126 urban areas of Southern Brazil, the same as in Chapter 5. Variable definitions are given in Table B1 in Appendix B to this chapter.

The results for equations 6.5 are given in Tables 6.4 and 6.5 based on Henderson (1986b). They are 3SLS results based upon the more limited set of instruments listed in Table 6.4. As for the United States the results are discussed by blocks of variables, combining the results for equations 6.5. Although, as noted earlier, the Brazil results and data set are not as impressive as for the United States, the results are suggestive and the methodology is important.

Wage variables. As for the United States, both wage variables have positive signs, indicating upward sloping supply curves in Figure 6.1. Unfortunately, neither coefficient is significant at a 5% level, which limits the interpretation of all results in terms of consumer willingness to pay. In the city equation, in different for-

Table 6.4. City Population Size and Composition: Brazil (All Variables Except D and Percentage of N_L Water and Sewer Are in Natural Logs)

	Size (N) 3SLS	Composition (N_H/N_L) 3SLS
N_H/N_L	2.732	
	(6.86)	
N		0.195
		(4.09)
w_L	1.588	
	(1.70)	
w_H/w_L		0.435
		(0.95)
Port distance (D)	-0.534×10^{-3}	0.182×10^{-3}
	(1.15)	(1.70)
Transf/Person	0.176	
	(1.15)	
Teacher education		0.828
		(2.03)
Pupil/teacher		-0.334
		(4.18)
Percentage of N_L water	-0.027	
	(0.04)	
Percentage of N_L sewer	-1.111	
	(0.82)	
Constant	6.380	-4.854
N	126	126

Source: Henderson, 1986.

Note: Absolute values of t-statistics are in parentheses.
Instruments are D, pupil–teacher ratio, teacher education, meso region urban population (excluding own urban area), meso region total population, urban area tax rate on industrial property, federal government employment in urban area, state dummies, labor force participation, percentage adult, and average temperature. Meso regions are an area such that a state such as Illinois would be divided into 6 to 8 meso regions.

mulations as well as in OLS estimation, the wage coefficient tended toward significance, so it is the most reliable. Its coefficient states that a 1% increase in wages is associated with a 1.6% increase in city size to maintain $\bar{U}_L$ along the supply curve.

Population amenities. The population amenity results for Brazil are in Table 6.5, based on equations 6.6 and 6.7 and the wage as well as population and composition coefficients in Table 6.4. These correspond to the U.S. results. The rise in wages necessary to compensate low skill workers for a 1% increase in city size is 0.63% (vs. 0.50% for the United States), while for high skill people it is only 0.18% (vs. 0.43% for the United States) indicating their much smaller aversion to larger cities. Second, low skill people greatly value better population composition, whereas, as in the United States, high skill people treat it as a disamenity. Again for low skill people, the presence of high skill people may result in better local public decision making, medical care, and so on.

These results reconfirm the notion that low skill people want to live near high skill people and may follow them into the larger cities preferred by high skill people, helping to make these cities large. These results are also supported by

Table 6.5. Brazil: Willingness-to-Pay Elasticities for Amenities $(-d \log w/d \log A)$

	Size (N)	Composition	Distance to port	Teacher education	Pupil–teacher ratio
Low skill	−0.63	1.72	−0.08	—	—
High skill	−0.18	−0.58	0.02	1.90	−0.77

Source: Henderson, 1986b.

growth rate results for Brazil, based on 1960–1970 changes in population size and composition.

Amenities. Other than educational variables discussed momentarily, the other variables in Table 6.4 are not statistically strong, although that in itself may have strong implications (see below). Second, all amenities except distance in the column for the size equation produced consistently zero coefficients in the composition equation, indicating that they have the *same* evaluation by high skill people. On the other hand, the schooling variables in the composition equation are not valued by low skill people.

The results in more detail are as follows.

Other price variables. Distance to the nearest port (i.e., regional market center) is negatively valued by low skill people, requiring as in the United States approximately a 0.08% increase in wages to offset the 1% increase in distance. As in the United States, there is a much lower aversion (essentially zero here) to greater distance by high skill people. For intergovernmental transfers to the city, the magnitude of the weak coefficient is consistent with the wage coefficient. Raising the transfer measure by one unit per person leads to an actual increase of 0.2 unit (see Appendix B). Thus the transfer coefficient should be 0.2 of the wage coefficient, which it is.

Local public services. Sewer and water facilities are set by local governments and financed out of local property taxes, in Brazil's quasi-democratic local government setting. In Brazil in 1970 city councils were popularly elected but mayors appointed. There are no measures for residential property taxes. Thus, *if these public output variables are optimally provided their coefficients should be zero*, or $dU_L/d\bar{A} = \partial U_L/\partial \bar{A} + (\partial U_L/\partial \text{ taxes}) (\partial \text{ taxes}/\partial \bar{A}) = 0$. The coefficients are zero, which could indicate that the preferences of local voters are satisfied, or that the marginal benefits of increased services $(\partial U_L/\partial A)$ are just offset by the implied marginal tax increases. On the other hand, the result could simply indicate that these measures are irrelevant.

State public services. Finally, there are the schooling variables, which are the only statistically strong amenities and then only for high skill people. Schooling variables are set by the state government and financed out of state taxes. Increases in state set public services in a community represent a straight gain for the community, given that they are financed out of national or state revenues; hence, they should have positive coefficients in the size equation. The list of characteristics of state set public services included variables related to the health, education, and transport system. The state also controls police and fire protection. For the city size equation none of the variables performed in any robust fashion with anticipated signs. It simply appears that the measures are not important characteristics of services to low skill people.

However, for high skill people, from the composition equation it appears that characteristics of the educational system are very important. This result is robust and also is very strong in growth rate equations for 1960–1970. The coefficients, however, do imply inordinately large consumer evaluations. In United States work, one would not find that such gross measures as pupil–teacher ratios and average education of teachers to have impacts. However in Brazil, the education system by reputation is very bad in terms of resources devoted to education in various cities in different states; it also appears that high skill people are strongly affected in their migration decisions by this phenomenon. It should be noted that the rate of participation in the education system is not included in the equations. That is an endogenous variable determined by the characteristics of the school system and of the population of an urban area. Such a regression is noted here.[5]

2.4. Summary of Supply Side

The Brazil and United States results support each other. The supply curves of population and of high to low skill workers in Figures 6.1 are upward sloping. There are a variety of amenities shifting the population supply curve. For the composition curve there are amenities that high skill people value differently from low skill people, as measured by the percentage compensating wage differentials. However, for the United States the differentials are modest, only being large for climate and perhaps murder rates. The former does represent a basis for Tiebout type stratification where high skill people would live disproportionately in more sunny climates in the United States. For Brazil it is schooling characteristics set by the state government that would lead to stratification, with high skill people living disproportionately in cities with better facilities. For the primary schools in the sample there is minimal correlation between city size and quality of schooling characteristics (Table B.3).

The complexity of the interrelationships between Figures 6.1a and 6.1b lies in population amenities. Relative to low skill people, high skill people have less aversion to larger cities. This does not reflect spurious correlation, since in the United States the correlation is zero. However, low skill people value high skill people as an amenity, perhaps because of their influence on the quality of life, public decision making, and shopping. In the absence of other considerations low skill people follow high skill people into larger cities, helping making these cities large. This is consistent with stability in the model.[6]

3. Econometric Results: The Demand Side

The demand side involves three basic issues. First, is it useful to think in terms of skill requirements in production? This is a question of whether high and low skill labor are highly substitutable, in which case notions of skill requirements are not useful, or whether they are complements or have a low degree of substitutability in production. In the latter case industries have little flexibility in their skill mix and skill requirements have a critical impact on a city's population composition. Second, do the skill requirements of different industries differ? Do industries that gravitate toward larger or smaller urban areas have greater skill requirements? Finally, are external economies of scale in production biased? In particular, are external economies of scale such that larger cities are relatively high skill using?

The estimation of the demand side employs conventional flexible form specifications of the cost function. Some restrictions are imposed on the general form of the cost function consistent with basic results from other work, based upon simpler specifications such as in Chapter 5. First, the firm's production function is constant returns to scale, but the industry function with external economies of scale is not. This allows estimation of the unit cost function rather than the total cost function. Second, external economies of scale may be ones of localization or of urbanization. Based upon extensive experimentation it is specified that the urbanization component of scale effects may be biased, and that localization effects are Hicks' neutral.

The focus of this section is on results for Brazil. In terms of estimating technology the Brazil data are remarkable. There are good data on skill mixes, capital stocks, and prices of capital and different skill groups. The data are uncensored at the three-digit level. Because the United States data are censored (see Chapter 5), many observations are missing and its coverage of variables is insufficient to specify technology fully.

3.1. Results for Brazil

For Brazil, the flexible functional form is the translog (see Fuss and McFadden 1978, for a review), where

$$\log c = A_0 + \beta_1 N_0 + \beta_2 N_0^2 + \beta_3 \log N + \sum_i \alpha_i \log p_i$$

$$+ \frac{1}{2} \sum_i \sum_j \gamma_{ij} \log p_i \log p_j + \sum_i \gamma_{iN} \log p_i \log N \qquad (6.10)$$

c is average unit cost of production, the p_i are factor prices of capital and high skill and low skill workers, N is urban area population, and N_0 is own industry employment in the urban area. The translog function is viewed as a second order Taylor Series expansion about the point where the logs of these variables equal zero (and our variables are so normalized). The quadratic form for economies of localization was chosen on the basis of extensive experimentation, and complements the quadratic form in Chapter 5. Symmetry is imposed on equation 6.10 so that $\gamma_{ij} = \gamma_{ji}$ and the function is linear homogenous in prices. This implies the following restrictions imposed during estimation:

$$\sum_i \alpha_i = 1, \qquad \sum_j \gamma_{ij} = \sum_i \gamma_{iN} = 0 \qquad (6.11)$$

Applying Shephard's lemma and partially differentiating (6.10) yields factor share equations:

$$S_i = \alpha_i + \sum_j \gamma_{ij} \log p_j + \gamma_{iN} \log N \qquad (6.12)$$

Given $\Sigma_i S_i = 1$, in estimation the number of independent share equations is the number of factors minus one.

The economic parameters of interest are as follows. First, there are the elasticities of substitution in production among capital, high skill, and low skill workers. For any pair of inputs the partial elasticity of substitution is

$$\sigma_{ij} = 1 + \frac{\gamma_{ij}}{S_i \cdot S_j} \qquad i \neq j \qquad (6.13)$$

where γ_{ij} is a parameter in (6.10) and (6.12) and S_i and S_j are factor shares. ($\sigma_{ii} = 1 + \gamma_{ii}/S_i^2 - 1/S_i$). σ_{ij} is evaluated at "representative" (average) values for S_i and S_j. If $\sigma_{ij} < 0$, factors are complements not substitutes. Note that in economic terms

$$\sigma_{ij} = \frac{\eta_{ij}}{S_j} \qquad (6.14)$$

where η_{ij} is the percentage of change in the ith input when the price of the jth input rises, holding output and other input prices fixed. Thus, $\sigma_{ij} < 0$ implies complementarity in the sense that if the price of an input rises, its use and the use of its complements falls, whereas the use of its substitutes rises.

Finally, there is the issue of nonneutrality of urbanization economies. These are reflected in the values of γ_{LN} and γ_{HN}, where

$$\eta_{L/H,N} = \frac{d \log (N_{OL}/N_{OH})}{d \log N} = \gamma_{LN}S_L^{-1} - \gamma_{HN}S_H^{-1} \qquad (6.15)$$

$\eta_{L/H,N}$ is the elasticity of relative factor usage with respect to scale, holding input prices fixed. Equation 6.15 will indicate whether urbanization economies are high skill or low skill labor using.

Given that stochastic components added to equations 6.10 and 6.12 will be contemporaneously related, equation 6.10 and the two factor share equations for high and low skill workers are estimated jointly by Zellner's approach for estimating seemingly unrelated regressions to achieve maximum likelihood estimates. This ignores any problems of right-hand side variables being endogenous, given the limited list of instruments for Brazil. Because the observations pertain to three or even four-digit industries within a city, it seems reasonable to assume that industry disturbances at this level of disaggregation do not usually affect city sizes and prices. For the United States 3SLS estimation has little impact on the results. Also the system of equations was estimated without and with equation 6.10, which is highly collinear. In all cases, the parameters of equations 6.12 are negligibly affected by including equation 6.10.

Data. The basic data are from the 1970 Industrial Census of Brazil. The data for high vs. low skill workers are from the 1970 Demographic Census. As discussed in Appendix B, Table B1, there are tabulations for full-time workers in the urban areas, giving the number of workers in each education category by two-digit industry and giving the average annual incomes by education and two-digit category. The figures on relative numbers in each education category divide total employees in the Industrial Census for the corresponding industry into two education groups. The figures on relative incomes (and numbers) of the two education groups are used to divide up total compensation, to obtain an annual compensation for high and low skill workers. For three-digit industries in the Industrial Census, numbers on incomes and skill division from the relevant two-digit industries of the Demographic Census are used. In doing so, it is assumed that relative annual incomes equal relative annual compensations for the two classes of workers, and that the numbers for two-digit industry divisions among high and low skill workers apply to three-digit industries. This latter problem does not appear serious: In most cases in the urban areas one three-digit industry accounts for most corresponding two-digit employment.

The system of equations was estimated for seven industries. All are three-digit industries except for traditional chemicals and spinning and weaving. Traditional chemicals is a collection of three-digit chemical industries primarily excluding petrochemicals. Spinning and weaving is the four-digit natural fiber component of the three-digit spinning and weaving category and omits the four-digit artificial fiber components.

The results for the estimated system of equations are presented in Appendix B, along with variable definitions taken from Henderson (1986b). The text focuses on the key results in Table 6.6 relating to the three sets of questions. The results are discussed in blocks. Note that in almost all cases the economic parameters in Table 6.6 are based on statistically significant coefficients in Appendix B, Table B4. Toward the end of this section there are other comments on the results in Appendix B.

Elasticities of substitution. The strong evidence in Table 6.6 states that high and low skill labor are complements in production or else very weak substitutes. This result is unexpected; but it is strong and persistent under all reasonable specifications. For example, if one does not like the cost of capital measure and would prefer to assume either that the cost of capital varies stochastically across space or that it is a function of distance from major metropolitan areas and of urban area size, the complementarity result and also the results concerning $\eta_{L/H,POP}$ hold just as strongly. Second, there are no peculiarities about the data. For example, the simple correlation coefficient between compensation of high and low skill workers in all manufacturing across urban areas is 0.58, which is quite low in this kind of estimation.

In summary, the results indicate that skill classes of labor are not substitutable so that skill mixes in industry cannot respond passively (i.e., to small wage variations) to the supply conditions in urban areas analyzed in Section 2.1. In short, skill requirements are an operational requirement.

Skill requirements. How do skill requirements vary across cities? In particular for Brazil, if requirements rise with city size, this would help explain the positive correlation between city size and the relative numbers of high skill people.

For a casual comparison the 126 Brazil urban areas are taken and classified by type, as described in Chapter 1. Table 6.7 gives the resulting ranking of the city types represented in Table 6.6. Chemicals and shoes are not in the ranking because, respectively, any large concentrations of chemicals employment are found in large diversified metro areas (typically the government owned petrochemical industry), and there is only one shoe city. The casual picture painted in Table 6.7 suggests that industry requirements for high relative to low skill labor may indeed rise, as the size of urban area type rises. That is, skill requirements mesh with a positive correlation between city size and population composition.

Nonneutrality of external economies. When we examine the second panel of results in Table 6.6, in all cases we see strong evidence that external economies of scale are relatively biased against low skill workers—that is, they are high skill

Table 6.6. Production Technology: Brazil

	Ceramics	Iron and steel	Agricultural machinery	Auto accessories	Traditional chemicals	Spinning and weaving	Shoes
σ_{LH}	0.04	−0.24	−.40	−0.27	−1.12	−3.04	0.16
σ_{LK}	0.88	1.13	0.67	1.27	0.79	4.65	0.85
σ_{HK}	1.29	1.16	0.69	0.96	1.41	6.05	1.04
$\eta_{IL/IH,POP}$	−0.19	−0.14	−0.09	−0.08	−0.10	−0.10	−0.01
N_{OL}/N_{OH}	5.08	3.28	2.27	2.20	1.64	5.98	4.67
ϵ_0 (mean)	−0.11	−0.34	−0.25	−0.24	−0.04	−0.08	−0.15
σ_{LL}	−0.64	−0.86	−0.33	−0.97	−0.17	−2.28	−0.44
σ_{HH}	−2.55	−1.63	−0.32	−1.00	−1.10	−3.80	−1.31
σ_{KK}	−1.93	−1.94	−1.25	−1.86	−1.47	−9.04	−2.87

Source: Henderson, 1986b.

Table 6.7.   Size Rankings of Types of Cities

Size ranking (starting with largest)	Percentage of decline in average size of type of city from transport type	N_{OL}/N_{OH} from Table 6.6 (for corresponding industry)
Transport type	n.a.	1.93
Machinery type	−4.6%	2.45
Steel type	−90%	3.28
Spinning and weaving type	−99%	5.98
Ceramics type	−235%	5.08

Source: Henderson, 1986b.

using. The elasticities of the ratio of low to high use with respect to urbanization effects were all nonpositive, controlling for wages. These appear to be *very* large effects, stating that a 10% increase in city population causes a firm to decrease its ratio of low to high skill workers by, say, 1% for the same factor prices and firm level of output.

This result suggests that even without skill requirement considerations, production in larger urban areas in a developing country is biased toward using high skill labor. Whatever are the source of scale effects such as larger general urban labor markets and a greater opportunity for specialization of industries and firms in their tasks within an urban area, they make high skill workers more efficient in relation to low skill workers. Perhaps this is not surprising. Specialization in tasks and communications in labor markets may go hand-in-hand with greater skills of workers. Finally, in Appendix B, scale effects appear to be neutral with respect to capital usage, confirming the result in Chapter 5.

Other results. As suggested in Chapter 5, localization economies appear to dominate urbanization ones. For urbanization economies, β_3 in Table B4 varies in sign and is only significant for one industry. Table 6.6 gives the localization elasticity evaluated at mean employment, where ϵ_0 is the percentage *decline* in unit costs for a firm when industry employment increases by 1%, holding firm inputs fixed. ϵ_0 is specified as quadratic and hence is only valid locally. (Note the declining elasticity form in Chapter 5, which was less robust in the translog form of technology used in this chapter.) Evaluated at mean employment, the elasticities are large. At median employment, which is typically one-half to one-third of the mean, elasticities would be smaller. However, evaluated at an employment of 500 as in Chapter 5, they would be much larger than the elasticities recorded there, given the difference in functional forms.

In terms of other parameters, the own factor partial elasticities of substitution all have the correct sign and have reasonable values. Second and most striking, the cross elasticities between capital and the two forms of labor are, first, close to each other and, second, generally close to one. Casually interpreted, there are rigid skill mixes of labor that display the same degree of substitutability with capital.

3.2. U.S. Results

The U.S. results are also based on a flexible form specification. Given the more limited data set (see later), only the factor share equations could be estimated. Because of problems with maintaining good global properties for a translog form, a generalized Leontief specification is used. Assuming perfect competition, the basic generalized Leontief representation of technology (Diewert, 1971) is

$$c = A_0 + f(N_0, N) + \sum_i \sum_j b_{ij} p_i^{1/2} p_j^{1/2} + \sum_i b_{iN} p_i^{1/2} N^{1/2} \qquad (6.16)$$

In equation 6.16, c are unit costs of production. $f(N_0, N)$ are Hicks' neutral external scale effects measured by own industry total employment (N_0) and urban population (N). p are input prices. The generalized Leontief can be viewed as a second order approximation of any function, where there is a second order Taylor series expansion in powers $\sqrt{p}$ and $\sqrt{N}$ about zero. The measures are thus normalized to be small numbers. In the expansion, the terms $\sum_i b_i \sqrt{p}$ disappear when linear homogeneity of the unit cost function in prices is imposed. The terms $\sum_i b_i p^{1/2} N^{1/2}$ represent nonneutral components of scale effects. N is used instead of N_0 or of both, because again, empirically for the United States, any effects seemed to arise from N rather than N_0.

Equation 6.16 is differentiated to get the estimating equations where, for example (see Denny, May, and Pinto, 1978):

$$N_{\text{OL}}/X = \sum_i b_{Li}(p_i/p_L)^{1/2} + b_{LN}(N/p_L)^{1/2}$$
$$(6.17)$$
$$N_{\text{OH}}/X = \sum_i b_{Hi}(p_i/p_H)^{1/2} + b_{HN}(N/p_H)^{1/2}$$

N_{OL} and N_{OH} are inputs of high and low skill labor, X is output, and p_L and p_H are the wages of low and high skill labor. Estimates of the b_{Li}, b_{Hi}, b_{LN}, and b_{HN} coefficients can be used to calculate the economic parameters central to the issues of this chapter.

For this functional approximation, the Allen–Uzawa partial elasticity of substitution between high and low skill labor is:

$$\sigma_{LH} = \frac{\frac{1}{2} b_{LH}(p_L^{1/2} p_H^{1/2})}{\rho_L \rho_H} \qquad (6.13a)$$

where ρ_i are factor shares. Nonneutrality of scale effects is reflected by the values of b_{iN}. For high and low skill labor,

$$\eta_{L/H,N} = \frac{d(\log N_{OL}/N_{OH})}{d(\log N)} = \frac{1}{2} N^{-1/2} \left(\frac{b_{LN} p_L^{1/2}}{\rho_L} - \frac{b_{HN} p_H^{1/2}}{\rho_H} \right) \qquad (6.15a)$$

Estimation is done for the two-digit industries which United States SMSAs tend to specialize in. From Chapter 1, these are food processing, textiles, apparel, pulp and paper, wood products, leather products, primary metals, nonelectrical and electrical machinery. Missing is transportation, which is so heavily censored at the SMSA level in the Census of Manufacturers that every major production center is a missing observation.

Given that stochastic components added to the equations 6.17 will be related contemporaneously, the equations are estimated jointly by Zellner's approach for estimating seemingly unrelated regressions to achieve maximum likelihood estimates, where $b_{LH} = b_{HL}$ across equations. An implicit assumption in estimation is that wages and urban area sizes are variables exogenous to the two-digit industries in each SMSA. Since in some cases these two-digit industries may dominate the city they are in, for some observations this may be a tenuous assumption. Thus, 3SLS estimates of relevant parameters are given for comparison, treating price and quantity variables as all endogenous.

Data. In terms of the data, the total employment figures and the measure of output are taken from the 1972 Census of Manufacturers. Skill level again is measured by educational attainment. Employment is divided between high (high school graduation or more) and low (less than four years of high school) skill workers, by combining tables from the Sixth Count of the 1970 Population Census. Prices of high and low skill labor are based on median earnings of males in each education group in each SMSA who were employed 50 to 52 weeks per year. Details of the calculations and all variable definitions are in Appendix A. Although, relative to the alternatives, the data on skill composition are excellent, data on quantities of materials and capital and prices of materials and capital are nonexistent. It is assumed that the prices of materials and capital are spatially invariant (apart from temporary stochastic fluctuations). However, the data only permit estimation of two equations in (6.17) rather than the cost function plus all factor demand equations.

The results for manufacturing industries based on Henderson (1985) are presented in Table 6.8. The actual coefficients and factor shares are in Appendix A. Table 6.8 indicates the absolute value of the t-statistics of the b_{LH} coefficient, upon which σ_{LH} is based. The top panel presents the Zellner results and the bottom panel the 3SLS results. The σ_{LH} and $\eta_{L/H.N}$ parameters for all industries are evaluated at typical values of p_L, p_H and N, which (before normalization) are \$3.85/hour, \$4.60/hour and 500,000, respectively.

Elasticities of substitution. As for Brazil, the results in Table 6.8 indicate that, in general, low and high skill labor are not strong substitutes. The Zellner and 3SLS give similar results on the question. For electrical and nonelectrical machinery they are *complements* in production, and for primary metals weak substitutes. For the second panel of industries (textiles, pulp and paper, and leather products) the partial elasticity of substitution is close to one. Only for wood products, apparel, and food processing is the elasticity significantly greater than one and even then the largest value in any situation is only 2.15. Another way of viewing the results is that, given factor shares in Appendix A, *all* cross price elasticities ($\eta_{LH} = \sigma_{LH}/\rho_H$) are *under* 0.33.

These results support the Brazil conclusions that high and low skill labor are not highly substitutable in production. Skill requirements of different industries will strongly influence population composition.

Table 6.8. Substitutability in Manufacturing (Parameters taken from Appendix A)

		Primary metals	Nonelectrical machine	Electric machine	Textile	Pulp and paper	Leather	Wood products	Apparel	Food processing
Zellner	σ_{LH}	0.59	−0.42	−0.38	0.92	0.92	1.31	1.41	2.15	1.90
		(1.15)	(2.07)	(1.32)	(1.39)	(2.25)	(1.41)	(3.28)	(4.62)	(3.71)
	$\eta_{L/H,N}$	−0.005	−0.004	−0.007	−0.008	−0.009	−0.017	−0.01	−0.012	−0.001
3SLS	σ_{LH}	0.89	−0.38	−0.53	1.11	1.21	0.92	2.13	1.95	2.12
		(1.48)	(1.52)	(1.57)	(1.39)	(2.56)	(0.91)	(4.03)	(3.34)	(3.51)
	$\eta_{L/H,N}$	−0.017	−0.002	−0.008	−0.030	−0.012	−0.017	−0.020	−0.021	−0.008
	N_{OL}/N_{OH}	0.84	0.64	0.57	1.22	1.93	1.15	0.86	1.29	0.86
	Sample size	98	168	110	61	108	31	128	118	212

Source: Henderson, 1985.
Instruments for 3SLS work are distance to regional and national markets, three regional dummies, coastal dummy, annual precipitation, heating degree days, percentage of public administration managers with a college degree, percentage female labor force participation, percentage of families in one unit housing, percentage of population that is black, percentage of population 18 years or older, percentage of population 65 years or older, percentage of houses built before 1950, and the cost of electrical power.

Table 6.9. City Size and Skill Usage Correlation: United States

	Average city size (Table 1.8)	Skill usage (N_{OH}/N_{OL}) (Table 6.8)
Nonelectrical machinery	0.36–0.77	1.56
Steel	0.43	1.19
Apparel	0.23	0.78
Textile	0.21	0.82
Pulp paper	0.16	0.52
Food	0.16	1.16

Skill requirements. The next question concerns whether skill requirements vary across industries and whether, given that variation, there is a relationship between skill requirements and city sizes for specialized types of cities. According to Table 6.8, skill requirements do vary substantially, particularly in the context of United States with the mean value of L_L/L_H rising from 0.57 for electric machinery to 1.93 for pulp and paper, a 340% difference. In terms of the relationship between city size and skill requirements, we take the average sizes from Chapter 1. The correspondence between sizes by city type and skill requirements for that type is presented in Table 6.9 for overlapping industries. As for Brazil, there appears to be a positive correlation between city size by type and skill usage, at least amongst smaller SMSAs in the United States.

Scale Elasticity Biases. As for Brazil, the impact of urban population on relative factor uses, controlling for factor prices and own industry scale, is to increase the use of high skill relative to low skill labor for all industries. Moving from the Zellner to 3SLS results generally only enhances this effect. Thus it would appear urbanization economies bias the use of high relative to low skill labor. This suggests the environment of larger cities is more conducive to the use of high skill labor given the altered nature of, say, labor markets and information flows in larger cities.

3.3. Summary

Given the existence of scale economies, the demand curves in Figure 6.1a may be upward sloping. They shift in and out with changes in industrial composition and city type, reflecting alterations in the degree of scale effects (and capital intensities).

Given own price effects as well as cross effects, the demand curves in Figure 6.1b for population composition should be downward sloping. They also shift with changes in industrial composition and skill requirements, as well as with changes in city size given biased scale effects. A basic issue concerns their elasticity. Given that substitution effects are weak, there is little flexibility in factor substitution and the curves should be quite inelastic.

4. Conclusions

What determines the skill composition of cities? Why in Brazil is there, for example, a strong positive correlation between high skill composition and city size, while in the United States there is not? This chapter econometrically uncovers the following information bearing on these questions. The U.S. and Brazil results support each other.

1. While there are many urban area level (as opposed to neighborhood level) amenities that consumers value generally, the differences in evaluation between high and low skill people are generally modest. An exception is schooling characteristics in Brazil and climate in the United States. Neither of these vary consistently with city size; thus, for example, better public primary schools do not draw high skill people into large cities in Southern Brazil. However, the same comment may not apply to high schools or colleges.

2. Population amenities are an important feature of tastes. High skill people have less aversion to large cities, perhaps because of the more sophisticated consumer markets there for both goods and services (such as health care). This could explain the correlation between city size and population composition in Brazil. However, in the United States such a correlation is zero.

Low skill people value high skill people as an amenity perhaps because of their impact on the local quality of life, shopping, and public decision making. In some sense low skill people may follow high skill people into large cities, helping make these cities large. What is surprising in the results is that high skill people do not appear to value increases in their relative numbers.

3. In production, high and low skill labor tend to be weak substitutes or even complements, indicating there is little flexibility in factor proportions in a city once industrial mix is controlled for. This permits relative Tiebout type stratification of the population through city specialization in high vs. low skill intensive industries. However, it also limits the extent of homogeneity in any city, given limited factor substitutability for any industrial mix.

4. In Brazil and the United States there casually appears to be a positive correlation between high skill intensity and size by type of city.

Result (4) on the demand side is consistent with result (2) on the supply side where high skill people want larger cities. Hence the demand and supply sides appear to reinforce each other. For Brazil, these two reinforcing factors could thus explain the positive city size–population composition correlation. However, the same two factors also reinforce each other in the United States, but there the correlation is zero. Why might this be? Several explanations are possible.

One explanation is that endogenous amenities related to large SMSAs and measured for the United States (but not Brazil), such as murder rates and certain pollution elements, drive high skill people out of large United States SMSAs. Note, however, these negative amenities are not sufficient to drive high skill people out of large Brazilian cities, despite their possibly even greater association with city size there.

Another is that the skill usage–city size relationship on the supply side is only examined in this chapter for specialized types of manufacturing cities, which in both Brazil and the United States are smaller types of cities. These relationships may not hold for larger cities, given their industrial patterns and high service component.

Finally, given these first two explanations of why the United States has a zero correlation between size and composition, Brazil could still have a positive correlation due to government policies there. First, government policies may favor the location of special amenities (e.g., good high schools) in larger cities and, second, it may force or favor the location of certain high skill industries in larger cities. This explanation is examined at length in Chapter 7.

While this chapter has investigated the determinants of city size and population composition, in making predictions for any specific city an element of the analysis may be missing in many cases. For any particular city to the extent both its size and population composition are influenced by industrial mix, we need to know the determinants of industrial mix. It may be that certain skill groups value certain exogenous consumer amenities (e.g., climate, schooling characteristics) at that urban site, so that they agglomerate there, drawing in particularly footloose (e.g., service and high tech) industries intensive in those skills. However, production amenities may determine industrial mix at a particular site, especially for industries requiring access to certain raw material deposits, natural harbors, cheap hydropower, agricultural produce from textile areas, and so on.

NOTES

1. Supply shifters can be incorporated into equation 6.1 in which case the parameters of (6.1) then reflect parameters of $U_L(\cdot)$, $p_L(\cdot)$, and the supply function. The directional impact of variables remains unchanged.

2. This evidence suggests that real wages for equal skill people (nominal wages deflated by costs of living) are approximately equalized across big and small cities and urban and rural areas. This suggests that people migrate to quickly eliminate real wage differentials (Williamson, 1977; Thomas, 1978; Henderson, 1980).

3. The ratio w_H/w_L is used rather than w_H and w_L separately. The supply function can be rewritten with w_L as well as w_H/w_L as arguments, or it can be assumed that w_H and w_L have similar coefficients (of opposite sign). Empirical work supports the latter interpretation.

4. The equations were reestimated, inserting three regional dummies (north central, south, and west). Their impact on the size equation is negligible, and their coefficients are insignificant. This would be consistent both with low skill people earning equal utility in all regions and with the assumption that there is a national labor market. Regional dummies in the composition equation are not insignificant. This may not represent disequilibrium in the high skill labor market, but rather a Rybcynski theorem effect where relative regional allocations of high and low skill differ, but utility levels are equalized across regions.

5. Participation in school for 5 to 11 year olds = $-0.701 - 0.666 \times 10^{-4}D +$
$$(2.06)$$
$0.218\ N_H/N_L + 0.021$ teacher education $+ 0.392 \times 10^{-3}$ pupil–teacher ratio. Adjusted
$(2.75) (2.19) (0.76)$
$R_2 = 0.16$, $N = 109$. Variable definitions are in Table B1.

6. To see this, examine the time rate of change of w_L and w_H/w_L as functions of excess demand. In calculating excess demand, ignoring the demand side (e.g., perfectly inelastic demands), the supply side is stable on its own. The first order expansion of supply accounts for both the direct effect of w_L and the indirect effect of w_H/w_L on N_H/N_L in the $\dot{w}_L$ equation, and for both the direct effect of w_H/w_L and the indirect effect of w_L on N_L in the (w_H/w_L) equation (from equation 6.4). For dynamic stability, the resulting adjustment matrix (see Chapter 4) is stable for point estimates of b_w, b_c, β_w, β_N in equations 6.5 for both the United States and Brazil.

Appendix A. United States

Table A1. Variable Definitions and Sources

Variable	Definitions and source
N	Urbanized population of SMSA in thousands from 1970 *Census of Population* (70 CEN) (normalized in production by further dividing by 1000).
N_H/N_L	Ratio of SMSA population over 25 years of age completing four years of high school or more, to those completing less than four years of high school. From 70 CEN.
w_H, p_H	Median income of adult (16 years or older) male civilian labor force working 50 to 52 weeks in 1969 with four years of high school or more. Calculated from Sixth Count of 70 CEN, as follows. For males for 51 occupations from Table 124D, calculate percent with four or more years high school. For each income category in Table 1240 multiply 51 occupations by a percent with four or more years of high school. In each income category sum across occupations to get the total workers in the income category with four or more years of high school. Looking across nine income categories, calculate the median income (assuming a uniform distribution in critical category). w_H for manufacturing is converted to hourly income by dividing by 2000 and further normalized by dividing by 5.
w_L, p_L	See w_H.
Annual precipitation	In inches per year for central city of SMSA. From 1972 City and County Data (72 CCDB). (Mean, standard deviation of 36.16, 12.66.)
Annual heating degree days	Total for season based on 65° F. From *Climatological Data* (National Oceanic and Atmospheric Administration). (Mean, s.d. of 4529.23, 2113.41).
Distance to regional markets	Distance to nearest of 27 Rand-McNally National Business Centers (based on volume of financing activity and wholesale and retail trade). Distance is in hours of driving time based on Rand-McNally estimates (gaps filled in based on likely routes and speeds of travel). (Mean, s.d., of 3.47, 3.25.)
Coastal dummy	Port located on seacoast, Great Lakes, or Mississippi basin. From Waterborne Commerce of the United States. (U.S. Corps of Engineers.) (Mean of 0.35.)
Tons of particulates per square mile	Tons of particulates per year in 1973. From *1973 National Emissions Report* (E.P.A.). Land area is carefully defined urbanized land for 1972 calculated in *1974 Transportation Report*. (Mean, s.d. of 0.72, 1.17.)
Buses per square mile	Number of operating buses divided by urbanized land both from *1974 National Transportation Report*. (Mean, s.d. of 0.41, 0.38.)
Murder rate	Number of reported murders per 100,000 people from 1970 and 1971 *Uniform Crime Report* (F.B.I.) (Mean, s.d. of 7.28, 5.30.)
Property taxes	Total property taxes (millions of dollars) for 1971 divided by SMSA population (1000s). From *1972 Census of Governments*. (Mean, s.d. of 0.19, 0.14.)
X	Output defined as value of production from *1972 Census of Manufacturers*.
N_{OL}, N_{OH}	For manufacturing from 1972 Census of Manufacturers. Total labor is annual production workers' hours plus 2000 hours/year × number of nonproduction workers. To get the education breakdown, combine the detailed matrix (Table 124D) of education by occupation from the 1970 Population Census (with 27 occupations relevant to each of durable and nondurable manufacturing) with the matrix (Table 1250) of occupation by 20 manufacturing industries to get for each SMSA a matrix of education by industry.

To aid in calculating elasticities the mean and standard deviation of the linear variables used in the population and size equations are noted.

Table A2. Coefficients for Manufacturing Industry Equations (Zellner Equations (Absolute t-statistics in Parentheses))

	b_{LL}	b_{LH}	b_{HH}	b_{LN}	b_{HN}	ρ_L	ρ_H
Primary metals	0.731×10^{-2} (0.38)	0.021 (1.15)	0.015 (0.87)	-0.595×10^{-2} (3.09)	-0.522×10^{-2} (2.35)	0.10	0.14
Electrical	0.050 (3.27)	-0.018 (1.32)	0.063 (4.88)	-0.362×10^{-2} (2.53)	-0.267×10^{-2} (1.20)	0.10	0.20
Nonelectrical machinery	0.049 (4.56)	-0.021 (2.07)	0.060 (6.36)	-0.261×10^{-2} (2.05)	-0.208×10^{-2} (1.35)	0.11	0.19
Leather products	-0.014 (0.27)	0.067 (1.41)	-0.016 (0.37)	-0.661×10^{-2} (1.54)	0.143×10^{-2} (0.33)	0.14	0.14
Textiles	0.013 (0.47)	0.034 (1.39)	-0.238×10^{-2} (0.11)	-0.782×10^{-2} (2.62)	0.110×10^{-2} (0.44)	0.13	0.12
Food processing	-0.339×10^{-2} (0.61)	0.019 (3.72)	0.239×10^{-2} (0.50)	-0.227×10^{-2} (2.43)	-0.271×10^{-2} (2.52)	0.06	0.07
Pulp and paper	-0.300×10^{-2} (0.22)	0.028 (2.25)	0.904×10^{-3} (0.08)	-0.201×10^{-3} (1.42)	0.986×10^{-3} (0.95)	0.10	0.12
Apparel	-0.053 (1.77)	0.125 (4.62)	-0.054 (2.17)	-0.022 (4.58)	-0.013 (3.19)	0.16	0.15
Wood products	-0.010 (0.73)	0.042 (3.28)	-0.125×10^{-2} (0.11)	-0.543×10^{-2} (2.80)	-0.264×10^{-2} (1.20)	0.10	0.13

Source: Henderson, 1985.

131

Appendix B. Brazil

Table B1. Variable Definition: Supply Side

Variable	Definition
N	Urban population of urban area.
N_H/N_L	Ratio of high to low skill adults. Skill level is determined by whether the adult has six or more years of schooling or has five or less years of schooling. The same basic results (except for the wage variable in OLS work on equation 4a where the coefficient becomes 0.132, $t = 1.18$) occur if the variable is defined by dividing households according to the educational attainment of the household head. The data indicate that, women are favored by higher primary school completion rates.
D	Distance in kilometers from nearest major coastal metro area. Coastal metro areas include São Paulo, which is actually about 100 km inland.
Transfer/person	Value-added tax revenues in manufacturing paid by the urban area divided by the urban population. 20% of these revenues are automatically returned to local governments. These revenues are the primary source of intergovernmental transfers. Tax revenue data are from the 1970 Census of Manufacturers.
w_i	Average annual income of people in the ith education group, based on the incomes of individuals working full time in manufacturing in an urban area.
Teacher education	Average education of all full-time school (not college) teachers in the urban area.
Pupil–teacher ratio	Total people ages 5 to 18 regularly attending a school in the urban area divided by total full-time school teachers. (Participation rates of people ages 5 to 18 in school vary widely.) One state had the data for the school system's presumably more precise measure of pupil–teacher ratios. For that restricted sample of 46 urban areas, the OLS results are similar to the results given in the text.
Percentage N_L water	The number of low skill households serviced by a water connection divided by total low skill households (as defined by education of the household head). Water connection means water from a public system piped into the house.
Percentage N_L sewer	See percentage of N_L water. A sewer connection means a connection to any type of sewage disposal system including a septic tank or pipes running into a roadside public sewage ditch only partially covered.

Table B2. Variable Definitions: Cost Functions

Variable	Definition
c	Total costs divided by output. Output is value added defined in the same way as in the U.S. Census. Total costs are total labor costs (wages and salaries plus firm contributions to social security and private pension, health, and other plans) plus capital costs. Capital costs are $K \times p_K$. K is the capital stock and is the response to the Census question, "What are your equipment and structures worth today?" with the verbal explanation to the effect. "That is, what could you get for them today if you sold them?" (see Appendix B, Chapter 5). p_K is defined below.
N_0	Average monthly employees in the industry (hours of work are not collected).
N	Urban area population.
p_L	Wage of low skill workers. This is calculated as total industry labor costs (see definition of c) multiplied by the ratio of average annual income of workers in the industry with less than six years of schooling to the average annual income of all workers in the industry. These annual income numbers are from the Demographic Census and are for full-time workers by two-digit industry.
p_H	Wage of high skill workers. Defined in corresponding fashion to p_L.
p_K	Opportunity cost of capital calculated to be $(0.23 + pt)$. 0.23 represents interest plus depreciation based for Brazil on a real rate of return of 0.08 and a rate of exponential decay of 0.15. Obviously these numbers are arguable but can be defended based on numbers in the literature (United States numbers are for decay, Brazilian numbers for real rate of return.) pt is the industry-urban area specific property tax rate and is calculated from industry property tax payments divided by K. Typically, $pt = 0.02$ but varies quite widely across space. The results are not sensitive to the choice of interest and depreciation rates.

Table B3. Simple Correlation Matrix for City Population and Composition Variables

	N_H/N_L	w_L	D	Transfer/House	Percent N_L Water	Percent N_L Sewer	w_H/w_L	Pupil/Teacher	Teacher Education
N	0.69	0.36	−0.11	−0.02	0.06	−0.19	0.33	0.05	0.14
N_H/N_L		0.29	−0.08	−0.16	0.01	−0.16	0.29	−0.27	0.28
w_L			−0.21	0.14	0.17	0.10	−0.07	0.25	0.07
D				−0.32	−0.15	−0.19	0.06	−0.06	0.03
Transfer/House					0.11	0.27	−0.01	0.33	−0.03
Percent N_L Water						0.56	−0.09	−0.21	0.31
Percent N_L Sewer							−0.16	0.01	0.00
w_H/w_L								−0.02	−0.07
Pupil/Teacher									−0.29

Table B4. The Parameters of the Cost Function[a]

	Ceramics	Iron and steel	Agricultural machinery	Auto accessories	Traditional chemicals	Spinning and weaving	Shoes
A_0	-0.045	-0.141	0.062	-0.277	-0.706	-1.387	0.387
	(0.34)	(1.38)	(0.44)	(2.69)	(6.71)	(4.61)	(4.38)
B_1	-0.185	-0.325	-0.95	-0.185	-0.077	-0.051	-0.214
	(1.53)	(4.20)	(2.08)	(2.00)	(0.38)	(0.88)	(3.14)
B_2	0.015	0.008	0.108	0.003	0.006	0.001	0.010
	(1.24)	(4.16)	(1.86)	(1.92)	(0.51)	(0.60)	(2.75)
B_3	-0.066	0.047	-0.037	0.040	-0.23	0.058	0.022
	(0.88)	(0.59)	(0.36)	(0.52)	(2.20)	(0.65)	(0.40)
α_L	0.080	0.129	0.562	0.373	0.429	-0.476	0.603
	(2.03)	(5.28)	(9.54)	(5.95)	(9.81)	(2.06)	(11.79)
α_H	0.328	0.427	0.230	0.196	0.085	-0.494	0.221
	(3.62)	(7.41)	(6.61)	(5.71)	(2.58)	(5.04)	(6.89)
γ_{LL}	0.102	0.086	0.186	0.096	0.181	-0.235	0.119
	(2.30)	(3.01)	(6.10)	(2.91)	(7.80)	(2.42)	(4.91)
γ_{LH}	-0.083	-0.107	-0.138	-0.121	-0.165	-0.353	-0.100
	(4.20)	(6.63)	(7.26)	(6.33)	(9.36)	(8.66)	(7.49)

134

γ_{HH}	0.065	0.095	0.164	0.125	0.111	0.017	0.108
	(4.46)	(6.83)	(8.33)	(6.93)	(5.39)	(0.69)	(8.16)
γ_{LN}	−0.027	−0.024	−0.028	−0.009	−0.014	0.013	0.003
	(2.08)	(1.72)	(1.86)	(0.54)	(0.92)	(0.43)	(0.33)
γ_{HN}	0.024	0.016	0.008	0.015	0.014	0.024	0.003
	(3.28)	(2.31)	(0.84)	(1.53)	(1.02)	(1.70)	(0.29)
Sample size	62	78	59	58	61	60	65
S_L	0.48	0.43	0.41	0.38	0.26	0.46	0.54
S_H	0.18	0.20	0.24	0.25	0.30	0.19	0.22
S_K	0.34	0.37	0.35	0.37	0.44	0.35	0.24
Mean employment (100s)	0.64	1.09	0.28	1.38	0.55	1.76	0.77
γ_{LK}	−0.019	0.021	−0.048	0.025	−0.016	0.588	−0.019
γ_{HK}	0.018	0.012	−0.026	−0.004	0.054	0.336	0.002
γ_{KN}	0.001	−0.033	0.074	−0.021	−0.038	−0.924	0.017
γ_{KK}	0.003	0.008	0.020	−0.006	0	−0.037	0

[a] t-statistics are in parentheses.

S_i are factor shares. The final panel of coefficients are calculated from the restrictions on equations. For these coefficients, the standard error of estimate is $\sqrt{\mathrm{var}_{ii} + \mathrm{var}_{jj} + 2\,\mathrm{cov}_{ij}}$ where var_{ii} and var_{jj} are the variances of the other coefficients used to calculate the residual coefficient and cov_{ij} is the covariance of the other coefficients. In practice approximating the standard error of estimate by $\sqrt{\mathrm{var}_{ii} + \mathrm{var}_{jj}}$ produces an estimate off by *less than* 15%.

Appendix C. Formal Modeling of Skill Composition

This brief technical note shows the procedure for incorporating skill composition into the model used in Chapters 2 to 4. On the production side, rewrite $X = g(N) N_{OL}^{\alpha_0} N_{OH}^{\alpha_1} K_O^{1-\alpha_1-\alpha_0}$, where N_{OL} and N_{OH} are the two skill groups. On the consumption side combine and simplify site and housing production, so that $H = \beta N^{-\delta} K_1$, or housing is subject to decreasing returns to scale (see Hochman, 1977), where now $N = N_{OL} + N_{OH}$. Following the methodology of Chapter 2 solve for indirect utility where $U_L = \hat{f}(q, r, N_{OL}, N_{OH})$ and $U_H = \hat{g}(q, r, N_{OL}, N_{OH})$. Then optimize to find efficient city size where now there are two equations $\partial U_L/\partial N_{OL} = 0$ and $\partial U_H/\partial N_{OH} = 0$. While these do not have a closed form solution, when solved jointly they will take parametric values

$$\overset{*}{N}_{OL} = N_L(\alpha_O, \alpha_1, f, \delta, b, \phi) \qquad \text{(C.1)}$$
$$\overset{*}{N}_{OH} = N_H(\alpha_O, \alpha_1, f, \delta, b, \phi)$$

Plugging back into U_L and U_H yields $U_L = f(q, r)$ and $U_H = g(q, r)$. This then presents a problem. If, for example, there are two types of cities, X_1 and X_2, where q_1 is the numeraire, to solve for q_2 as a function of r as in Chapter 2 involves equating utilities across types of cities. Doing that for type L labor yields $q_2 = \bar{f}(r)$ and for type H labor $q_2 = \bar{g}(r)$. The two equations are not consistent. To avoid that problem the housing side of the model needs to be respecified not to be log linear so as to get in (C.1) $\overset{*}{N}_{OL} = N_L(\cdot, k)$ and $\overset{*}{N}_{OH} = N_H(\cdot, k)$, where k is the city K/N ratio, as in Henderson (1977b, Chapter 3). In such a model, city sizes, capital rentals, output prices, and capital-to-labor ratios are solved simultaneously (in nonclosed form solution in multisector models), with no consistency problems.

CHAPTER 7

Government Policies Creating Unintended Spatial Distortions

Chapter 2 demonstrated that any change in the economic environment that alters the composition of national output will alter a country's system of cities and the degree of urban concentration. This chapter reviews a variety of common central government policies in developed and developing countries, which have, perhaps unintended, spatial impacts. Some of the policies reviewed in this chapter may have locational aspects such as favoring specific firms in specific cities or favoring specific cities, but their intent is not to affect the spatial allocation of resources per se. This is to be contrasted with policies enacted with intended specific spatial impacts such as urban deconcentration and industrial location policies. Such policies are reviewed in Chapters 8 and 9. In this chapter the concern is with more traditional national policies, such as export–import restrictions, minimum wage laws, and public and private capital market restrictions. These are implemented with, for example, particular development, benevolent social, power enhancing, or profiteering motives and goals. The concern is neither with these motives nor per se with the usual welfare distortions or gains associated with these policies. Some comments on the welfare analysis of these types of situations are made in Chapter 9. The concern here is with their implicit spatial impacts, which may be unintended and their cause not understood by national policymakers. An excellent review of this problem is given by Renaud (1979).

This chapter argues that in general the impact of these traditional policies particularly in developing countries is to enhance the degree of urban concentration. If this is so, it suggests that the traditional welfare cost analysis of such policies (e.g., Little et al., 1970) misses a critical component of welfare distortions (see Chapter 9). Unnecessarily increasing the degree of urban concentration may sound innocuous. However, in practice it involves the uprooting of millions of people and erosion of their social fabric as people move from traditional towns and villages to larger urban areas. Without advocating the joys of rural life per se, we suggest that if people would have been better off economically by staying in their traditional residences under a better policy regime, it is unclear that there are any other offsetting social gains from their movements to large cities. Indeed, one could view the erosion of social "capital" and the unnecessary tearing of the traditional social fabric as a probable loss.

Moreover, the population movements from smaller to larger cities (or in fact amongst *any* cities) places an administrative and fiscal burden on the growing cities. Public infrastructure (such as roads, water works, and parks), not to mention housing, are immobile and must be abandoned and left to deteriorate in places losing population. Places gaining in population then must build a new housing and urban infrastructure for immigrants out of the country's scarce resources. In some countries,[1] the largest metro areas have grown at rates averaging over 8% a year, leading to doubling or even tripling of city sizes every decade. Administratively and fiscally these cities seem unable to plan and cope with the population invasions, leading to haphazard spatial layouts of cities and the social conflicts created by urban squatter settlements and residents' quasi-legal efforts to obtain public utilities.

These problems have led to explicit or implicit urban deconcentration policies. Explicit policies are reviewed in Chapters 8 and 9. Implicit policies may simply discourage large city immigration by making living conditions for immigrants intolerable; this is done, for example, by refusing to provide public utilities, uprooting squatters, and so on. That is, the attempt of either explicit or implicit deconcentration policies is to offset the distortional gains of the migration to larger cities that was unintentionally created by national policies. The offset may be done by creating other (again perhaps distortional) gains in living outside larger cities by carrying out explicit deconcentration policies (see Chapter 9). Or it may be done by creating or allowing to fester offsetting costs that must be borne by immigrants attempting to take advantage of the initial benefits of national policies unintentionally provided by the migration to larger cities.

The obvious point is that many countries would generally have been better off if these traditional national policies had never been enacted in the first place. The urban problem is revealed either innocuously through unnecessary increases in measures of urban concentration or vividly through treatises on the deplorable conditions of certain metro areas. It is one aspect of the welfare costs of such policies, usually overlooked by economists. However, that is not to stress evils of large cities. At least initial and substantial increases in urban concentration appear from the data in Chapter 3 to be a normal and natural part of the economic development process. As such, the role of governments of larger cities should be to plan for and accommodate growth with proper provision for urban infrastructure and services. The concern here is with unnecessary increases in concentration—the overconcentration of population in the largest cities in developing countries.

The chapter reviews some traditional national government policies, which have impacts on the spatial allocation of population. Each policy is discussed in terms of why there is a presumption that it will increase rather than decrease urban concentration.

1. Trade Protection Policies

Virtually all countries have an array of trade protection policies. The intent of the policies is to reduce the imports of certain products so as to spur the domestic production needed to meet domestic demands. There seem to be at least four bases for the policies. The first is to protect certain "infant" industries from import competition. The hope is that, if industries are protected so that they can expand, sufficient scale (assuming either intrafirm or national interfirm economies of scale) and level of technical expertise (fostered by scale) may result, enabling them to compete effectively with imports and perhaps even to export on the world market. One entrepreneur alone may not be able to finance or may be unwilling to bear the risks either of setting up an industrial operation on the necessary initial scale or of incurring losses during an initial start-up period while necessary technical expertise is acquired through training and learning by doing. The government gives import protection to foster the needed development of scale, with reduced risk of financial loss by providing a protected domestic market for the initial high cost production. One obvious national issue is whether such infant industries ever grow up and achieve low cost production rather than remaining high cost, often monopolistic producers. Another issue is whether protection is in fact necessary for industries to grow up or whether there are indeed entrepreneurs who would finance and risk product development without protection. It is, of course, in the financial interests of entrepreneurs to argue that they need import restrictions.

The other bases for import restrictions are less central to this chapter. One is to protect faltering industries (e.g., cotton, shoes, and autos in the United States) from international competition, where a national government is responding to intensive lobbying of interest groups bearing the brunt of perhaps natural changes in national production patterns. A third is to develop domestic capabilities in certain industries for national defense purposes, so as to not be reliant on (subject to manipulation by) foreign producers. The fourth basis is strict profiteering, where favored families may be granted a monopoly right to domestic production of a good yet to be domestically produced and granted a protected domestic market.

In many cases the first or third and the fourth bases for trade protection may be combined. A national government may view as critical to its economic development process or defense the domestic establishment of certain key typically heavy manufacturing industires. At the same time, it may satisfy nepotism and profiteering motives by discretionary granting of production licenses.

Nevertheless, in many developing countries, the commonly believed scenario is that trade protection policies favor development and expansion of "modern" heavy industries such as iron and steel, autos and other transport equipment, petrochemicals, weapons production, and heavy electrical and nonelectrical machinery and appliances, at the expense of traditional industries such as textiles, nonmetallic minerals, food processing, wood products, and agriculture. Governments in many countries appear to believe that artificially stimulated development of modern industries is critical to rapid economic growth. The welfare costs of such programs resulting from costly shifts in national output patterns (Little et al., 1970) and underinvestment in research and development of traditional industries (Evenson and Kister, 1975) have been heralded by many economists. The focus here is on the likely urban impacts of such policies.

Import restrictions may take the form of either tariffs on imports or quotas on imports. While the two forms have different distributional impacts and import quotas may additionally create wasteful rent-seeking behavior (Kreuger, 1974), the directional and urban impacts of the two forms are basically the same. There are also similar export promotion policies, where typically modern heavy industries in developing countries are subsidized not just to protect them domestically but to enable them to expand in order to compete on international markets. Again the directional impact of such a policy is the same. As such, the formal exposition need only cover import tariff impacts—the others have similar impacts.

The analysis uses the international trade model presented in Chapter 4. There are two traded good industries in the country, X_1 and X_2, with two corresponding types of cities. X_2 is a traditional labor intensive export product while X_1 is a modern heavy industry import product. The government enacts import tariffs on X_1, raising its relative domestic price above the world terms of trade (TOT). This has two impacts.

First, assuming a locally concave national transformation curve between X_1 and X_2, which would be guaranteed by national constant returns to scale (which is consistent with localization economies from Chapters 2 to 4), trade theory tells us that X_1 production will rise and X_2 production will fall. This result is implicit in the stability conditions developed in Chapter 4. Thus the number of X_1 type cities will rise and the number of X_2 cities will fall.

Chapters 1 and 6 for the United States and Chapter 6 for Brazil suggest that type 1 cities, housing modern industries, are significantly larger than type 2 cities, housing traditional industries. This means that with the enactment of the policy the total number of cities required in the economy falls. That is, some sites of former type 2 cities are abandoned. People from these abandoned sites migrate to other former type 2 cities that convert to X_1 production. In this scenario the increase in urban concentration and migration to larger cities occurs when some former type 2 cities expand to become type 1 cities. Implicit in the conversion of type 2 to type 1 cities, rather than abandonment of all unneeded type 2 sites and the creation of entirely new type 1 sites, is the conservation of immobile public capital of former type 2 cities (where such immobility is considered in Chapter 3). Section 4 of this chapter notes that trade protection policies can be implemented in such a fashion as to also (or only) encourage growth of existing X_1 cities. The simple general tariff implemention here leaves efficient city sizes for each type of city unchanged, so that increased concentration is simply the expansion of the number of larger in relation to smaller cities. However, the social upheavals and urban growth (of some former X_2 cities) discussed in the introduction of the chapter are one result of the tariff protection policies.

The second basic impact of trade protection policies follows from the Stolper–Samuelson trade theorem. For an open economy, if the relative (domestically received) price of a traded good increases, the return to the factor used intensively in producing that good will rise and return to the other factor will fall. From equations 2.24 and 2.17

$$\partial r / \partial(q_2) < 0 \quad \text{iff} \quad \alpha_1 < \alpha_2$$
$$\partial U / \partial(q_2) > 0 \quad \text{iff} \quad \alpha_1 < \alpha_2$$

Given that the relative price of X_2 falls (X_1 rises), this implies r rises and U falls. In summary, under the assumption that typical "modern" industries in developing countries are more capital intensive than traditional industries, the owners of capital will gain at the expense of laborers. This result should not be overlooked in assessing the political motivations and sources of lobbying for the domestic protection of "modern" industries in developing countries.

2. Minimum Wage Policies

Most countries have some type of minimum wage policies, based perhaps on notions of social fairness. Often minimum wage policies are poorly enforced or easily evaded legally. For example, they may only apply to full-time workers

or to workers employed for over a year. In many cases it is easy to define workers as part-time or to fire all workers every New Year's Eve and rehire them New
Year's Day. The concern here is with enforced fully effective minimum wage
policies.

In a partial equilibrium context, the impact of minimal wages is to raise the
pay of those remaining at work and leave others unemployed. The general equilibrium impacts can be quite different—they can, for example, distort national
output patterns and shift factor rewards toward labor with no unemployment. The
impacts depend on how minimum wage policies are defined. In a general equilibrium context wages must be defined relative to something or by some standard.
For example, in a country where minimum wages may be defined in nominal
monetary units at a point in time, they are typically regularly reassessed and adjusted not just for inflation but according to some social norm. Thus effectively
a minimum wage policy sets long-run minimum wages according to some norm.
This section examines the impact of minimum wages on a system of cities, for
minimum wages set according to one particular social norm.

Prior to minimum wage legislation, from Chapter 2 wages rise monotonically
with city size. Again, city types are indexed so that $N_1 > N_2 > \ldots N_n$, and hence
$w_1 > w_2 > \ldots w_n$. Examining a closed economy, minimum wage legislation is
implemented to effectively fix all nominal wages to be no less than the level
prevailing in some visable industry, say, the k industry in city type N_k. That is
the social norm assumed. Before legislation, $N_1 > \ldots > N_k > \ldots > N_n$. What
happens after legislation?

This is seen by examining the impact of the law on factor returns. By law, for
all cities smaller than type k, which are city types $i = k + 1, \ldots, n$, regulated
wages $\hat{w}_i \geq w_k$. If $w_i < w_k$ before legislation, after legislation w_i's must rise to
(the new equilibrium) w_k. To solve for the impact on city sizes, examine U defined
in Chapter 2 in terms of wages (w) and capital rentals (r) (see equations 2.4 and
2.7). In the U expression for each type of city, capital market equilibrium requires
equal r's across city types and the law requires $\hat{w}_i \geq w_k$. Labor market equilibrium
requires $U_i = U_k \ \forall i \geq k$. In the utility expressions, given equalized w's and r's,
equal utilities then require that under regulation city sizes $\hat{N}_i$ be determined by

$$\hat{N}_i^{\beta b(\gamma - \delta)} = N_k^{\beta b(\gamma - \delta)}$$

or

$$\hat{N}_i = N_k \ \forall i \geq k$$

That is, the size of all type i cities must rise to that of type k cities.

Why is the impact of this legislation to raise the sizes of all cities, initially
smaller than type k, to the size of type k cities? Effectively the government has
intervened on the production side in type i cities to make their wages equal to
those of type k cities, so that the work benefits of living in type i cities are made
equal to those in type k. Equilibrium of population allocation through utility equalization then requires that type i cities have the same *consumption conditions* as
type k cities, which requires city sizes to be the same. Since type k cities are not
regulated, their sizes are unchanged and are determined by the condition $\partial U / \partial N_k$
$= 0$. So it must be that sizes of type i cities for i equal to $k + 1$ through n increase
to N_k. But then sizes of type i cities can no longer be determined by the condition
$\partial U / \partial N_i = 0$. Figure 7.1 depicts the resulting situation in type i cities, assuming
that entry to type i cities is not restricted.

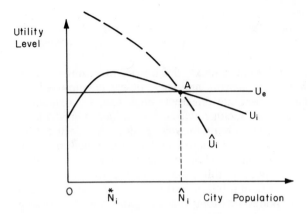

Fig. 7.1   Impact of Minimum Wage Laws on City Sizes

U_i is utility for city type i that would exist if i cities paid unregulated competitive wages, given (new) equilibrium prices; $\hat{N}_i$ is equilibrium city size. Regulated utility is $\hat{U}_i$. Given a fixed w, $\hat{U}_i$ declines continuously for $N_i \geq 0$ because consumption conditions deteriorate continuously. Equilibrium is at A where (1) utility in type i cities equals the opportunity value, U_e, (2) producers can pay the minimum wage (i.e., $\hat{U}_i = U_i$), and (3) $\hat{N}_i = N_k$. $\hat{U}_i$ lies above U_i to the left of A, since, for unregulated wages, w_i, $w_i < \hat{w}_i = w_k$; and $\hat{U}_i$ lies below U_i to the right of A since $w_i > \hat{w}_i = w_k$.

What happens to the relative numbers of cities? For $j = 1, \ldots, k - 1$, m_j/m_k is unchanged in equation 2.29. For $i = k + 1, \ldots, n$, things are different. In equation 2.29 since $\hat{N}_i = N_k$ for $i = k + 1, \ldots, n$

$$\frac{\hat{m}_i}{m_k} = \frac{a_i}{a_k} \frac{\alpha_i}{\alpha_k}$$

Comparing this with the expression before the minimum wage, which included a N_i, N_k term greater than one, $\hat{m}_i/m_k$ declines given N_i has risen. This is not surprising.

In summary, the impact on a system of cities of a completely enforced minimum wage policy that standardizes minimum wages to those prevailing in a visible medium wage industry is to increase urban concentration unambiguously. There are two reasons. First, the numbers of cities engaged in the production of goods located in small types of cities are reduced. Second, the sizes of surviving cities of this type are all increased. The minimum wage policy effectively imposes a minimum city size policy. The result is an unambiguous increase in urban concentration.

Of course, minimum wage policies in practice are not well enforced as noted earlier, especially in traditional industries where firm sizes are smaller or in household industries. In developing countries, to the extent that these industries are located in smaller cities, the spatial impact of minimum wage policies is ameliorated. However, the direction of the impact is clear.

3. Subsidies in the Public Capital Market

The model in Chapters 2 to 4 assumes that local governments are autonomous, that local public services levels are chosen in a full information local democratic environment, and that public service production is priced at opportunity cost to localities. The democracy assumption per se may not be unreasonable. Even under quite authoritarian national political systems, local public decisions are made in a somewhat democratic fashion (e.g., Brazil and even parts of China). However, the other two assumptions often do not prevail. First, autonomy of local governments may be quite restricted so that the scope of local public decision making is narrow with higher levels of government setting many local service levels. Second, central governments may intervene to alter the costs facing localities by subsidizing provision of certain locally set public services. For example in the United States there are literally hundreds of local public service subsidy programs available to localities through the federal government.

Chapter 10 considers empirically the impact of restrictions on local autonomy by comparing federal with centralized systems of government. It shows that centralized systems tend to have much higher degrees of urban concentration, ceteris paribus. Speculation suggests that central governments may be biased toward providing public services in national capital regions (where policymakers live) and may be ignorant of the needs of outlying areas as well as politically insulated from and insensitive toward these regions.

This chapter focuses on government intervention in local decision making through, in particular, subsidization of public capital. Such intervention may have a benevolent base. For example, in countries where capital markets are undeveloped, localities may be unable to float long-term bonds to finance public construction, and financing out of current taxes only may be fiscally impossible. The national government can borrow nationally or internationally and then relend the money to cities at perhaps opportunity cost.

The question is what happens if such loans are subsidized or offered on some type of discriminatory basis. Since these types of capital market programs and explicit or implicit subsidization are widespread, these are critical issues in examining urban concentration. Even if explicit subsidy programs are not as widespread or as generous as in the United States, regular forgiving of loans (e.g., India) may make them implicitly as generous. And discriminatory provision can be the rule in centralized systems of government.

The technical analysis of various types of subsidy programs is in Henderson (1982a) and is adapted here based on the model in Chapter 2. In terms of that model, subsidies are paid on infrastructure investments $\hat{K}_2$ in cities. They are paid by the national government from revenue raised by a national income tax. This alters the per person income, y, in equation 2.7, to that it becomes

$$y = w(1 - t) - r(1 - s)\,\hat{K}_2/N \tag{2.7a}$$

w is the wage rate, t is the national income tax rate, and s is the matching rate, or the proportion of local public infrastructure costs the national government will pay. The remainder $r(1 - s)\hat{K}_2/N$ is paid out of local income taxes. This program affects the local demand for infrastructure investment and local utility levels, as well as other variables. Specifically, in equations 2.10 and 2.12, postsubsidy demand for infrastructure $\hat{K}_2^*$ and postsubsidy utility level U^* become

$$\hat{K}_2^* = \hat{K}_2 (1 - s)^{-1} \qquad\qquad (2.10\text{a})$$

$$\overset{*}{U} = U(1 - t)^{f+\gamma\beta b} (1 - s)^{-\gamma\beta b} \qquad\qquad (2.12\text{a})$$

where $\hat{K}_2$ and U are the nontax expressions in equations 2.10 and 2.12, respectively. For unchanged factor prices, the subsidy causes the use of $\hat{K}_2$ to rise, while t and s have, respectively, a negative and positive impact on utility levels.

What is the overall impact of a subsidy on the system of cities? Three cases are considered.

3.1. Uniform Subsidy to All Cities

Suppose all cities face the same subsidy rate for infrastructure investment. This is the case for many U.S. programs. First, in terms of the "urban system" the subsidy passes neutrally through the system, leaving city sizes and the relative numbers of each type of city unaffected. Note that in (2.12a) the subsidy does not affect the N terms in U that are critical for solving for equilibrium city size. Second, because each city faces the same subsidy rate, the impact on each city type is the same and their relative positions are unchanged. Of course, prices and the national allocation of capital between urban infrastructure and other uses will be adversely affected as with any distortion of this type. But traditional welfare analysis captures completely the impact of the subsidy.

3.2. Uniform Subsidy to Just One Type of City

Suppose the national government decides to favor any location that specializes in the production of a good it favors, such as iron and steel or autos. So it offers a subsidy on infrastructure investments to only this type of city, say the jth type of city producing X_j, financed out of national income tax revenues. Given that $\overset{*}{U}$ for j type cities remains as in equation 2.12a, the efficient sizes of j type cities are unchanged. However, the numbers of j type cities are affected. Resolving for q_j in equation 2.18 yields

$$q_j = (Z_1/Z_j)^{\alpha_j} r^{(\alpha_1 - \alpha_j)/\alpha_1} (1 - s_j)^{\alpha_j\gamma\beta b/[(f - b\beta(1 - \gamma)]}$$

indicating that the relative cost of producing the output of the favored type of city falls, which leads to an increase in the numbers of that type of city. With appropriate substitutions (Henderson, 1982a),

$$(m_j/m_1)^* = (m_j/m_1)(1 - s_j)^{-\gamma\beta b/[f - b\beta(1 - \gamma)]}$$

where (m_j/m_1) is the equilibrium presubsidy ratio of j type cities and $(m_j/m_1)^*$ the higher equilibrium ratio after subsidization.

Apart from distorting the use of $\hat{K}_2$ in j type cities, the impact of subsidizing infrastructure in j type cities is the same as subsidizing X_j production per se. One implication is that any one j type city does not benefit in the long run from the subsidy, because the value of the subsidy is not capitalized into higher wages (or land rents). Through competition among cities to become j type cities in order to get the subsidy, its benefits are dissipated.

What is the impact on urban concentration of expansion in the relative numbers of X_j cities? If these favored cities tend to be willing to engage in the production

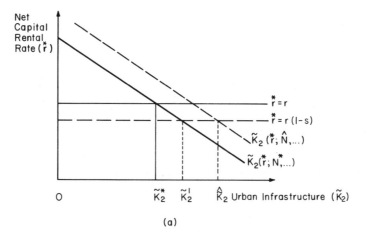

(a)

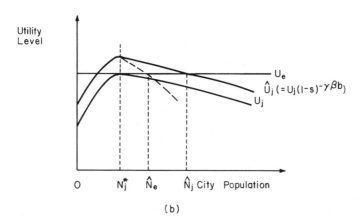

(b)

Fig. 7.2   (a) Subsidy Impact on Urban Infrastructure (b) Subsidy Impact on Size of Favored City

of modern manufactured products, as suggested in Section 1 on tariff protection, this expansion at the expense of traditional product cities will lead to an increase in urban concentration.

3.3. Subsidy to Just One Particular City

Suppose the national government offers the subsidy rate s to only one particular city of type j, and to no other cities. An example would be a country favoring a national capital region, or one particular urban area as a center of commerce. This subsidy is paid out of the national income tax, although it benefits only one small part of the country. As illustrated in Figure 7.2a, the subsidy first lowers the cost of capital in the local public capital market, increasing the use of public capital in the favored city to $\hat{K}_2^1$ from $\hat{K}_2^*$ for the same city size. If U_j is the utility in any other j type city, from (2.12a), utility in the favored city $\hat{U}_j$, given the subsidy and increased use of public capital, is shifted up in Figure 7.2b so that

$$\hat{U}_j = U_j (1 - s)^{-\gamma\beta b}$$

This shift may be viewed in absolute or relative terms, if we allow that general equilibrium changes in all prices $\hat{U}_j$ for any city size is higher than the new U_j. However, because the subsidy only affects the demand for one use of capital in just one city (in contrast to Sections 3.1 and 3.2), a partial equilibrium view of the process can be used, where the impact of the subsidy on the national capital rental rate is negligible. Given that any city's share of the national tax cost of the subsidy to this one city is also negligible, then U_j is essentially unchanged and the shift up in $\hat{U}_j$ is absolute. Regardless, the central analysis of concern, the impact on city sizes, is the same.

What are the impacts on city sizes, as well as the ultimate impact on realized utility after the feedback effects of changed city sizes? For other j type cities, in Figure 7.2b equilibrium city sizes remain at N_j^* where $\partial U_j / \partial N_j = 0$. At that point, in equilibrium $U_j = U_e$, where U_e is the equilibrium utility level in national labor markets. However, in the favored city, although $\partial \hat{U}_j / \partial N_j = 0$ at N_j^*, at N_j^* the shifted up $\hat{U}_j$ curve lies above U_j. What happens to the favored city size?

The analysis of this was given in Chapter 4, Section 4.2, by examining a city favored with a special amenity bundle. There are two possible polar solutions. First, there is the free-entry solution. With unrestricted entry the favored city will expand in size to $\hat{N}_j$ in Figure 7.2b, where U_j declines to U_e. This also results in a feedback effect in Figure 7.2a, shifting out the demand curve for $\hat{K}_2$ to $\hat{K}_2(\hat{r}; \hat{N})$, resulting in a final infrastructure of $\hat{K}_2$. In terms of city size, the impact of the subsidy is to attract people to this favored city, driving up costs of living relative to wages, until the potentially beneficial effect of the subsidy on this one city is dissipated through in-migration. This is a caricature of national capital regions in many countries, which are favored with special infrastructure investments, and which then attract immigrants.

Second, there is a restricted entry solution, where landowners (who can be owner occupiers if subsidies are unexpected) restrict city size to maximize the surpluses generated because potential utility (the $\hat{U}$ path) lies above opportunity costs of labor supply (the U_e line). The surpluses are collected by charging entry fees, such as premiums on prices of residential lots (the purchase of which is required to "enter" the city). Following Chapter 4, Figure 4.2 and equation 4.3, there is a curve marginal to $\hat{U}$ indicated by the dashed line in Figure 7.2. Profits are maximized by restricting city size to $\hat{N}_e$. Restricting size occurs by refusing to permit land development and by strictly zoning density of developed land, so that the population is fixed. In practice, such restrictions partially break down, and population may expand beyond $\hat{N}_e$ toward $\hat{N}_j$, through the development of squatter settlements. Alternatively, inferior living conditions for new entrants (say beyond N_j^*) could be viewed as an indirect way of imposing entry fees (see Chapter 9). In either case the development of inferior conditions for new entrants is a caricature of certain national capital regions.

The extent of favoritism of some national capital regions may be so great (e.g., Bangkok in Thailand, Lagos in Nigeria, traditionally Paris in France), that primacy ratios can be extraordinary. Primacy is the ratio of the largest city's population to the population contained in the next size group of cities (next 3, next

10, next n largest). While in a partial equilibrium sense only one city is involved, the general equilibrium impacts on spatial population allocation can be very pronounced, if the favoritism is extreme.

4. Capital Market Restrictions

Many developing countries have immature or nonexistent capital markets. Investment funds for firms come from several sources. First are family or very small consortium funds. Second are loans from banks—typically, government owned banks, against which substantial collateral may be required. Moreover, banks may be formally restricted in the magnitude of venture capital loans, because collateral (machinery, for example) can only be resold after initial purchase at less than the purchase price. Third are direct government investments typically involving some degree of government ownership. Finally there are private lenders—at rates and terms that are not conducive to long-term financing. Because a formal stock market and perhaps the proper legal structure (for contract enforcement) for extensive shared ownership by venture capitalists do not exist, typically the government plays a substantial role in the capital market, for firms attempting to develop modern large-scale plants with assembly lines and multistage processing. There is, of course, a cause and effect problem here. The government may institutionally structure the economy so that private capital markets and private banking cannot properly develop, creating a vacuum that it then fills.

Typical of government intervention in the capital market is to focus on the development of what it views as key heavy industrial products "essential" for rapid economic development. Just as for import restrictions, the policies tend to favor products such as steel, petrochemicals, and transport equipment, at the expense of traditional goods. In analyzing the spatial impacts of such policies, this chapter considers only policies with no direct locational components. Chapter 8 examines capital subsidy and other policies designed to force producers to locate in certain specific cities. For private capital subsidies, just as for public capital, there are general loan–subsidy policies available to all firms engaged in particular types of manufacturing vs. particular loan policies available to select (perhaps government-owned) firms. The general and spatial impacts of these policies are quite different.

4.1. "Nonlocational" General Subsidy Policies

These are policies where the government provides "subsidized" loans to firms engaged in the production of certain types of goods. The policy may simply be a subsidy policy by which firms can borrow at less than the "prevailing" rate from private lenders such as private banks or family funds (based on the opportunity cost of family funds). However, quantity aspects usually exist, because even private loan policies rationally involve both price and quantity aspects. The quantity aspect would be to increase the magnitude of possible loans beyond the quantity restrictions in the private market.

In either case, the impacts of the policies on urban concentration are the same as under tariff protection and as under public capital subsidies to one type of city. Industries favored with subsidized loans expand domestic production given their lowered domestic costs and increased competitive edge in international markets.

Thus the number of cities engaged in the production of favored products increases, while the number of other city types declines. If favored production typically occurs in larger types of cities, then urban concentration increases. From Chapter 1, as suggested in Sections 1 and 3 of this chapter, favored products are typically produced in larger types of cities.

4.2. "Nonlocational" Specific Subsidy

These are policies where particular firms but not the general industry are favored with subsidized loans. Nonlocational means that favored firms are chosen randomly in space from among existing firms. While such randomness in spatial choices may be unlikely, this is a useful benchmark.

Favors to a specific limited number of firms in particular industries may have negligible impacts—both general and spatial. In partial equilibrium terms, the impacts are intramarginal. Favored firms earn excess profits, given the costs/ prices set by the bulk of competitive unfavored firms operating at the margin. There are distributional costs to the policies and there will be welfare costs if favored firms are less efficient than unfavored ones, so that their potential excess profits are dissipated by inefficiency. For example, one type of subsidy policy may be for the government to cover all losses of an inefficient firm operating in a competitive market.

If favored firms are spatially scattered and within each of their cities are one of many firms, the spatial impacts are also negligible. City wages, utility levels, and equilibrium sizes are determined given the actions of the bulk of unfavored firms, so that favored firms have only intramarginal distributional impacts. This is not to deny that changes in income distribution and intramarginal efficiency losses have general equilibrium impacts; but they are usually viewed as second order impacts whose directional impact may be uncertain.

Substantial spatial impacts only arise if a favored firm is the single traded good producer in a city. Then the employment decisions of that firm essentially determine local wages, total employment, and costs of living. This case is reviewed although, in practice, it may not be particularly relevant since even in developing countries the number of "one-company" towns is very small.

For the analysis let us return to Figure 7.2b. Prior to favored status the firm is one of many operating in a national competitive product market for its output and in a national competitive labor market. As such it has no inherent monopolistic or monopsonistic power. Prior to favoritism, the city has utility path U and its equilibrium size is at $\overset{*}{N}$ where it just pays out U_e, the prevailing utility level in national labor markets.

The subsidy to its dominant firm raises the utility level the city could pay out, as pictured by the $\hat{U}$ curve in Figure 7.2b. If the firm passively expands output, ignoring its local monopsonistic power and continuing to employ labor simply so that wages equal the value of the marginal product, city size would expand to N_e, as the favored city analysis in Section 3 suggested.

However in a "one-company" town, the firm has the power to restrict city size by restricting its own employment. Doing so, moving back from N_e so that $\hat{U}$ lies above U_e, the firm can pay wages less than the value of marginal product and hence earn a profit. Thus, as before, in allowing its own employment and hence city size to expand beyond $\overset{*}{N}$, the firm chooses employment to maximize profits—

the surplus of labor marginal products over wages needed to meet U_e. Thus in Figure 7.2b, again there is a curve marginal to $\hat{U}$ and an equilibrium restricted city size $\hat{N}_e$, where the firm maximizes its profits by restricting employment. These profits go to firm owners if the unusually large firm size (relative to other cities) is due to the entrepreneurial talents (in terms of utilizing specific large firm technologies) of the owners, which could be exercised at any urban site. However, if the size is due to some specific locational amenity (affecting firm technology) which any firm could exploit, the profits will go to rentiers—the owner(s) of the urban site.

5. Conclusions

The theme of this chapter has been that government policies without explicit spatial components have unintended spatial impacts. These impacts typically can be expected to unnecessarily increase urban concentration in a country. This increase means massive migration and uprooting of the traditional social fabric in rural areas and smaller towns, as well as massive reinvestment in urban infrastructure in expanding locations.

The conclusion that policies lead to increased urban concentration is based on the observation that policies tend to favor expansion of output of modern manufacturing products at the expense of traditional industries. Based on the average sizes of different types of cities observed in Chapters 1 and 6, this shift in the composition of national output results in a shift of the population from smaller cities and towns to larger cities.

The favoritism can take the form of trade protection policies for favored products or subsidization of their capital inputs on a nationwide basis. They can also take the form of general concessions on financing of urban infrastructure to localities that choose to shift production toward favored products. This type of favoritism may raise the return to capital at the expense of labor, which could be important to understanding the motivations in political lobbying of various groups.

These policies available to *all* firms or types of cities engaged in production of favored products are to be distinguished from favors granted to *specific* firms or cities. In terms of specific *firms* the impacts are intramarginal to the industry and even to the city, leading to expansion and increased profits for the specifically favored firms, but little overall impact on the particular industry or city the firm is located in.

However, favors to a specific *city* can result in large-scale immigration to the city by people attracted by the potential increase in quality of life. The immigration, of course, dissipates the benefits of the favors by increasing costs of living and disamenities (crime, pollution, congestion, etc.) Even if the city attempts to restrict immigration by restricting formal land development and expansion of urban infrastructure and services, the result is often the development of squatter settlements and social conflicts between favored "original" residents and immigrants who are denied basic urban services and legal residence. This scenario is a caricature of certain national capital regions or large metro areas in some developing countries, where central governments have favored certain urban areas with public services and government sector employment opportunities not available in other locations.

The chapter also examined minimum wage policies. For the population in small cities initially paying wages less than the minimum, higher legislated wages imply a potential increase in utility. This increase is dissipated through increases in city size and hence costs of living, so that utility levels are equalized across cities. In essence, then the minimum wage policy becomes a minimum city size policy, increasing urban concentration.

NOTE

1. For the period 1970–1975, the capitals of Nigeria, Thailand, Bangladesh and Zaire grew at respective rates of 7.3, 5.3, 11.6, and 8.5% annually (Dillinger, 1979).

CHAPTER 8

Industrial Location Policies: Illusion and Remedy

This chapter examines two sets of common industrial location policies found in some developing, as well as developed, countries. The policies have opposite objectives, are typically based on different interpretations of the facts, and have opposite welfare implications. The first set of policies encourage concentration of heavy industry and standardized light industry in very large metropolitan areas. They include state decisions to locate state owned industries in large metropolitan areas, policies that are found in Brazil and China, for example. They also include indirect policies, such as providing only the public infrastructure essential for particular industries in large metropolitan areas or only public services demanded by high skill workers in high skill intensive industries in large metro areas. Both sets of policies are pursued in many parts of the world.

The second set of policies encourage decentralization of manufacturing from metro areas to perhaps nearby small and medium size cities. The motivation is in fact to stem the overconcentration of resources and the resulting congestion and consumer disamenities in large metro areas. In terms of the two sets of policies, there can be a sequence of events. First, the government directly and indirectly encourages high concentrations of industrial resources in large metro areas at early stages of economic development. Over time there is corresponding population growth in the metro areas, which ultimately results in the development of substantial disamenities and a decline in the quality of metro area life. To stem or even reverse the flow of resources into the metro areas, policies are enacted to deflect resources into smaller cities, often nearby satellite cities. That is, deconcentration policies are enacted to offset some of the impacts of the original policies.

Deconcentration policies include loan subsidies to firms locating in smaller cities and subsidized land sites in industrial parks with perhaps subsidized utilities and the provision of required infrastructure. They are aimed primarily at private producers. Only a few countries such as Korea have strong deconcentration policies, but a number such as Brazil, India, and Mexico have weak ones.

Section 1 of the chapter examines the first set of policies, which encourages the location of heavy industry in large metro areas. The view here is that generally

151

such policies are grossly inefficient. However, paradoxically they may appear to be very efficient to planners, because typical productivity measures may be much higher in metro areas compared to smaller cities when small city locations are more efficient. Section 1 focuses on why this is the case and why the reasoning used by planners is fallacious. The problem is explored using a hypothetical example. The example also serves to point out that the welfare losses of mislocation as a fraction of output are potentially enormous.

Section 2 presents a framework for evaluating deconcentration policies. Typical instruments used in countries such as Korea are reviewed. A major issue is into what towns different industries should decentralize. The answer depends on the particular technologies of production in different industries and the amenities offered by different towns. A methodology for estimating these technologies and answering these questions is developed.

1. Metropolitan Location of Heavy Industry

Chapters 1, 5, and 6 argue that heavy industries will be found in specialized smaller and medium size cities because their external economies of scale are ones of localization, not urbanization. Although it benefits firms of these industries to agglomerate with similar producers in small and medium size cities, it does not benefit them, ceteris paribus, to locate in large diversified metropolitan areas and pay the very high wage and land costs there. One exception is industries such as publishing, certain types of chemicals, apparel, and furniture, and certain specialized machinery products that, according to the discussions in Chapters 5 and 6, may experience significant urbanization economies. Another exception is manufacturing goods largely nontraded across cities, such as bottling of beverages or certain nonmetallic minerals (e.g., cement production). A final exception concerns the product cycle, where the early stages of product development (see Chapter 4) may require metro area location for efficient progress. Product development for developing countries may mean adoption and appropriate adaptation of existing technologies from developed countries.

However, standardized manufacturing products that are transportable and tradable across cities typically have no inherent bases for metro area location, apart from historical considerations (such as emplacement of immobile plant and equipment in the earlier stages of product development when metro area location was beneficial). This is particularly so for heavy industries for two reasons. Large metro areas in many countries tend to be port cities. Natural resource deposits tend often to be located somewhere in the hinterlands. Heavy industries such as iron, aluminum, and to some extent steel, tend to be weight-reducing. Thus they are optimally located for reasons of transportion near natural resource deposits rather than near consumer markets (Beckmann, 1968). Accordingly, heavy industries in the United States, Canada, the United Kingdom or the private sector for Brazil tend to be found in the hinterlands. Second, hinterland location of heavy industries in smaller specialized urban areas keep the worst polluting industries away from high concentrations of victims, as would be found in metro areas.

Despite these natural tendencies there are government policies that can induce metro area location of heavy industries. First are direct policies such as state location of state-owned industries or licensing of private producers to metro area locations. Second are indirect policies, many of which were noted in Chapters 6 and 7. For example, there are private and public capital market subsidies. These include reduced loan charges or granting of loans only to metro area locaters. They include subsidized or sole provision of particular infrastructure in metro areas, including provision of reasonable cost reliable power. As another example, there are subsidies for public services demanded by high skill workers (good schooling) or sole provision of such only in large metro areas, precluding viable location of high skill intensive industries outside metro areas. Another example may be excessive regulation of industry and concurrent centralization of bureaucracy so that producers must remain in capital cities to maintain required day-to-day contact with bureaucrats. Of course, large firms may avoid some of the problem by deconcentrating production activity while maintaining central head offices. Finally, regulation and provision of transport facilities may affect location decisions. For example state-owned raw material extractors may have access to state-owned rail systems to ship ore to coastal cities, while processors and other intermediate producers may be denied adequate access to rail systems for shipping their products forcing them to locate near the consumers of their products. To some extent this situation exists in China.

Unfortunately, such policies and the resulting metro area location of heavy industry may be viewed as being efficient by economic planners. This occurs because even when such location is inefficient typical productivity measures such as output per worker may remain substantially higher in metro areas. This also fosters a belief among planners in the existence of essentially urbanization economies. In Brazil it is phrased in terms of how the environment of metro area locations is a prerequisite to the success of industrial production. In China it is phrased in hierarchy terms, where it is viewed that basic industrial production belongs at the top of the hierarchy in large metro areas. In China that view is reinforced by giving large metro area producers the best managers and the newest technologies, indeed artificially creating a more productive environment. The result is that in China and Brazil the concentration of heavy industry in large metro areas is much higher than in, say, the United States. From Chapter 11 the ratio of the share of national heavy industry output (and components such as primary metals) to the share of national urban population is more than 3 for Shanghai and Beijing combined, compared with less than 1 for Chicago and New York combined, both currently *and* historically (e.g., 1914). Similarly, in Brazil Grande São Paulo's ratio is more than 2. For Brazil this concentration is based on policies governing state-owned or subsidized producers (see Henderson, 1987b for a review). Private iron and steel producers are located in the hinterland in Minas Gerais where resource deposits are found.

1.1. Interpreting Productivity Figures

This section takes a hypothetical example and explores the following questions. What is the magnitude of urbanization economies required for it to be *equally* efficient to locate a heavy industry in a large metro area of 10 million compared to a smaller city of, say, 100,000? What relative differences in output per worker are consistent with *equal* efficiency, and the ability of the industry to *just* meet the higher wage and land costs of the large metro area? If such magnitudes of urbanization economies do not exist in fact, what are the magnitudes of subsidies (and welfare costs) needed to maintain metro area location of heavy industry? Even with such subsidies, will true output per worker remain substantially higher in metro areas, perhaps still indicating to planners the efficiency of metro area locations? This would particularly be the case if proper financial accounting is divorced from the planning process, as in China and perhaps to some extent in Brazil.

In the hypothetical example, the metro area vs. small city location of an industry of several thousand employees is considered. It is assumed that infrastructure, public services, technologies, and access to input and output markets are the same for the two locations so there is no artificial or even inherent bias toward one location or the other. Moreover, because own industry employment is held constant, localization economies are the same in both locations. The locations differ in only two respects.

First, labor costs in the metro area are significantly higher. These are compensating wage differentials for the higher costs of living in larger metro areas documented in Chapter 6. Compensating wage differentials for low skill workers holding amenities fixed suggest wages must rise by about 0.6% for each 1% increase in city size. Accounting for variation in endogenous amenities that improve with city size, raw data on low skill workers in iron and steel industries in Brazil suggest that wages must increase by 2.5 to 3 times between a city of 10,000 and one of 10 million to compensate for cost-of-living increases. This is supported by cost-of-living data for Brazil and Peru (Thomas, 1978), indicating a more than doubling of costs of living across urban areas. Between a city of 100,000 and one of 10 million the compensating wage differential seems to require a doubling of wages.

Second, the locations will differ in their extent of potential urbanization economies, because of their population differences. This issue revolves around how great these economies must be to finance the labor cost differentials and what happens if they are not great enough.

For the example a Cobb-Douglas technology is assumed where

$$X_i = SN_{0i}^{\beta}K_{0i}^{1-\beta} \qquad (8.1)$$

for N_0 and K_0 being labor and capital inputs in the X industry in city i. S is a production function shifter of the form (see Chapter 5)

$$S = A_0e^{-\phi/N_0}N^{\epsilon} \equiv AN^{\epsilon} \qquad (8.2)$$

In the illustration only city size varies across the two cities because N_0 is held constant. ϵ is the urbanization economy elasticity.

As in Chapter 2, equilibrium is solved by imposing equilibrium in national output and input markets. The price of X is normalized at 1 and is spatially invariant. Capital moves across cities to equalize its return and hence its value of marginal product. However, for labor it is utility levels that are equalized by factor movements. Thus, as noted above, wages in the metro area must be twice those in the city of 100,000 for equalized utility levels. Then the value of the marginal product of labor in the metro area must be twice that in the city of 100,000 for *equal* net efficiency. With that differential, capital and labor will earn the same net returns across cities with no profits left over. In summary, where w_i and r_i are, respectively, wages in city type i, in equilibrium

$$\frac{r_1}{r_0} = 1 = \frac{S_1}{S_0}\left(\frac{k_1}{k_0}\right)^{-\beta} \qquad (8.3)$$

$$\frac{w_1}{w_0} = 2 = \frac{S_1}{S_0}\left(\frac{k_1}{k_0}\right)^{1-\beta} \tag{8.4}$$

The metro area is indexed 1 and the other 0. k_i is the capital-to-labor ratio in X production in city type i.

There are unique S_1/S_0 and k_1 for k_0 normalized at 1 and a given value of β for which (8.3) and (8.4) are satisfied. β is set at a typical labor distribution parameter of 0.75. Solving yields $S_1/S_0 = 1.68$ and $k_1 = 2$. However, $S_1/S_0 = 100^\epsilon$; thus, $\epsilon = 0.11$. For $\epsilon = 0.11$, the location of the X industry in the big and large city is equally efficient. Note that $k_1/k_0 = 2$. $k_1 > k_0$ with equal efficiency because labor costs are higher in the larger city so that labor is conserved. Given that k_1 is much higher and that $S_1/S_0 = 1.68$, then the higher labor costs can be met. But this implies that output per worker is much greater in the larger city. In particular, for

$$\frac{AP_1}{AP_0} = \frac{S_1}{S_0}\left(\frac{k_1}{k_0}\right)^{1-\beta}$$

then output per worker in the metro area is twice what it is the smaller city. But at double output per worker, the locations are only equally efficient.

If ϵ is not 0.11, then firms in the metro area will not be able to meet factor costs. From Chapters 5 and 6 we know that for heavy industry in Japan, United States, and Brazil the point estimates of ϵ lie well below 0.08. The highest ϵ is for primary metals in the United States with a value of 0.073; for other heavy industries across the three countries values are all below 0.03.

Suppose $\epsilon = 0.075$. X-industry firms will face potential losses in metro areas. To sustain metro area location, inputs or outputs must be subsidized. The exact subsidy critically affects welfare losses. From the relevant optimal tax literature (Murray, 1983; Brooks, 1987) the most efficient subsidy is on output, since it induces only a "location distortion." Relative subsidization of one factor compared to the other also induces a factor usage distortion.

An output subsidy program would raise the price of X in the metro area, p_1 relative to p_0 (= 1). In equations 8.3 and 8.4 S_1/S_0 is rewritten as $S_1^*/S_0^* = (S_1/S_0)(p_1/p_0)$. Given with $\epsilon = 0.075$, $S_1/S_0 = 1.41$, to sustain equilibrium S_1^*/S_0^* must be raised to 1.68 (for the solution where $\epsilon = 0.075$). This implies that $p_1/p_0 = 1.19$ or that the output subsidy rate is 19%. The k_1 is unchanged from the equal efficiency solution, since it is consistent with the true opportunity costs of factors that are unchanged.

The actual AP_1/AP_0 evaluated at the true $p_1 = 1$ is still high being 84% of the original, or 1.68. Thus despite an output subsidy rate of 19% of unit output and a corresponding welfare loss of the exact same amount (the shortfall of factor productivity from opportunity costs), output per worker is still much higher in the metro area. This could be misinterpreted as an indicator of greater locational efficiency, if financial accounting is divorced from economic planning and the planners ignore the welfare losses. The basic problem is that in using output per worker alone as an indicator of greater efficiency planners ignore net efficiencies and the less commonly documented differences in opportunity costs.

Typical government explicit or implicit location subsidies are not on output but often tend to favor one factor at the expense of another. Chapter 11 will argue that in China the subsidy is implicitly on labor. For Brazil the policy is difficult to decipher. However, it appears that firms must compete in labor markets and pay competitive opportunity costs, with the government adjusting the capital-to-labor ratio k so as to enable firms to meet competitive wage costs. Thus the subsidy is a capital subsidy policy. From equation 8.4 for $w_1/w_0 = 2$ and $S_1/S_0 = 1.41$, k_1 must be 4.05 to meet the wage payments. That is, given the insufficient ϵ and S_1/S_0, k_1 must be four times k_0 to meet wage payments. This is not surprising. k at the state-owned COSIPA operations near Grande São Paulo in 1970 was 18 times the (unweighted) average for iron and steel production for urban areas in Minas Gerais state, where private sector production is concentrated. Given the higher k_1/k_0, despite the shortfall in S_1/S_0, AP_1/AP_0 is again very high at 2.

While output per worker is very high in the metro area, the marginal product of capital in the metro area is a fraction of that in the smaller city. From (8.3) $MP_K^1/MP_K^0 = 0.50$; thus the industry in the metro area can only pay a fraction of capital costs. Subsidies per unit of output are

$$(MP_K^1 - MP_K^0)K_1/X_1 = \left(\frac{MP_K^0}{MP_K^1} - 1\right)(MP_K^1 K_1/X_1) = 0.25$$

Now welfare losses are higher than under an output subsidy because of the addition of factor distortion costs to location costs.

If labor rather than capital is subsidized, welfare costs will be lower because labor is the more intensive factor in production and hence the price wedge (subsidy rate) needed to transfer sufficient revenue to induce metro area location is smaller. For example, if the state invests to equalize the marginal product of capital across cities, then $k_1 = 1.58$. Given the shortfall in S_1/S_0, k_1 falls so that competitive r_1's may be paid. For $k_1/k_0 = 1.58$ and $S_1/S_0 = 1.41$, MP_N^1/MP_N^0 only equals 1.58. This implies a welfare cost as a fraction of output revenue of $[(M\hat{P}_N^1/MP_N^1) - 1](MP_N^1 N_{01}/X_1) = 0.20$, where MP_N^1 is the actual marginal product of labor and $M\hat{P}_N^1$ the required value to cover opportunity costs.

In summary, output per worker in metro areas may generally be significantly higher than in smaller cities even if metro area locations are inferior. In constructing other examples where the elasticity of substitution in production is significantly lower than the value of 1 assumed in (8.1), the problem was only accentuated. Planners must determine how much higher output per worker must be in metro areas for an industry to cover opportunity costs of factors before deciding on the superiority of metro area locations. This question will arise again in Chapter 11 in the context of examining location decisions for heavy industry by state planners.

2. Deconcentration of Manufacturing into Smaller Cities

A country considers that it has an excessive concentration of resources in a large metro area. As noted earlier, the potential excess could be the inadvertent result of existing government policies encouraging centralization such as spatially biased provision of public services or location policies governing state-owned firms. Alternatively, in the innovative stages of product development in a developing country, manufacturing firms may have agglomerated into one metro area. Regardless, the government decides there is overconcentration, perhaps based on notions of excessive negative externalities such as congestion and pollution. Policies are implemented to encourage decentralization of existing metro area firms or at least to divert new firms or plants to decentralized locations.

Such policies are followed in a number of countries such as Brazil, India, and Korea. The Korean situation of overconcentration was reviewed in Chapter 3, Section 2.2. There the central government has instituted a number of policies encouraging deconcentration from the Seoul urban area into outlying parts of the national capital region or province. These include tax and credit breaks, building of serviced industrial sites allocated on a subsidized basis, prohibition of new firms in the Seoul area, and relocation orders for some existing urban area firms. Song and Choe (1981) and Murray (1983) conclude that many of the policies are not especially effective, in that most relocators planned to move even in the absence of inducements. The inducements tend simply to distort factor usage, encouraging capital usage. In choosing where to locate, however, several factors are critical. Foremost is quick access (a half-hour drive) to Seoul. Also important are good quality local public services for the families of high skill workers and local autonomy in public service decisions to meet the particular needs of the locality.

These statements raise some of the general issues involved in evaluating decentralization policies. What is the best way to induce decentralization: lump-sum grants, investment in urban infrastructure, earnings guarantees, provision of better residential conditions for workers so that they require smaller compensating wage differentials, and so on. Second, is it best to induce decentralization of a particular industry into towns where that industry is already found, or is it best to select entirely new sites? In choosing among industries for decentralization (especially in giving relocation orders or relocating state-owned firms), which type of production is most ripe for decentralization, needing the amenities of the main metro area the least? Into what localities with what features should various industries relocate?

These questions require an examination of the location decision process of industries and the issue of whether a particular industry is found in a particular city or not. Critical are the notions that some relative degree of specialization and a lack of diffusion of production in any industry are efficient aspects of the spatial allocation of resources across cities. To model the problem of firms in any one industry decentralizing into a few of the outlying localities and analyzing which localities are chosen requires a microeconometric analysis of firm behavior. If firms decentralize will they go to localities with already existing firms of the same type? Will they occupy localities en masse that previously had no such firms? If so, how many will locate there? This latter question assumes that firm size is determinant, which may appear at odds with the constant-returns-to-scale assumptions and cost function approach of Chapters 5 and 6. One can argue that constant-returns-to-scale are an approximation, which is locally accurate at the bottom of an average cost curve.

Imposing determinacy of firm size suggests a profit function approach (Diewert 1973, Lau 1976, Fuss and McFadden 1978), which presumes increasing marginal costs of production. A firm has a profit function

$$\pi = \pi(\mathbf{P}; \mathbf{A}, S) \tag{8.5}$$

where $\mathbf{P}$ is a vector of input *and* output prices. $\pi(\cdot)$ is linear homogeneous in $\mathbf{P}$ (if *all* prices double, nominal profits double). $\pi(\cdot) > 0$, indicating, for example,

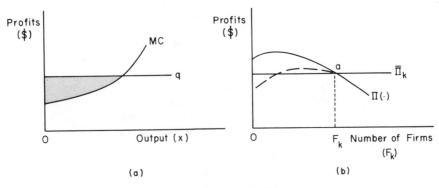

Fig. 8.1   Determinants of Profits

the presence of a fixed factor earning rents (e.g., entrepreneurship) in a constant returns to scale production function. Where p_i is the price of input i and q_j the price of output j

$$\frac{\partial \pi}{\partial q_j} = x_j \qquad \frac{\partial \pi}{\partial p_i} = -l_i \qquad (8.6)$$

x_j is output of j and l_i is input of i. $\pi(\cdot)$ is increasing and convex in q_j (i.e., $\partial x_j/\partial q_j > 0$ or $\partial^2 \pi/\partial q_j^2 > 0$) and $\pi(\cdot)$ is decreasing and convex in p_i (i.e., $\partial l_i/\partial p_i < 0$ or $\partial^2 \pi/\partial p_i^2 = -\partial l_i/\partial p_i > 0$).

For a competitive firm with one variable input the situation is pictured in Figure 8.1a. The firm has an upward sloping marginal cost curve and faces a horizontal demand curve. Per firm profits are the shaded area. A shift up in q increases output and profits. An increase in p rotates the marginal cost curve upward, reducing output and profits. All this is standard.

The location issue dwells on the shift arguments in $\pi(\cdot)$, the A and S. A is a vector of public service inputs and amenities that may affect profitability. Towns endowed with better amenities have marginal cost curves rotated or shifted down and yield higher per firm profits, ceteris paribus. That, of course, raises the following question. Why do all firms in an industry simply not locate in the single city with the best amenity vector for them? One answer would be efficiency limits imposed by city size considerations in a general equilibrium context, as discussed in Chapter 2. But often for three- or four-digit industries the number of firms and level of local employment in a particular industry in any city are well below levels exhausting potential employment in the export base sector of that city. That is, a number of perhaps interrelated industries coexist in the same city. For microanalysis of detailed industry employment patterns, this suggests that a partial equilibrium approach becomes feasible at three- or four-digit levels. (In fact, simultaneity problems in estimation based on the general equilibrium effects in Chapters 5 and 6 only appeared for a few two-digit industries and seem to disappear for three- or four-digit industries.)

Then to determine the number of firms in one particular industry in a city some type of industry scale effects must be considered. Interactive scale effects with other industries are a possibility but appear too weak in the econometric work in Chapter 5. An alternative raised in Chapter 5 is own industry, or localization economies that are quadratic in form. Initially increases in the number of firms in an industry in the local area bring scale benefits, rotating the MC curve in Figure 8.1a down to increase per firm profits. However, as the number of firms increases, perhaps congesting relevant amenities and infrastructure or exhausting skill supplies in local labor markets, profits per firm start to decline. What then determines the equilibrium number of firms in a city?

For any city, there is a minimum acceptable level of profits $\bar{\pi}_k$, which would be, for example, the compensation necessary to induce entrepreneurs to live in city k. $\bar{\pi}_k$ could be a function of local costs of living, and amenities relevant to entrepreneurs as consumers. Thus, for example, from Chapter 6

$$\bar{\pi}k = C(N_k, \tilde{\mathbf{A}}_k) \tag{8.7}$$

where N_k is population of city k representing cost-of-living and other population effects, and $\tilde{\mathbf{A}}_k$ includes arguments such as educational level of the adult population, access to coastal markets, quality of schooling, local infrastructure, etc. Thus $\partial C/\partial N_k > 0$ and $\partial C/\partial \tilde{a} < 0$ for $\tilde{a}$, a positive amenity.

Firms may be in a city if from equation 8.5

$$\pi(\mathbf{P}_k; \mathbf{A}_k, S_k(F_k)) \geq \bar{\pi}_k \tag{8.8}$$

That is, for some number of firms $F_k > 0$, per firm profits are as least as great as the minimum acceptable level.

With free entry, in cities with the industry, F_k should adjust until scale effects are such that excess profits are dissipated. That is, F_k adjusts until the shaded area in Figure 8.1a adjusts to $\bar{\pi}_k$. The process is also pictured in Figure 8.1b where $\pi(\cdot)$ plots per firm profits against the number of firms F_k in the city. Equilibrium is at a where the number of firms is $\overset{*}{F}_k$. a is a stable point; or, at a, $\pi(\cdot)$ is downward sloping. Imposing a strict equality in (8.8) and inverting, the number of firms is

$$\overset{*}{F}_k = F(\mathbf{P}_k, \mathbf{A}_k, N_k, \tilde{\mathbf{A}}_k) \tag{8.9a}$$

$\mathbf{A}_k$ and $\tilde{\mathbf{A}}_k$ are, respectively, consumer and producer amenities and there may be overlap in the elements of the vectors. In (8.9a)

$$\frac{\partial \overset{*}{F}}{\partial z} = \frac{\partial [\pi(\cdot) - C(\cdot)]/\partial z}{-\partial [\pi(\cdot) - C(\cdot)]/\partial F} \tag{8.9b}$$

for z the arguments in (8.9a). In Figure 8.1b, for any locally stable equilibrium $\partial \pi(\cdot)/\partial F < 0$, or the denominator of (8.9b) is positive, assuming that $\partial C(\cdot)/\partial F = 0$. Therefore from the numerator of (8.9b), arguments that increase $\pi(\cdot)$ increase $\overset{*}{F}_k$ in (8.9a) and arguments that increase $C(\cdot)$ decrease $\overset{*}{F}_k$.

Two final comments are in order. In Figure 8.1b the solid $\pi(\cdot)$ curve represents a simple situation where $\pi[\mathbf{P}_k; \mathbf{A}_k, S_k(F_k \to 0)] > \bar{\pi}_k$ or at the axis $\pi(\cdot) > \bar{\pi}_k$. Suppose, instead, $\pi(\cdot)$ is the dashed curve in Figure 8.1b where there is a recrossing interior to a and $\pi[\cdot S_k(F_k \to 0)] < \bar{\pi}_k$. Then, if city k has no firms in the industry, a single firm would not find it profitable to enter. However, if firms entered en masse (e.g., a number in the neighborhood of $\overset{*}{F}_k$), entry would be sustained. This lumpiness problem in establishing an industry in a city presents an interesting public policy basis. If it is assumed that either the private institutions or entrepreneurial skills among private land and industrial developers do not exist

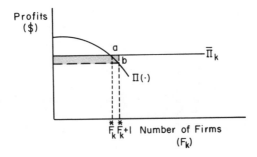

Fig. 8.2   Per Firm Subsidy To Induce Extra Locater

to facilitate the en masse movement of firms into a city, when the dashed $\pi(\cdot)$ curve in Figure 8.1b is relevant, atomistic entry will not occur.

The second comment concerns "long" vs. "intermediate" run effects. These could be separated out with an analysis of an adjustment mechanism in a time series model. Unfortunately, existing samples tend to be cross-sectional. As such, one might assume that in the number of firms equation 8.9, arguments are long-run ones in which firms enter based on, say, expectations as to "permanent" or long-run prices and labor force quality. These are the arguments in a long-run profit function. However, the arguments in the current profit function (8.5) may be intermediate. That is, current profits are based on current, not permanent, prices, where it might be assumed that capital stocks are sufficiently flexible to adjust to current prices (and to readjust as current prices move to permanent ones). Conceptually the idea is that (re)location decisions are less malleable and flexible than capital stocks and investment.

2.1. Locational Policies

The location policies analyzed here are inducements to private firms to relocate. The focus is on potentially efficient, or least costly inducements—whether they may be required infrastructure investments or lump-sum relocation grants, which do not distort factor choices. For expositional purposes in this section the discussion concentrates on lump-sum grants. Location policies have two sides—the social costs and the social benefits. Two locational situations are examined. In the first, additional firms are induced into a city that already has firms from that industry. In the second, entry is induced into a city that has no existing firms in the industry. The policies have distinctly different social costs and benefits.

Suppose the starting point is a in Figure 8.2 with $\overset{*}{F}$ firms in a city. To induce an additional firm to the city and move to point b with $\overset{*}{F} + 1$ firms, a lump-sum grant equal to the shaded area in Figure 8.2 must be made to the new firm. It must *also* be made to *each* existing firm to retain each existing firm in the city. This cost of the shaded area times $\overset{*}{F} + 1$ firms is also the social cost of the program—the externality or amount by which marginal costs exceed revenue for all firms in the city.

For cities without the industry two possibilities exist, as shown in Figures 8.3a and 8.3b. Before proceeding it is important to note that either situation may be

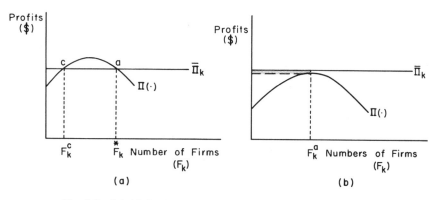

Fig. 8.3 Subsidizing Location of a New Industry in an Urban Area

difficult for policymakers to identify, in terms of identifying cities where the $\pi(\cdot)$ curves have the shape and *height* in Figure 8.3. Figure 8.3*a* represents a situation with, at least in partial equilibrium terms with instantaneous adjustment, no social costs but only the benefits of relocation. To induce location into this city k, all that is required is a guarantee of profits $\bar{\pi}_k + \epsilon$, $\epsilon \to 0$ to any entrants. As soon as the number of firms passes F_k^c, the guarantees can be removed for further entrants. In practice, the guarantees will be costly during the period of adjustment while the number of firms grows to F_k^c. Such a situation exists if nonatomistic movement of firms is lacking because of, for example, an inadequacy of entrepreneurial talent or resources in land and industrial development markets or nonfunctioning local land and capital markets.

Figure 8.3*b* represents a "more normal" situation where there is no F_k that can support the industry in the locality without ongoing lump-sum grants. In Figure 8.3*b* F_k^a firms in the city may be achieved by offering a guarantee of $\bar{\pi}_k$ profits to the first F_k^a entrants. The financial and social cost of the guarantee for the F_k^a firms will be that number of firms times the shaded area in Figure 8.3*b*. In comparing Figures 8.2 and 8.3*b*, it seems at least for the welfare cost in Figure 8.3*b* F_k^a movers result, whereas in (8.2) only one mover results. However, in evaluating the costs a primary consideration is the gap between $\bar{\pi}_k$ and, for example, the maximum point of the $\pi(\cdot)$ curve. If that is very large, then per mover welfare costs can be very high.

Moreover, it is on the benefit side where the two situations differ most radically. What are the benefits of deconcentration supposed to be? They are presumably a reduction in externalities in the major metro areas, caused by overcrowding. The externalities are thus primarily population externalities as discussed in Chapter 9, although deconcentration could also contribute to a reduction in environmental externalities in major metro areas. The issue then is how effective are relocation subsidies at inducing population relocation. It is here that the two types of policies differ. In Figure 8.2 inducing additional firms into a city with an existing industrial base in the subsidized product has marginal impacts. From Chapter 7, subsidies to particular cities of various kinds in a general equilibrium context do raise potential utility levels and lead to an expansion in city size. Here that may occur as a second order effect not represented in the partial equilibrium context of Figure 8.2. But the effect may be minimal: A marginal expansion of a one industry may marginally displace some other industry in the city, with little overall population impacts.

The situation in Figure 8.3 is quite different. There the subsidies lead to the establishment of an entirely new industrial base in a city. The general equilibrium impact of this may be to change the nature of the city and its type, potentially altering its size radically. Thus a shift in a city's industrial base from, say, traditional textiles to machinery manufacturing could lead to a doubling or tripling of city size, thereby having large population impacts. Of course, the displacement of textiles presumably alters the composition of national output as textiles perhaps displace something else somewhere else.

That raises issues analyzed in Chapter 9. If the problem is the spatial allocation of population, that is best solved by population policies, directly aimed at reallocating population. These could involve residency tax or subsidy policies aimed at, respectively, over- and underpopulated cities, or simply a reduction in the degree of bias in the spatial allocation of public services, favoring large metro areas. Subsidizing particular industries to alter their locational patterns is also a subsidy in general to that industry, encouraging expansion of its output. Thus while desired population relocation may occur, there is a new distortion created in terms of the composition of national output.

Despite these normative comments, there is still the policy issue that if relocation is to be induced, what industries can be most easily deconcentrated, what cities are the best targets, and what inducements are most attractive. To answer that requires estimation for different industries of the two equation model, described by equations 8.5 and 8.9. This is done by estimating equations 8.5 and 8.9 jointly by full information maximum likelihood methods, directly modeling the simultaneity, truncation, and sample selection problems inherent in the problem.

Estimation would yield parameters in the profit function for various amenity and scale arguments. This would serve several purposes. First, we could calculate the probability that a given industry would be found in a given city and thus potentially identify a few cities (with currently no firms in that industry) that have high probabilities and hence are likely targets. Second, we could predict the magnitude of firm movements into a city, where location of a new industry is targeted. Third, we could identify what urban characteristics are important for what industries. This would allow sensible matching, targeting cities with industries valuing the characteristics of those cities. It would also tell us what urban infrastructure measures we should invest in.

3. Conclusions

Because of higher average productivity figures in large metro areas, planners may be led to locate heavy industry there rather than in smaller cities. However for larger metro areas to be as efficient as smaller areas, output per worker must be sufficiently greater to compensate for the much higher social costs of living in larger cities. In general, we expect the level of urbanization economies needed to generate sufficiently higher productivity of workers in larger cities not to exist for heavy industries. Hence, such locational policies may be grossly inefficient.

If concentration of heavy and some light industries in a few large metro areas has historically been induced, some type of decentralization policies may eventually be viewed as desirable. For decentralization, it is necessary to decide which industries should be decentralized into what cities and with what particular characteristics. This requires estimation of technology based upon a discrete choice model of whether an industry is in a city or not plus a continuous choice model of industry size and profits in cities having a particular industry. The estimation will tell which urban characteristics are important for different industries and hence how to match cities to industries. One policy issue is whether to focus on expanding the industry size in cities already having an industry or whether to focus on new urban locations, transforming a city with an existing traditional industry into a larger modern industrial town. The later policy may generally have a greater population decentralization impact.

CHAPTER 9

City Size Policies and Laissez-Faire

Chapters 7 and 8 evaluate the spatial impacts of some typical governmental tax, subsidy, import restriction, and wage regulation policies and of governmental industrial relocation policies. The motivation and analysis of population relocation policies in this chapter are somewhat different. First, only some economies with strong central planning (see Chapter 11 on China) and a few federal multilingual countries have comprehensive national population location policies. Moreover, these existing policies, as will be noted, are not based on typical economic considerations. The scope for positive analysis of national population location policies is thus somewhat limited, although in Section 2 of the chapter some informal analysis is conducted.

However, a normative analysis is very useful. First, it gives an economic basis for population relocation policies as a conceptual basis for countries engaging in such policies. Second, it provides a general framework for evaluating piecemeal or localized policies with intended population location effects. Such policies are widespread. In particular, individual cities enact policies restricting entry and city size. Third, and related, regions enact policies trying to deflect migrants to large metro areas into smaller satellite cities. A framework for welfare analysis of national population allocation allows us to evaluate whether individual city size policies or other piecemeal policies are consistent with national welfare maximization. Finally, a welfare economics framework can be used to make further normative comments on the positive analyses in Chapters 7 and 8.

The first section of this chapter analyzes the theoretical welfare economics basis for population relocation policies, uncovering the set of circumstances in which such policies are relevant, as well as examining implementation problems. A basic theme is that, despite the presence of various population externalities as well as perhaps other types of unpriced externalities, the situations requiring first, second, or even nth best national policies to alter population allocation are quite narrowly defined. Having isolated these situations allows us to examine the more practical issue of piecemeal policies. For any level of government in dealing with a particular city on a particular issue, what (if any) are population policies for that single city that are consistent with national welfare maximization? What is the context in which partial equilibrium policies for altering a city's size have strong conceptual foundations? Finally, there are the implementation problems of such policies.

The second part of the chapter examines existing types of population relocation and city size policies followed in different countries. Some countries pursue vigorous policies aimed either at deconcentration of population from the major metropolitan area(s) or at general national decentralization of population, which, for example, might maintain a slow national rate of rural-urban migration. One objective is to identify the conceptual bases for these policies and determine if there is any link to the conceptual analyses of Section 1 of the chapter. Another is to identify the various population location instruments that are pursued in developing primarily market economy countries. We focus on the instruments used in India. These may be contrasted with instruments used in planned economies such as China (Chapter 11). Evaluations of the effectiveness of different instruments are typically casual, based, say, on opinion surveys of businesses. Econometric work trying to sort out the effectiveness of different instruments such as industrial location subsidies reported in Chapter 8, Section 2 is quite limited.

1. The Theoretical Foundations for Population Relocation Policies

To isolate the issues, this section starts by examining population relocation policies in the simplest situation, a large economy with a single type of city. In that context, even in the presence of population related externalities, of unpriced other externalities such as pollution, or of distorting national government policies, the best population relocation policy is none at all. Moreover, relaxing the large economy assumption, generally no population relocation policies are justified. Next, multiple types of cities in a large economy are introduced, but to no avail.

Only when differentiated kinds of cities in a "small" economy are considered is there a basis for national population policies. Differentiated kinds of cities can be different types of cities specialized in production of different traded goods or the same types of cities endowed with, say, different exogenous consumer or producer amenities (Chapter 4).

Section 1.3 examines the set of circumstances in which local policies advocated to alter the sizes of individual cities in a partial equilibrium context are consistent with the optimal national allocation of population, as discussed in Tolley et al. (1979). In these circumstances, it is possible to explain and perhaps even justify the implicit (squatter settling) or explicit (zoning) population policies of some large metro areas in various parts of the world.

1.1. Population Allocation in a System of Identical Cities

This section starts with a benchmark case to identify the issues and to outline the basic approach. The theoretical analysis is carried out in a general functional form version of the specific model described in Chapters 2 to 4. It is an adaptation of the general framework outlined in Buchanan and Wagner (1972), formalized and developed in Flatters, Henderson, and Mieszkowski (1974), and extended by Berglas (1976) and Stiglitz (1977). The adaptation to a system of cities model was introduced in Mirrlees (1972), developed in Henderson (1977), and extended by Kanemoto (1980) and Arnott (1979). All these papers contain land as a specific factor of production and the urban papers contain explicit spatial dimensions. Although the model in Chapters 2 to 4 is an "as if" model without explicit incorporation of land resources, there will be direct analogs to the spatial model results, and the conclusions generalize completely.

What are the potential problems with the free market allocation of population, which suggest the need for welfare analysis and population policies? That is, what unpriced externalities are present? Foremost in a system of cities, cities exist because of external economies of scale in production. Given the specification of these scale externalities, when people migrate, they affect the level of scale efficiencies and the productivity of other factors in the cities they leave and enter. In making their location decisions they do not account for these external effects; therefore, they could be making socially inefficient location decisions.

Second, as in Chapter 6 people may have preferences about city size per se—population amenities. When more people enter a city they may directly affect the utility of existing residents, but this externality imposed on others does not enter their migration calculus.

Finally, there are fiscal externalities created by the operations of local governments. For example, there may be local pure public goods, a consumption basis for agglomeration. By definition, the addition of another person to a city does not affect other people's consumption benefits from a given level of government expenditures on pure public goods. However, an additional person does reduce everyone else's tax cost, since there is now an additional person to share in taxes. For example, if the cost of a unit of public goods is $1 and tax shares are equal, the per person tax price of a unit of public goods is $1/N$, where N is city population. As population grows, the per person unit tax price declines, a benefit to all residents from adding population. This phenomenon is a fiscal externality, since people do not account for the positive or negative effect they have on other people's tax costs in the cities they enter or leave. Again, this might lead to situations where people's location decisions may not be socially optimal.

Fiscal externalities are potentially pervasive, arising from the presence of any "nonproductive" income in a city. Nonproductive income could be locally redistributed tax revenue from a Henry George tax by the city government (or "land trust") on all "surplus" land rents above agricultural opportunity costs, locally redistributed proceeds from pollution taxes, or redistributed royalties from natural resource deposits, as well as taxes to finance pure or quasi-public goods. Entrants to a city, in making their location decisions, do not account for their impact on other people's shares of these redistributed monies or tax liabilities.

The ultimate example in a regional context concerns the royalties of an oil rich province or state of a federal country with free population movements. The regional legislature enacts a royalty policy collecting revenue to be redistributed either directly to local residents (given a short length of residency requirement) or indirectly redistributed by public financing of private services. Citizens of the rest of the country can partake of these benefits only by moving into the region. However, there is no productive basis for any population movements, assuming an original efficient allocation, since, for example, in-migration to the region only reduces marginal products in productive activity there, and raises them elsewhere in the economy. Movements occur until the negative aspects (e.g., diminished marginal products) of overpopulation dissipate the royalty benefits. The point is that a better redistribution policy is national redistribution of revenue so that the citizens of the country do not have to mass in one region to pick up their royalty checks and thereby distort the allocation of productive resources. This is the essence of a fiscal externality, based on the existence of locally redistributed "non-productive" income (royalties, rents, taxes).

To obtain criteria for the efficient allocation of resources in an economy, the usual welfare-maximization problem facing a social planner is to maximize the utility of a representative individual subject to production and resource constraints, holding the utility level of all other individuals constant. Here an additional constraint is placed on the social planner, which is designed to make planning solutions directly comparable to market solutions. People with the same utility functions and opportunity sets must have equal utility levels. This constraint ensures that planning solutions are consistent with stable-market solutions where, with nondiscriminatory government intervention, identical perfectly mobile people must achieve identical utility levels.

In maximizing utilities, the planner is concerned with the welfare of two basic groups of people in the model: laborers and capital owners. Given two differing groups of people, by definition, a planner's Pareto-efficient solution is one that either maximizes the utility of laborers while holding the welfare of capital owners fixed or maximizes the welfare of capital owners while holding the utility of laborers fixed. In the planning solution, the utility of laborers is a function of their consumption of produced goods and any amenities. On the other hand, capital owners need not live in the cities where their capital is employed. It is assumed without consequence that for the planner the only variable affecting the welfare of capital owners is their consumption of market goods. Therefore, the planner's problem is to maximize the utility of laborers either for a fixed total consumption of capital owners or, equivalently, for a fixed real return per unit of capital (given a fixed capital stock).

The planner's problem starts with the simplest case, population allocation in a world in which only population externalities are present: any other externalities are optimally priced and all other government policies are optimal.

Population allocation with only population externalities. As in Chapter 2, a consumer's utility is a function of housing h and, with only one type of city, one export base good x. Given the equal utility constraint for our identical residents in a system of identical cities (see later), the planner's objective is to maximize utility from per capita consumption or to maximize

$$U = U(X/H, H/N) \tag{9.1}$$

where X and H are total local consumptions and N is the representative city's population.

The planner's opimization problem is then

$$\max J = U(X/N, H/N)$$
$$+ \lambda_1[H - F(N) h(\hat{N}_1, \hat{K}_1, \hat{K}_2)]$$
$$+ \lambda_2[X + p_K(\hat{K}_0 + \hat{K}_1 + \hat{K}_2) - G(N)x(\hat{N}_0, \hat{K}_0)] \tag{9.2}$$
$$+ \lambda_3(N - \hat{N}_1 - \hat{N}_0)$$
$$+ \lambda_4[\bar{C} - (\hat{K}_0 + \hat{K}_1 + \hat{K}_2)/N]$$

In the λ_1 constraint, housing consumption H is constrained to equal local production $F(N)h(\cdot)$. Relative to Chapter 2 in defining production, equation 2.3 for

l is substituted into equation 2.2 where H would equal $N^{-\delta\beta}(\beta D^{\gamma\beta}\hat{K}_2^{\gamma\beta})(\hat{N}_1^{\beta}\hat{K}_1^{1-\beta})$. $F(N)$, which is $N^{-\delta\beta}$ in Chapter 2, is the spatial complexity factor representing the increasing average commuting times necessary in a spatial model to utilize the increasingly distant land sites on an expanding city edge. Thus $F' < 0$. $\hat{K}_2$ is a *public* intermediate input of urban infrastructure used in "site" and hence housing production, and $\hat{N}_1$, $\hat{K}_1$ are private inputs, as in Chapter 2.

In the λ_2 constraint, the city's export base production $G(N) \cdot x(\hat{N}_0, \hat{K}_0)$ is used for local consumption X and to pay capital owners the planner's fixed return p_K on locally employed capital. With λ_3 there is a local full employment condition. The λ_4 constraint represents a carefully defined national full employment constraint where the representative city must employ the same ratio of capital to labor as nationally $\bar{C}$. However, no bound is placed on the number of cities nor are absolute national endowments specified. This is a large country case where at the limit the number of cities approaches infinity. In fact, as analyzed later, except under special circumstances, the same population (non)relocation policies will also apply in a small country with a single type of city.

The planner maximizes (9.2) with respect to X, H, $\hat{K}_0$, $\hat{K}_1$, $\hat{K}_2$, $\hat{N}_0$, $\hat{N}_1$, and N. Except for N, we get standard welfare results that the marginal products of factors should be equalized in all uses and that marginal rates of substitution in consumption should equal ratios of marginal costs or the marginal rates of transformation. For N, after substituting in for multipliers, there is

$$\left[G(N)x_N - \left(\frac{X}{N} + \frac{U_H}{U_x} \cdot \frac{H}{N} \right) \right] + \left\{ [G(N)x_K - p_K] \left(\frac{\hat{K}_0 + \hat{K}_1 + \hat{K}_2)}{N} \right) \right\}$$

$$+ \left(\epsilon_X \frac{X^s}{N} - \epsilon_H \frac{U_H H^s}{U_x N} \right) = 0 \qquad (9.3a)$$

or

$$SMC \equiv \left(\frac{x}{N} + \frac{U_H}{U_X} \frac{H}{N} + \epsilon_H \frac{H^s}{N} \frac{U_H}{U_x} \right) = SMB$$

$$\equiv G(N)x_N + \epsilon_X \frac{X^s}{N} + [G(N)x_K - p_K] \left(\frac{\hat{K}_0 + \hat{K}_1 + \hat{K}_2}{N} \right) \qquad (9.3b)$$

Each of the three bracketed terms in (9.3a) represents the *net* benefits of adding one resident to the representative city. The first is the excess of the private marginal product of the resident $G(N)x_N$ over the value of his private consumption (with H/N evaluated at U_H/U_x). The second is the excess (or deficit) of the private marginal productivity of capital $G(N)x_K$ over cost p_K, for the additional capital that comes with each laborer in maintaining $\bar{C}$. The third is the excess of marginal scale economy benefits in X production from an additional resident over the marginal scale diseconomy costs in H production. $\epsilon_X \equiv (G'/G)N$ and $\epsilon_H = (-F'/F)N > 0$ are the respective elasticities, given X^s/N, H^s/N are per capita production. Then $\epsilon_X X^s/N$ is the value of the increase in per capita production, and $\epsilon_H H^s/N$ is the value of decreases both due to scale effects alone.

Equation 9.3a may be expressed as (9.3b) where the left-hand side is the social marginal cost of an additional resident—his consumption plus the negative production externality. The right-hand side is the social marginal benefits of an additional resident including his private and external contributions to output.

Optimal city size occurs for the representative city when $SMC = SMB$, holding consumption of capital owners fixed. A criterion such as this should, of course, be anticipated. The question is whether efficient city sizes satisfying (9.3) are achieved in a market economy without policy intervention. For example, are the city sizes achieved in Chapter 2 in the presence of scale and fiscal externalities Pareto-efficient?

To determine this, the Pareto-efficiency criterion in (9.3) is interpreted in a market context where factors are paid the value of marginal products, goods are priced according to marginal rates of substitution, and urban infrastructure $\hat{K}_2$ is financed out of a local tax on wages, as in Chapter 2. Hence, $p = U_H/U_X$, $w = G(N)x_N$, and $r = p_K = G(N)x_K$, so that capital gets no surplus in (9.3). For taxes $twN = r\hat{K}_2$ and $w(1 - t) = X/N + pH/N$, so that after-tax income equals the value of private consumption. Substituting all of these into (9.3) yields

$$wt + \epsilon_X \frac{X^s}{N} - \epsilon_H \frac{H}{N} = 0 \qquad (9.4)$$

In market terms optimal city size is achieved when the marginal benefits of an additional entrant to existing residents which is his tax share, wt, plus the external increase in X output just equals the marginal cost, the external decrease in H output. In spatial models the term $(-\epsilon_N H/N)$ is typically replaced with (a negatively valued) land rent share where new residents claim a share in urban land rents above rural opportunity cost.

Note the presence of a public intermediate input, K_2, that creates through its financing a fiscal externality, wt. This is "nonproductive" income, as are the land rents in a spatial model. That is, adding a person to the city does not detract from others' K_2 usage per se, but generates new tax revenues.

Do market solutions to city sizes in the current context satisfy (9.4)? The answer is yes. For example, interpret (9.4) using the specific functional form model in Chapter 2. This involves evaluating $[(\gamma\beta b)/(f + \gamma\beta b)]w + G'x(\cdot) - F'h(\cdot) = 0$. Substitute for $h(\cdot)$ from (2.2) and (2.3), for p from (2.9), for $\hat{K}_1$, $\hat{N}_2$, $\hat{K}_2$ from (d) and (e) in note 5 of Chapter 2 and (2.10), for y from (2.11), and for w from (2.4). Normalize $q = 1$, evaluate F' and G' from (2.2), (2.3), and (2.4), cancel terms, and rearrange to get

$$N = \frac{\phi}{\alpha} \frac{[f - b\beta(1 - \gamma)]}{\beta b(\delta - \gamma)} \qquad (9.5)$$

That is, if (9.4) is satisfied, N is defined in (9.5). But this is the same N as equilibrium size in (2.15).

It is also important to note that in equations 9.3 and 9.4 the stability of market city sizes noted in equation 9.5 as well as second order conditions will require SMB to decline relative to SMC costs (e.g., increase at a slower rate) as city size increases. In (9.5) and the model in Chapter 2, that is ensured by having ϵ_X decline.

The equivalency of equilibrium and Pareto-efficient city sizes makes sense for two reasons. First, the statement of the planner's problem, which is to maximize laborers' utility for a given return to capital, is consistent with the way in which market solutions are defined in Chapter 2. In a partial equilibrium approach to city size, developers set city size so as to maximize laborers' utility given a fixed borrowing rate on capital. In a general equilibrium approach, equilibrium city size occurs when the sum of total capital rental income and monetized utility levels is maximized. This sum can only be maximized when, while holding one element constant, the other is maximized. Accordingly, under the current assumptions, the market determination of city size and the planning solution are simply different ways of stating and approaching the same maximization problem.

The equivalency also makes sense from an externality perspective. Laborers in a market economy move to equalize the private marginal benefits of moving among cities. From a social perspective, they should incorporate into their calculus any external effects from their location decisions and move to equalize the social marginal benefits of moving among cities. However, if all cities are identical, the magnitude of these external effects will be equal between all cities; and when laborers move to equalize private marginal benefits they will incidentally equalize social marginal benefits. Therefore, the fact that laborers do not account for migration externalities does not adversely affect the allocation of resources in this situation.

Equations 9.3 and 9.4 and the conclusions generalize to situations with other population externalities. There are already scale and fiscal externalities. To these could be added population amenity externalities where N is a direct argument in utility and, say, pollution externalities resulting from the employment of $\hat{K}_0$ in X production. Then utility would be

$$U = U(X/N, H/N, \hat{K}_0, N) \qquad (9.6)$$

where $U_3, U_4 < 0$. The optimal allocation of resources is now altered so that for $\hat{K}_0$ usage, redefined social marginal products of capital are equalized; or

$$\frac{U_H}{U_X} Fh_{K_1} = Gx_{K_0} - \frac{(-U_3)}{U_X} N \qquad (9.7)$$

Second, to the left-hand side of equation 9.3a is added the term $-(-U_4/U_X)N$. Reinterpreting the new (9.3a) in a market context, (9.4) becomes

$$wt - \left(\frac{-U_3}{U_X}\right)\frac{\hat{K}_0}{N} + \left[\epsilon_X \frac{X^s}{N} - \epsilon_H \frac{H}{N} - \frac{(-U_4)}{U_X} N\right] = 0 \qquad (9.8)$$

where $\hat{K}_0$ usage is optimally taxed at a rate $(-U_4)/U_X$ according to the marginal disutility of the pollution it creates. Relative to before, an additional resident now imposes a new fiscal externality, his share of pollution tax proceeds; and he imposes population disamenities marginally valued at $[(-U_4)/U_X]N$. Note that pollution itself is not a population disamenity; therefore, it does not directly appear in (9.8), other than through the distribution of tax proceeds from pricing pollution.

If city size in the equilibrium model in Chapter 2 is resolved incorporating population disamenities and priced pollution externalities, the resulting equilibrium size will be consistent with (9.8). The reasons are as before—adding on a string of new population externalities does not affect the result that maximizing utility holding capital rentals fixed in a market equilibrium duplicates a Pareto-efficient solution.

The remaining issues in the single type of city case are whether this conclusion is altered in second or nth best worlds or in small economies.

Second and other less than best worlds: Unpriced nonpopulation externalities. Consider a second best world with, for instance, unpriced pollution externalities. Furthermore, assume the identical cities are all heavily polluted from an excess allocation of K to $\hat{K}_0$ usage in X production (where $\hat{K}_0$ could be any resource). By reducing city sizes per se and the concentration of pollution in any one city, can residents' welfare improve? That is, reducing city sizes and dividing the population among more cities reduces the magnitude of $\hat{K}_0$ in any one city and hence local pollution (the size of $\hat{K}_0$ in utility functions). Despite the appeal of this idea, the answer is no.

To analyze this, assume that no second best pollution policies are in place, although that is of no consequence to the city size results. With no pollution policies, all factors including $\hat{K}_0$ are paid values of private marginal products. To calculate the equilibrium city size achieved in the competitive development market, differentiate utility totally (holding r fixed) to account for the impact of N on all internal variables, *including* the impact on $\hat{K}_0$ employment and disutility from such. At equilibrium city size, the marginal benefits of increasing city sizes are equated to the marginal costs, *including* the costs of the indirect effect on $\hat{K}_0$ employment. That is, by setting city size to maximize utility (and correctly "calculating" that point) markets do the best that can be done—to maximize the welfare of laborers holding capital rentals fixed. There are no second best population policies to be enacted.

An an example, to the function for U in equation 2.10 add a multiplicative term $\hat{K}_0^{-z}$. The new equilibrium size becomes

$$N = \frac{\phi}{\alpha}\left[\frac{f - b\beta(1 - \gamma) - z}{\beta b(\delta - \gamma) + z}\right] \qquad (9.5a)$$

This *equilibrium* size is unambiguously smaller than the size without pollution in (9.5) and equals the optimal city size consistent with the welfare maximization problem for this nth best situation. Further reductions in size below the equilibrium in (9.5a) would *by derivation of (9.5a)* reduce utility holding capital rentals constant. From the way in which the competitive development market for cities operates, in achieving equilibrium city sizes the required nth best reductions in city size with the introduction of unpriced pollution relative to a no-pollution world occur naturally without the need for government intervention.

Second best pollution policies involve not changes in the total allocation of population to cities per se, but rather changes in the *allocation* of total employment of labor and capital within cities. In particular, assuming $\hat{K}_0$ employment cannot be taxed, a second best policy will involve subsidizing $\hat{K}_1$ and $\hat{K}_2$ usage to draw K out of polluting $\hat{K}_0$ usage and subsidizing N_0 employment to substitute $\hat{N}_0$ for $\hat{K}_0$ usage in producing X. This policy in itself alters the magnitude of fiscal and pollution externalities in the city and hence equilibrium city size. That change is optimal. The point is that altering city population per se does not directly impact the relative allocation of resources to polluting activity, as altering the prices of substitutes and competing uses does. The market already accounts for desired reductions in city size; or, in achieving equilibrium, city size *within the confines of the relevant institutional environment* maximizes the utility of residents for a given rental rate on capital. Population externalities are all internalized in reaching equilibrium size.

Distortionary national government policies. Suppose there are a variety of national government policies distorting the allocation of resources. By various tax-subsidy and quantity restriction policies the government might directly influence the output of H relative to X, the use of $\hat{N}_0$ vs. $\hat{K}_0$ in X production, or the use of $\hat{N}_1$ vs. $\hat{K}_1$ vs. $\hat{K}_2$ in H production. In a multiple type of city context the government through trade and development policies might influence the allocation of resources to different types of traded goods and hence cities. There are two issues. First, do such policies affect city sizes and urban concentration? Second, does this suggest that second best population allocation policies are needed?

The first issue is the subject of Chapter 7. In general, national government policies "distort" city sizes and in Chapter 7 we argue that they tend to bring about "unnecessary" increases in urban concentration. This raises the second issue. Should offsetting second best policies be instituted? The answer to that really depends on the role of the economist in the particular situation.

The notion that policies *distort* the allocation of urban resources is based on an economist's goal of maximizing "real national income," or the welfare of residents based on bundles of market goods and personal amenities. However, that specification of the objective function for a sovereign nation can be presumptuous. A nation representing itself to the rest of the world may include in its objective function items such as "beauty" of cities, extent of heavy industry, size of standing army, and so on. An economist-technician cannot say that these are bad items to include in an objective function per se. Accepting the government's objectives behind certain policies after giving earnest advice on the pure economic welfare costs of those policies means that no offsetting second-best population allocation policies are required.

That is, given the government's deliberately "distorting" policies, the allocation of resources across types of cities and city sizes as determined in the distorted market place is efficient. Given the government-distorted prices, city sizes are chosen to maximize residents' utility when the welfare of other economic agents is held fixed. So, if the government favors heavy industry at the expense of traditional industry, the increase in urban concentration appropriately complements the switch in national resource allocation.

At the other extreme, suppose in a typical uncoordinated national government the semiautonomous ministry of construction and public works subsidizes urban infrastructure or the ministry of metals subsidizes construction of heavy industry plant and equipment. The finance ministry wants to mitigate the costly policies of these other errant autonomous ministries. Then there is a second best problem of finding optimal offsetting sets of tax-subsidy and quantity restriction policies.

However, as under second or nth best pollution control policies, while offsetting policies will affect city sizes, it is difficult to think of general circumstances where *direct* city size policies are part of a second best solution. However the government manipulates prices, for those new prices, the resulting urban allocation of resources is efficient. The exception in Section 1.3 is national policies directly targeted at and impacting particular individual cities relative to the general mass of cities.

Small economy case. So far this section assumes identical cities whose number approaches infinity. First, let us keep the assumption that cities are potentially identical but remove the large country assumption. In particular, in Figure 9.1 suppose there is a small economy equilibrium with two cities each of size N_e, as in Chapter 4, Section 3. Does this change the welfare analysis?

In equation 9.2 replace the λ_4 constraint with two new constraints:

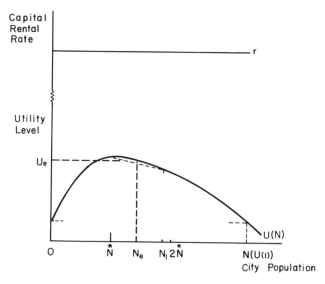

Fig. 9.1   City Sizes in Small Economies

$$+\lambda_4'(\bar{N} - mN) + \lambda_5'(\bar{K} - mK)$$

m is the finite number of cities and $\bar{N}$ and $\bar{K}$ are national endowments. Remaximizing in equation 9.2, the new welfare criteria as detailed in Section 1.2 to follow is that the *gap* in (10.3) of *SMB − SMC* be *equalized* across all cities. However, if cities are identical, by definition the gaps will be equalized and the allocation of resources will be efficient. Again this applies to all second and nth best situations with a limited number of *identical* cities. Only two issues can arise. These are detailed in Henderson (1986c) in a regional context.

First, can there be gains from making cities nonidentical? That is, if "utility transfers" were possible, relative to both cities being size N_e with utility U_e, heuristically, "total utility" can increase by having one city of size $\overset{*}{N}$ with $\overset{*}{U}$ and one of size N_1 with utility U_1. The basis for such a policy would be the nonconvexities inherent in small economies with scale effects. Noting the larger number of people with U_1 than $\overset{*}{U}$, in terms of averaging utility, it is sufficient that the U path be concave to rule out such a policy as dominating the market solution. The "averaged" utility (for N_e people) along a straight line between $\overset{*}{U}$ and U_1 is lower than U_e. Note with an infinite number of cities, this is no issue since all cities and people are at $\overset{*}{U}$.

The second issue was raised in Chapter 4. The city solutions assume the existence of either informed or experimenting land developers/entrepreneurs, who set up new cities. In a growing economy the issue is whether new cities form at the time that is optimal. In particular, starting with only one city, will a new city form with the resulting mass relocation of people when the first city reaches a size such as $2\overset{*}{N}$, or will a new city only form when the atomistic movement of one individual results in his gain? That is, must the first city grow to $N\{U[N(1)]\}$ for the population to start to relocate? In small economies without properly developed land markets and land titles and without capital markets for land developers to utilize, this could be a real problem. In that case subsidized migration may be needed to initiate the required population relocations for a second city to form at a optimal time (and size of the first city). These types of policies are detailed in Henderson (1986c) in a directly applicable regional context.

1.2. Population Allocation with Differentiated Cities

Section 1.1 assumes situations in which all cities are identical. As such there are no circumstances in which population relocation policies are justified. The basis for population relocation policies lies in situations in which cities are not all identical. But the justification for such policies when cities are not identical depends critically on a small economy assumption. The main basis for differentiated cities will be specialization in production of different types of goods. Another basis also considered will be cities enjoying different exogenous amenity bundles.

Different types of cities. Consider a "small" economy producing two traded goods X_1 and X_2, where there are m_1 (endogenous) cities of type X_1 and m_2 of type X_2. The planner's problem in (9.2) must be revised to include a new type of city and consumption good. The new problem is

$$\max U\left(\frac{X_1^1}{N_1}, \frac{X_2^1}{N_1}, \frac{H_1}{N_1}\right) + \lambda_1\left[U\left(\frac{X_1^2}{N_2}, \frac{X_2^2}{N_2}, \frac{H_2}{N_2}\right) - U\left(\frac{X_1^1}{N_1}, \frac{X_2^1}{N_1}, \frac{H_1}{N_1}\right)\right]$$

$$+ \lambda_2[H_1 - F(N_1) \cdot h(\hat{N}_1^1, \hat{K}_1^1, \hat{K}_2^1)]$$

$$+ \lambda_3[H_2 - F(N_2) \cdot h(\hat{N}_1^2, \hat{K}_1^2, \hat{K}_2^2)]$$

$$+ \lambda_4(N_1^2 - \hat{N}_0^1 - \hat{N}_1^1)$$

$$+ \lambda_5(N_2 - \hat{N}_0^2 - \hat{N}_1^2) \tag{9.9}$$

$$+ \lambda_6(K_1 - \hat{K}_0^1 - \hat{K}_1^1 - \hat{K}_2^1)$$

$$+ \lambda_7(K_2 - \hat{K}_0^2 - \hat{K}_1^2 - \hat{K}_2^2)$$

$$+ \lambda_8[m_1 X_1^1 + m_2 X_1^2 + p_K(m_1 K_1 + m_2 K_2)$$

$$- m_1 G_1(N_1) X_1(\hat{N}_0^1, \hat{K}_0^1)]$$

$$+ \lambda_9[m_1 X_2^1 + m_2 X_2^2 - m_2 G_2(N_2) X_2(\hat{N}_0^2, \hat{K}_0^2)]$$

$$+ \lambda_{10}\left[\frac{m_1}{m_2} - \frac{N_2}{N_1}\left(\frac{\frac{K_2}{N_2} - \bar{k}}{\bar{k} - \frac{K_1}{N_1}}\right)\right]$$

Superscripting refers to type 1 vs. type 2 cities for local inputs ($\hat{N}_0$, $\hat{N}_1$, $\hat{K}_0$, $\hat{K}_1$, $\hat{K}_2$) and traded good consumptions (X_1, X_2). The λ_1 constraint is an equal utility constraint for laborers across all types of cities. The λ_2 and λ_3 constraints equate nontraded good production and consumption within each type of city. λ_4 and λ_7 represent local full employment constraints. X_1 is the numeraire good. In λ_8 national consumption of X_1 plus payments to capital owners are equated to national output of X_1. λ_9 is a similar production equals consumption constraint on X_2. From equation 2.23 the λ_{10} constraint is a particular national full employment constraint, where k is the national capital-to-labor ratio.

Differentiating (9.9) with respect to all allocations and solving for the city size yields the general condition, which is a revised version of (9.3b) that

$$(SMB^1 - SMC^1) = (SMB^2 - SMC^2) \tag{9.10}$$

where

$$SMB^i - SMC^i = G_i(N_i)x_N^i - \left(\frac{X_1^i}{N_i} + \frac{U_H^i}{U_{X_1}^i}\frac{H_i}{N_i} + \frac{U_{X_2}}{U_{X_1}}\frac{X_2^i}{N_i}\right) + \epsilon_{X_i}\frac{U_{X_i}}{U_{X_1}}\frac{(X_i^s)}{N_i} - \epsilon_H^i\frac{U_H^i}{U_{X_1}^i}\frac{H_i}{N_i}$$

given that capital allocation now has a separate constraint. Equation 9.10 states that the gap between the social marginal benefits and social marginal costs of adding a resident in any city type 1 should equal that in city type 2. While the precise terms of $SMB^i - SMC^i$ correspond to those in (9.3a), altering the context only adds or subtracts additive terms as in the market economy version (9.8). If there are more than two types of cities, (9.10) reads $SMB^i - SMC^i = SMB^j - SMC^j$ for all i,j. In (9.10) if, for example, $SMB^1 - SMC^1 > SMB^2 - SMC^2$, type 1 cities are underpopulated. Since the gap between per person productivity and consumption is greater in type 1 cities, a person could be moved from a type 2 city to a type 1 city with utility levels unchanged and have a residual of goods left over.

Will equation 9.10 be satisfied in a free-market economy? If the economy is small, the answer is no and national government intervention is required. The problem in attaining efficient city sizes given more than one type of city is due to the existence of different degrees of external economies of scale in traded good production between cities. If economies of scale differ between cities, the external effect of labor migration decisions will differ among cities. Laborers will move to equalize the private marginal benefits of moving among cities; but given different marginal scale effects, the social marginal benefits will be equalized. Given the resulting differences in efficient city sizes, the tax share and scale diseconomy terms also will probably differ.

To determine under- or overpopulation (9.10) is interpreted in a market context. We follow the derivation of (9.4) to get

$$w_1t_1 + \epsilon_{X_1}\left(\frac{X_1^s}{N_1}\right) - \epsilon_H^1\left(\frac{H_1}{N_1}\right)p_1 = w_2t_2 + \epsilon_{X_2}\left(\frac{X_2^s}{N_2}q_2\right) - \epsilon_H^2\left(\frac{H_2}{N_2}\right)p_2 \tag{9.11}$$

Note that p_i is the price of housing in city type i, and q_2 the price of X_2 in terms of units of X_1. From (9.4), the left-hand side is the net benefits (positive or negative) of adding a person to city type X_1 and the right-hand side for city type X_2. In a small economy, in general (9.11) will not be satisfied. It is difficult to predict which type (smaller vs. larger) of city will be under- vs. overpopulated. That requires precise evaluation of the terms in (9.11)—see Section 1.4. After evaluation, some type of federal intervention would be required to tax people living in the overpopulated type of cities or subsidize those living in the underpopulated type of cities. This cannot be a general subsidy to labor in one type of industrial usage vs. another, which would only alter the numbers of one type of city to another (see Chapter 7), rather than city sizes. They must be population allocation subsidies based on city size per se, which hence alter city sizes.

These statements and the general approach to the problem of population allocation in general but not always (Section 1.3) reject a partial equilibrium approach to determining whether cities are optimal in size in a small economy. Under a partial equilibrium approach, viewing one city on its own, when the social marginal benefit of labor exceeds the private marginal benefit of labor, it might seem desirable to subsidize immigration to that city. From a general equilibrium perspective, however, this is incorrect. Subsidizing labor to migrate to one city would draw population away from other cities where the social marginal benefit of labor may also exceed the private marginal benefit. This is not to deny that one way of satisfying (9.10) is to tax/subsidize to set $SMB - SMC$ in all cities to zero with equal national redistribution of the resulting national budgetary surplus/deficit. It is simply that pursuing this policy in only one city in a small economy is inappropriate.

The result that the allocation of population across different types of cities may be nonoptimal *depends on a critical assumption*—that the economy is "small." In a large economy, as in Section 1.1, the market allocation of population is optimal. As the number of each type of city becomes very large, the gap between the SMB and SMC of population for each type of city in equation 9.10 approaches zero, just as it did in section 1.1. At the limit both gaps are zero, so both equations 9.10 and 9.11 are satisfied. That is, with no lumpiness in city size solutions, all cities approach their individual efficient sizes, and there is no longer a problem of population allocation at the margin. Chapter 2 assumed this in solving for equilibrium city sizes.

Alternatively viewed, in the maximization problem in (9.9), maximizing with respect to m_1 and m_2 yields conditions such as

$$\lambda_8\left[X_1^1 + \frac{U_{X_2}^1}{U_{X_1}^1}X_2^1 + p_K K_1 - (X_1^s)\right] + \lambda_{10}/m_2 = 0 \qquad (9.12)$$

Then as $m_2 \to \infty$, this implies

$$\left[X_1^1 + \frac{U_{X_2}^1}{U_{X_1}^1}X_2^1 + p_K K_1 - (X_1^s)\right] \to 0$$

This imposes a "balanced budget" for each city where traded good production (X_1^s) just covers the consumption of traded goods plus capital rentals. This "balanced budget" implies that there are no federal taxes or subsidies to the city that transfers resources to or from other types of cities to encourage population relocation. This means the gaps between SMB and SMC in different types of cities must be equalized, but generally equalization will only occur if both cities have optimal populations where the gaps are zero. This result is intuitively appealing.

When the number of cities becomes very large and they approach their most efficient size, a constant-returns-to-scale world is approached. That is, doubling the economy's endowments would double the numbers of each type of city, leaving city size unchanged, and would double production, without affecting utility levels or capital rentals. In this de facto constant-to-returns-to-scale world at the economywide level, the problem of misallocation of resources from urban external economies of scale vanishes.

Different amenity bundles. The other basis for differentiated cities following Chapter 4 is different exogenous amenity bundles offered by differing qualities of urban sites in an economy. Then, for example, the $U(\cdot)$ function could have an argument A_j where, given limited availability of sites for the n cities in an economy, $A_1 > A_2 > \ldots > A_n$. The indexing also represents the equilibrium order (with population growth) in which the cities are occupied, so that from Chapter 4 the best sites are occupied first. Then equation 9.9 is revised with equal utility and different production-consumption-resource constraints for all n cities. The result for population allocation, however, is simply a repeat of (9.10), or $SMB^1 - SMC^1 = SMB^2 - SMC^2 = \cdots = SMB^n - SMC^n$. Again given the exogenous shifts in utility paths with A_j, *free entry* city sizes will generally not satisfy equation 9.10 and population allocations will not be optimal. The restricted entry case is considered next in Section 1.3 (see also Chapter 4, Section 2.2). Determination of under- and overpopulation again requires precise evaluation of the magnitudes in a market economy of the $SMB^j - SMC^j$ for all n cities (see Section 1.4).

While the analysis again assumes a "small" economy, in this case it is difficult to specify the large economy situation. The problem is allowing for the existence of amenity bundles and an infinite number of cities. For example, if amenities are distributed uniformly on the line [0,1], that allows for an infinite number of cities and population. However, it is then difficult to describe the discrete allocations to different sites, which involves balancing a limited population across a limited number of sites (see Chapter 4). This remains an unsolved problem.

Summary. Differentiated cities in a "small" economy present the basis for national policies to redistribute population optimally. The policy calls for national population tax subsidies based on the relative and not absolute gaps between SMB and SMC in all cities. Under what circumstances does the typically advocated (see Tolley et al. 1979) partial equilibrium welfare analysis of the optimal size of any particular city apply, and when are size restriction policies of individual cities consistent with national welfare maximization.

1.3. Partial Equilibrium Optimal City Size Policies

This section examines one city of many in an economy and attempts to design policies to optimally reduce (or increase) its population. The partial equilibrium approach to this problem first adds up all the marginal external benefits and costs of an additional resident to the city holding all external (traded good and capital rental) prices fixed. Then it imposes an entry, or residence tax equal to the gap between $(SMC - SMB)$. Under what circumstances is such a policy optimal, in the sense that it is consistent with national welfare maximization?

Section 1.2 argues for a small economy that the optimal policy is to equalize the gaps between SMC and SMB in all cities. If taxes are imposed in *all* cities equal to the absolute values of their respective gaps, this result would be achieved (although the national population allocation budget generally would not be balanced and monies would have to be raised or redistributed at the national level to meet, respectively, the shortfall or excess). However, imposition of the tax in only one city or subset of cities would be incorrect, since that would not equalize the gaps between SMC and SMB in *all* cities. In general, it could make the situation worse.

For the treatment of just one city (or cities) to be first best, it must be the case that in all untreated cities $SMB - SMC = 0$. Then imposition of taxes equal to the absolute value of $SMB - SMC$ would equalize the gaps at zero in all cities. In what situations will there be a subset of cities (all but one in the pure partial equilibrium version) in which $SMB - SMC = 0$? There are only two possibilities.

First, the untreated sector of the economy can exhibit no population externalities, so that the terms in, say, (9.4) or (9.8) are nonexistent. That is, there could be a sector without scale effects or public goods—unfortunately even the farm sector exhibits both scale effects and consumes public intermediate inputs.

Second, because there could be one sector where the number of cities approaches infinity, $SMB \rightarrow SMC$: for example, in either the traditional service sector in rural areas or farms. This basically returns us to a large economy situation. In that situation "most" cities are at the maximum point of their utility paths where $SMB - SMC = 0$. However, there may be either a "few" cities with special amenity bundles whose utility paths are shifted above the norm or a few cities specialized in products requiring only one or two cities of that type to service the very large economy. This last situation represents an economy in which for most types of cities there is no lumpiness problem in setting equilibrium size, but for a few types there is (i.e., a "large-small" economy). In these cases then it is optimal to impose a residency tax equal to $SMB - SMC$ at efficient size in all of the oddball cities. However, this situation does not necessarily require national government intervention. Again in large economies the private actions undertaken in individual cities and in the land development market will be sufficient to ensure efficient city sizes if there are no restrictions on such actions. Before turning to this point, there is one other question. If there are n oddball cities, is it an improvement to impose an entry tax of $SMB - SMC$ in one (i) of them, even if the other $n - 1$ [$n - i$] of them have no entry restrictions?

The answer to that question lies in the old debate on second best policies. In general, correcting an externality on a partial equilibrium basis in just one sector where there are many sectors that have externalities is not a second best policy (Lipsey and Lancaster, 1956). Under particular additivity assumptions, such as are probably met in Chapter 2, such a policy however can be second best (Davis and Winston, 1966). Moreover, even if such a policy is not second best, in a nth best world, it may still improve national welfare (Harberger, 1971) relative to no policy.

Returning to the central question, is national government intervention required to alter city sizes of those "few" potentially overpopulated (oddball) cities in a large economy? That is, are individual cities motivated to pursue optimal city size policies when their $SMB - SMC \neq 0$? This question is examined in some detail, since it critically highlights the (non)role of central governments in population location policies. It also highlights the partial equilibrium methodology, problems with the methodology, and generalizations of the methodology.

The setting for examining individual optimal city size policies is stylized as follows. Consider an economy of $(m - 1)$ identical cities where $m \rightarrow \infty$ and one city which, relative to the others, is favored with either an unusually good exogenous amenity endowment or subsidized urban infrastructure ($\hat{K}_2$) investments. An example would be a national capital region. The situation is then as in Chapters 4 and 10, and is represented in Figure 9.2a.

The prevailing utility level in the economy is U_e, as set by the $(m - 1)$ cities whose sizes $\overset{*}{N}$ put them at the maximum of their utility paths. The favored city has a utility path $\hat{U}$ shifted up relative to other cities. With free entry equilibrium city size would be N_e $(<\overset{*}{N})$. However, this equilibrium size is neither Pareto-efficient nor sustainable under certain assumptions.

In particular, just as in Chapters 4 and 7, assume that there is a monopolist (land developer) who controls entry to the city through the imposition of entry fees (e.g., a fixed surcharge on sales of a fixed number of land plots in a spatial model). The monopolist sets a per resident fee, F, to maximize his profits, FN, subject to the constraint that $U_e - U(-F,N) = 0$. The constraint states that, after fees, residents realize the going utility level in national markets. Maximizing and solving yields

$$F = \left(\frac{-\partial U/\partial N}{\lambda} \right) N \tag{9.13a}$$

where λ is the marginal utility of income. As noted in earlier chapters there is a curve marginal to $\hat{U}$, where $\hat{U}$ represents "average" utility. "Total utils" are $N\hat{U}$ and hence marginal utils are $\hat{U} - (-\partial U/\partial N)N$. Restricted city size occurs at $\hat{N}$ where

$$\hat{U} - (-\partial U/\partial N)N = U_e$$

or

$$\hat{U} - F\lambda = U_e \tag{9.13b}$$

$F\lambda$ is the utility value of the fee. This is all expressed in general terms because the actual imposition of fees affects incomes and all local prices, details of which we ignore with no loss of generality. The fee in utils, $F\lambda$, is equal to the distance between the population supply curve U_e and the average utility paid curve $\hat{U}$ at efficient size $\hat{N}$ in Figure 9.2a.

Imposing this fee results in Pareto-efficient city size. This can be viewed in two ways. First, $(-\partial U/\partial N)$ is the decline in net utility for an existing residents of a new entrant, and $(-\partial U/\partial N)N$ is this decline summed over all residents. This in essence is the gap between SMC and SMB in utils holding U_e and nonlocal prices fixed. As such, imposing the fee, F, in monetary units prices the gap between SMC and SMB. F is the charge for net population externalities.

The second way of viewing (9.13a) is that, holding U_e and r fixed, imposing the fee maximizes the income of a third party for others' welfare unchanged. In partial equilibrium terms, maximal consumers' surplus is being extracted. Note that a city cannot impose a fee on itself per se and redistribute the proceeds locally, unless entrants beyond $\hat{N}$ are denied redistributed income.

However, in the real world, city imposition of entry restrictions may indeed result in a separation of entrants before and after $\hat{N}$. In particular, assume size $\hat{N}$ represents a long-run equilibrium achieved by population growth overtime. Entrants purchase their lots and house (or residency certificates). No restrictions are anticipated. However, beyond some point, say, $\overset{*}{N}$, existing residents realize that new residents impose losses on them, given a declining $\hat{U}$. They then impose (zoning) restrictions limiting final city size to $\hat{N}$ and impose an entry fee, F, for further entrants based on that. Ultimately, each existing resident will then collect a fee $(\hat{N} - \overset{*}{N})F/\overset{*}{N}$. The problem for the $\overset{*}{N}$ existing residents is then to choose

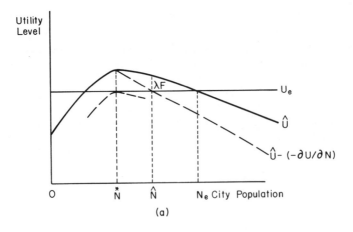

(a)

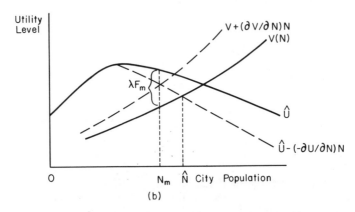

(b)

Fig. 9.2 Efficient and Inefficient Restrictions on City Sizes

$\hat{N}$ to maximize realized utility including the entry fee income, or $U[F(\hat{N} - \overset{*}{N})/\overset{*}{N}, \hat{N}]$ subject to paying newcomers U_e, or subject to $U_e - U(-F, \hat{N}) = 0$. The solution ignoring the differences in income effects is the same as in (9.13), again the efficient city size. Entrance fees, while not present in a direct form in the real world, may be indirectly imposed in other fashions. One such fashion is to decrease the public services offered to new vs. existing residents or to raise their tax liabilities by overassessment of property taxes (or by forced overconsumption of housing). Note that without entrance fees of an implicit or explicit form, entry would be restricted at $\overset{*}{N}$ so as to maximize realized utility for homeowners. (However, for renters whose rents reflect the "benefits" of restrictions this would be a disaster.)

Figure 9.2a assumes that the supply curve of entrants is horizontal. This is critical to the efficiency of the monopolist solution. Suppose the curve is upward sloping as in a general partial equilibrium case. To attract entrants with limited population mobility, a city must pay higher and higher utility levels to attract residents from further away or from better opportunities. Assume, then, in Figure 9.2*b*, a supply curve based on alternative utilities $V(N)$. In maximizing profits, the monopolist now maximizes FN s.t. $V(N) - U(-F,N) = 0$ yielding

$$F = \left(\frac{-\partial U/\partial N}{\lambda}\right)N + \frac{\partial V/\partial N}{\lambda}N \qquad (9.14)$$

To a monopolist, an additional marginal cost of entrant besides declining average utilities payable is the increase in the best alternative utility level along $V(N)$, which must be met (Figure 9.2*b*). There is also a curve marginal to $V(N)$ equal to $V(N) + (\partial V/\partial N)N$. Equilibrium is at the intersection of the two marginal curves, resulting in a fee of F_m and equilibrium city size N_m. However, N_m is not Pareto-efficient. $V(N)$ itself is a marginal curve of best alternatives, so that $(\partial V/\partial N)N$ represents a "pecuniary externality." Pareto-efficient city size is at $\hat{N}$ where $V(N)$ intersects the marginal utility offered curve. This solution could only be realized by a discriminating monopolist who charges at the margin a fee equal to the distance between the $\hat{U}$ path and $V(N)$. At $\hat{N}$ in Figure 9.2*b*, as in Figure 9.2*a*, the marginal fee income for a discriminating monopolist then equals the externalities at $\hat{N}$, or $[(-\partial U/\partial N)/\lambda]N$.

Again the basic aspects of such a solution may in practice be present with initial residents collecting entry fees from later entrants through calibrated discriminatory provision of services. The calibration can range from inferior schools in some new neighbors all the way down to squatter settlements where no public services exist.

This entry fee analysis has other applications. The widespread imposition of entry fees describes the restricted entry solution to all city sizes in the situation described in Chapter 4, Section 3 where amenity bundles differ across all cities. There it is assumed that in a "large" economy there is a "base" city on the worst occupied site whose size generally approaches that corresponding to the maximal point on its utility path. This becomes the base utility level in the economy. Then all other cities could have entry fees imposed according to their net marginal population externalities. This would maximize the "surplus" collected from each city and hence the economy for redistribution on a national basis. While from Section 1.2 of this chapter, imposition of fees to close the gap between *SMB* and *SMC* is generally optimal if done for every city, the general equilibrium impacts are hard to model and assess. For example, entry fees and the decline in city sizes would mean new cities must form on lower quality urban sites, lowering the base utility level and altering all factors prices.

Finally, as discussed in Chapter 4, this analysis of entry fees assumes one of the following for viability. Developers are free to impose entry restrictions (assuming one development corporation has all development rights). Existing owner-residents can impose entry restrictions (e.g., restrictive zoning and land development ordinances) *and* either charge owners of vacant land development fees (hence indirectly collecting the F's in equation 9.13) or in a discriminatory manner tax and service new entrants. If at least one of these situations does not pertain, then localities cannot achieve efficient sizes and federal government intervention will be required. With free entry, city sizes will be too large (N_e in Figure 9.2*a*). With restricted entry by owner-residents, if entry fees cannot be collected in any fashion, restricted city sizes will be too small ($\overset{*}{N}$ in Figure 9.2*a*).

There remains an issue of whether imposed entry restrictions, typically in practice as opposed to in theory, can be expected to lead to efficient sizes. This is examined next, taking the perspective of a national government attempting intervention.

1.4. Implementation Problems

Optimal population policies when justified face critical implementation problems, more serious than the problems facing typical externality correction policies. For a single city the way to proceed is to "calculate" the efficient size $\hat{N}$ and impose an optimal entry tax F equal to the monetized difference between $\hat{U}$ and U_e at $\hat{N}$ in Figure 9.2a. Note the optimal policy requires a fee equal to the externality at $\hat{N}$, not at the current existing size N_e. The information requirements for this policy are formidable. They require knowledge of the shape of the U_e and $\hat{U}$ curves, or all the parameters of the city size model. Small economies with tax subsidies on all cities, require the information to calculate efficient sizes and to impose for those sizes the correctly calibrated tax subsidies on entry to equalize the gaps between SMB and SMCs across all cities. Again this implies that the shapes of U-curves for all cities are known. If national urban planners are doing the calculation of the shapes of the U-curves (as opposed to their being "intuited" by experienced land developers), they need to utilize an algorithm where they know all the parameters of the city size model.

Even if one had econometric estimates of all such parameters, the most serious difficulty remains. The calculation of, say, $\hat{N}$ and the magnitude of externalities is very sensitive to the values of parameters. For example, consider the scale parameter ϕ, estimated in Chapter 5 for Brazil and the United States. Typically, in Chapter 5, estimates of ϕ had a 95% confidence interval of, for instance, 5 to to 145 for a point estimate of 75 and a 68% confidence interval of 30 to 120. When we calculate the basic equilibrium city size in the large country case, for example, the result is a direct multiple of ϕ, so even with a 68% confidence interval there is a fourfold variation in possible city size. For externality terms similarly there is a fourfold variation in the possible magnitude of the $\epsilon_x(X/N)$ term in (9.3b) for any city. In short, typical city size and externality calculations are very sensitive to precise magnitudes of parameters, and econometric tools do not allow us to pinpoint these parameters.

In practice, given that the parameters cannot be pinpointed to identify the overall shapes of $\hat{U}$ and U_e, the seat-of-the-pants way to proceed is to calculate the magnitude of the externalities at N_e. Good back-of-the-envelope calculations for this are illustrated in Tolley et al. (1979). Then the procedure is to impose a fee based on externalities at N_e, watch city size drop, readjust the fees for the new level of externalities (instantaneously recalculated) for each new city size, and iterate until at the final fee no further changes in city size occur. If the externalities are correctly calculated at least for the final move, efficient city size will be realized.

The problem remains that the calculations of marginal externalities at N_e or anywhere may be off by severalfold. As illustrated in Tolley et al. (1979), existing estimates are back-of-the-envelope examples for academic consumption. Second, iterating on fees raises the problem of anticipations. If entrants recognize the game being played and that the current fee is not a permanent exogenous variable, then their responses to fees will no longer be optimal. In short, at present, there is no practical way to calculate optimal city size. The nth best alternative is to attempt to recognize situations where city sizes are "too large" and advocate a "reasonable" seat-of-the-pants reduction in size through entry restrictions and possible implicit or explicit fees.

There remains a final issue: What are the welfare costs of an excessive city size? In theory they are equal to the fees collected at the efficient size—the surplus over U_e that can be extracted by moving to an efficient solution. Again, that calculation involves knowledge of the shapes of the U_e and $\hat{U}$ curves. The usual alternative approximately equivalent method (in a constant-returns-to-scale world) is to calculate the sum of the marginal population externalities over the distance from N_e to $\hat{N}$. Again, that requires knowledge of the magnitude of the parameters to calculate externalities. In short, the range of reasonable guesses may contain a severalfold variation, just as the calculations of optimal city size or final fees do.

2. Decentralization and Deconcentration Policies

A number of countries pursue population location policies, apart from individual city size policies. Two types of policies are most common—decentralization and deconcentration policies. Although the two types of policies can be closely linked, they have distinctly different bases and intents. Decentralization policies refer to the interregional dispersion of population and economic activity, while deconcentration refers to intraregional dispersion of activity. In practice, decentralization means the maintenance of significant population in remote areas of a country, either by inhibiting rural-to-urban and interregional migration of indigenous populations (e.g., India) or by encouraging settlement in more sparsely populated areas (e.g., Brazil). In practice, deconcentration means inhibiting the buildup of population agglomerations in a few core metro areas by deflecting migrants or existing residents to nearby satellite towns. These latter policies are more directly linked to the discussion in Section 1, since they can be interpreted as having an externality base.

Decentralization policies appear to have other bases. The focus is on large "federal" countries such as Brazil, Canada, China, and India where there are diverse regional populations often speaking different languages and having distinctly different ethnic or racial origins. Some of these countries may have national objectives, even constitutionally stated ones, of maintaining diversity and the traditional social characteristics of their distinctive regions. That is, in popular language, the ideal may be to maintain a national mosaic, to use the Canadian term, as opposed to, for instance, the American melting pot ideal. Maintenance of mosaics is generally thought to require some spatial separation and especially limited mixing of regional populations. With free population mobility that in turn requires standards of living cannot vary dramatically across regions. Otherwise, some regions' populations will migrate for significantly better economic alternatives, resulting in a mixing of regional populations and perhaps either a destruction of traditional regional social fabrics or long-term social conflicts and tensions, or both. A critical ingredient of economic policy then becomes the maintenance of regional balance and balanced growth interregionally.

In Section 1 of this chapter, national population location policies were based on traditional externality arguments. The regional balance argument to maintain national character has been little explored by economists (an exception is Scott, 1950). The arguments have the most force in countries such as Canada and India, where there are strong constitutional foundations. For countries where regional diversity and mosaics are not part of their constitution and are not important objectives, the basis of national population location policies must lie in Section 1. Then a desire for decentralization, or a restriction on the degree of centralization, must typically be based on the notion of subsidizing populations to stay in less developed regions where net externalities (net $SMC - SMB$) are low, in order to keep those populations from moving to more developed regions where net externalities are high.

Unfortunately, for nonfederal countries, typical decentralization policies have only vaguely stated externality bases or none at all. The presumption that less developed regions are in a better externality position certainly has no empirical backing (because of lack of investigation) and has no intuitive basis given the strong external economies of scale that appear to be part of industrial production processes. In short, apart from arguments concerning national character, decentralization policies from an economist's viewpoint have no solid empirical bases. Why then are such policies implemented? Possible reasons include the following. Decentralization may be consistent with maintenance of political stability for some less than democratic governments. Rapid centralization may be difficult for some governments to handle managerially given the required shifts in public infrastructure. Decentralization may be part of national defense policy. Decentralization may be an objective of a dominant, rich region trying to restrict immigration from a poorer region predominantly containing people of a different ethnic-racial group.

While decentralization policies typically have weak or unexplored economic bases, deconcentration policies do have an economic basis. However, as often implemented they may produce perverse results. As explained in Chapter 8, the stereotype for deconcentration policies is the national capital region or the major metropolitan area of a country. Such cities may be international "showplaces" as well as the residence of policymakers. As such they may typically be favored with relatively high levels of urban infrastructure investments (roads, parks, walkways, utilities, etc.) as well as special public services (higher quality schools and colleges). The relative attractiveness of these metro areas following high levels of infrastructure investment draws in migrants from local and other areas of the country. At the limit in the long run such immigration would dissipate the entire relative benefits of the higher infrastructure investment. To protect their amenity position, the existing residents of the metro area and their local government may enact city size restriction policies. These include refusing to zone vacant land for new residential development, density zoning on existing land, higher tax burdens for new entrants, denial of public services to new entrants, and so on. As discussed in Section 1.3, these policies have welfare economics foundation in at least an nth best setting.

The other way of protecting the amenity position of the core national capital city is to try to deflect migration elsewhere. One way, of course, would be widespread infrastructure investment and better quality public services throughout the country. That may or may not be both too expensive given taxing capacities of the national government, and inconsistent with an efficient national allocation of resources. The frequently adopted alternative is local deflection of migration to planned satellite towns and residential centers in the outer rings of the national capital region. The attempt then is to deconcentrate population from the core metro area to outlying localities, so as to try to protect the core metro area amenities from dissipation and to limit the extent of negative externalities. Chapter 3 noted the example of Korea.

Unfortunately, it is not clear that true protection is possible. Deflection also increases the regional area over which amenities are provided at a higher level in relation to the rest of the country. That in turn draws in even more migrants to the national capital region, potentially creating a massive overpopulated region. That is, while such policies may allocate population more efficiently within a region, based on the conceptual notions of Section 1, they may have a negative impact interregionally. The problem is that they are piecemeal policies rather than comprehensive national policies.

Since deconcentration policies are reviewed in Chapter 8, this section in terms of illustrating policies, focuses on decentralization policies.

2.1. Decentralization in India

By any standard India is an unusually decentralized country. Decentralization is a constitutional objective and, in contrast to many other countries, an ongoing priority. India has a low rate of urbanization (24% in 1981) and, compared with many other less developed countries, its urban population growth rate (3.86% per year for 1971 to 1981) in relation to its rural rate is not high. While class I cities (over 100,000 people) are growing fast (4.6%), class VI cities (under 5,000) are growing faster. Within class I cities, growth is balanced with existing 1971 cities of 1 to 4 million, 250,000 to 500,000, and 100,000 to 250,000 all growing at about 4% a year. Interregional urban growth rates are not highly variable. Industrial concentration is very low (see Chapter 1) and even declining. The share of the big four industrial states (Maharashtra, West Bengal, Gujarat, and Tamil Nada) in manufacturing value added fell from 67% in 1961 to 55% in 1976. Correspondingly, manufacturing value added as a share of net domestic product is growing fastest in less industrialized states. (These figures are all from *Planning of Urban Development,* published by the Task Force on Housing and Urban Development of the National Planning Commission, September 1983.)

The obvious question is how India has largely escaped these tendencies, given that, in most less developed countries entering a phase of fairly rapid industrialization, centralization and concentration are typical and natural. India has a multiple of long-term decentralization policies. There is much disagreement on their effectiveness and no hard economic study of them. However, it may be that India's high degree of decentralization is maintained by the combination of both these policies, as well as more naturally by its unusual degree of regional population diversity. Following Sekhar (1983), the above mentioned Task Force reports, and Datta (1981), this section reviews some of the key policies based upon the constitution and subsequent legislation. Some of these policies are also enhanced by monies allocated to support objectives of the five year plans. However, the five year plans appear to be focused on deconcentration more than on decentralization.

Key policies

1. Octroi taxation. The overwhelming local source of local government revenues is octroi taxation. This is a tax by weight on goods imported into cities (typically easily collected because of the predominance of rail shipping). In essence, it is a local import tariff, albeit based on weight. The tariff has two perhaps conflicting effects. Ignoring population mobility, as an import restriction it encourages local self-sufficiency and broad-based local economic development. However, given population mobility it encourages clustering of population to reduce tariff costs of intercity trade, drawing population away from small towns into agglomerations. Thus in net it may contribute to centralization of population.

2. *Uniform delivered prices on industrial products.* Apart from local sales taxes, raw or semiprocessed materials (e.g., iron and steel inputs) sell at a fixed price to the producer and to the purchaser regardless of location. Transport charges are the same regardless of distance shipped. The stated notion is that this encourages location of raw material processers in backward regions with mineral deposits because it doesn't matter how far away their customers are. However, given the weight-reducing nature of processing, the natural location of such producers is near the deposit site anyway. The real impact of the pricing policy is to encourage *intermediate* users of raw materials (say, auto manufacturers) to locate near consumer concentrations rather than at some more efficient intermediate location (based on Weberian triangle notions), since their input (but not output) transport costs are invariant to location. That in turn may encourage centralization (away from intermediate locations), not decentralization (see Mills and Becker, 1986.

3. *Uniform delivered prices on consumer products.* Apart from local taxes, prices to consumers for a number of consumer products are fixed nationally regardless of distances from production sites. This permits centralized production because there is no locational advantage to decentralizing to be near medium-size population concentrations. However, in terms of population location, it also means the populations of remote areas where decentralized production of these products would be unlikely can remain there at a relatively lower consumption cost. Thus again, intermediate locations (between more centralized producers and distant rural locations) may be adversely affected compared with central and distant locations.

4. *Location of public sector plants.* There has been an emphasis on locating plants of public sector manufacturing enterprises in low income regions. The decentralization impact of this is unambiguous.

5. *Protection of traditional small-scale industries.* Various traditional small-scale producers are protected by financing advantages and the banning of large plant production. An example is traditional handloom textiles protected through licensing and excise and export duty differentials. This protects village and small-town producers at the expense of modern mill towns.

6. *Backward region policies.* Firms locating in designated backward areas are favored with low interest loans, income tax concessions, shipping subsidies, and so on, both from national and local agencies. These policies, which are also utilized in Brazil and Canada, are controversial. Two usual issues are how many location decisions are affected at the margin (as opposed to how many producers collecting subsidies would have located there anyway) and whether induced-firm relocations are symbolic. For the latter (in particular in Brazil) the problem is that a firm may relocate only some small part of its production process to the backward region, typically labor intensive assembly. For India the additional problem is the liberal designation of "backward" to cover rural districts next to already large metro areas. Under 10% of the qualifying districts received 90% of concessionary investment funds in the late 1970s and most of these funds seemed to go to metro

area regions (*Planning of Urban Development,* Task Force on Housing and Urban Development of the National Planning Commission, September, 1983). Thus not only may such policies have limited effectiveness, they may inadvertently encourage centralization through misdesignation of districts.

7. *Ineffective policies.* Two ineffective policies are thought to be rural industrial estates to which private industries undersubscribe and licensing of locations for private producers. Political impediments are thought (Sekhar) to eliminate the decentralization impacts of the latter, and the former involve often unserviced ill-conceived projects at too distant locations.

A summary of the overall impact of India's decentralization policies is difficult. Only public sector location policies and the protection of traditional small-scale industries have unambiguous strong impacts. Both are very sector specific policies (focused, for example, on iron and steel and textiles). The uniform pricing policies appear to favor both centralized and far decentralized localities at the expense of the intermediate. Other policies appear weak or defective in implementation. It could be that India's high degree of decentralization is better explained by its diverse regional populations with their unusually inherent disaffinity to centralization.

3. Conclusions

In large economies, equilibrium city sizes achieved in competitive development markets for a given institutional environment are efficient sizes; and there is no justification for population relocation policies at a national level. This statement holds up in the presence of other unpriced externalities or "distorting" national government policies. In these cases there are no second best population location policies. The economic environment in which such policies are justified are "small" economies with differentiated types of cities. Then the appropriate policy is population location tax subsidies to equalize the gaps for all cities between the social marginal benefits and social marginal costs of adding people to those cities.

This, in principle, rejects a partial equilibrium approach where for any one city we tax or subsidize entry to set the gap between social marginal benefits and costs to zero. However, that partial equilibrium approach can be valid for a city if there is another base group of cities in the economy where the gap is already zero either because those cities have no externalities (not realistic) or because of their number is very large.

In that situation, potentially overpopulated cities may be expected to impose their own optimal city size restrictions, without national government intervention. Existing residents of a growing city may impose indirect entry fees on new entrants through discriminatory tax assessments and provision of public services, limiting their city populations to approximate efficient sizes.

In summary, the true basis for national population relocation policies is small economy situations, with differentiated types of cities. Not only are population relocation policies found in large countries (e.g., India, Brazil), but when imposed in small countries they are often at odds with the welfare analysis of this chapter. It is true that in some large federal countries, decentralization policies have appropriate foundations in national and constitutionally defined objectivities of regional diversity and maintenance of traditional ethnic groupings. But in many developing countries the current focus is on deconcentration policies, where the intent is to deflect migrants to large metro areas into nearby satellite cities. Such a policy in itself will attract even more migrants to the metro area regions from other parts of the country. The end result may be mammoth overpopulated metropolitan regions.

CHAPTER 10

Empirical Determinants
of Urban Concentration

This chapter examines the empirical determinants of urban concentration using a cross section of countries. Having discussed theoretically the market and government policy determinants of urban concentration in Chapters 2 to 4 and 7 to 9, an empirical evaluation is critical. Unfortunately such an analysis presents many difficulties and the attempt to resolve them here, while suggestive, represents only a beginning and points the way to future work. Among the problems are defining a measure of urban concentration, settling on a definition of urban area size, and collecting data relevant to national characteristics likely to affect urban concentration. Before proceeding to a discussion of the empirical formulation, data, and results, let us consider the conceptual issue of how to define urban area size.

There are political and geographic definitions of urban area size, neither of which necessarily corresponds to the relevant economic definition. A political definition is often historically based, taking the land incorporated into an original small town plus any subsequent annexations. In the United States this is an urban place definition. However, urban places have limited economic and even geographic significance. In many cases the agglomerated urban place population has spilled over these political boundaries, or the population of two or more adjacent original political cities may have overrun each other. A geographic definition may then include the whole spatial area of some number of original smaller cities, whose population density exceeds some critical number. In the United States this is an urban area definition. Finally a political-geographic definition for the purposes of data collection may utilize a collection of political units one step up from the city, such as a county in the United States or municipio in Brazil. Then the relevant definition, while based on urban area notions of contiguous areas exceeding some critical density, incorporates the rural as well as the urban parts of counties. In the United States this occurs because much data are collected at the county level. The relevant definition for the data in this chapter would be the Standard Metropolitan Statistical Area (SMSA), which for non-New England areas is the county population centered around an urban place(s) or the counties' population centered around contiguous cities with overlapping populations.[1]

The choice of definitions can be critical both in terms of quantifying city size and characterizing production patterns. For example, there are several definitions of the New York area, starting from its five central boroughs and expanding west and north to incorporate outlying urbanized areas. The population range of these definitions goes from 7.5 million up to 18 million or even more. Historically, as New York City's economy expanded, its labor and housing markets essentially overran other outlying and previously independent urban areas. Thus, while the core urban area may be service and commerce oriented with also a market oriented apparel industry, as its economy overruns outlying areas (such as Newark and Paterson), it may incorporate a diverse set of heavier manufacturing industries. The same problem exists in examining, for example, Chicago. If we look at the core urban area compared with its incorporation of parts of the state of Indiana, we get a different picture of its industrial base.

Moreover, from the theoretical point of view of this book, it is not clear what to do. The analysis in Chapters 2 to 4 relates to economies composed of cities that are conceptually monocentric, although the critical site production equation 2.3 can be interpreted more generally. While many cities remain primarily monocentric with one key industrial base, a large proportion of the urban population does reside in multinucleated metropolitan areas, where the populations of some original adjacent monocentric cities have spilled over and overrun each other. The question is how to interpret these areas economically. For reasons to be developed conceptually below, they are basically interpreted as clusters of the economic cities discussed in Chapters 2 to 4, which in other circumstances (see below) could be spatially separate monocentric cities.

Using the terms of Chapters 2 to 4 to examine urban concentration in a pure economic form, one still might want to use urban place definitions to focus on the key centers of multinucleated urban areas; in practice, however, this is not possible. First, data are not readily available in that form. Second, once cities become clustered together the metro area takes on a life of its own. For example, massive intrametropolitan transport networks contribute to massive cross commuting among the multicenters and a blending of economic bases of contiguous centers so that defining where one center's activity ends and another's begins becomes arbitrary and perhaps not particularly meaningful. From another perspective, the original urban place political units have their boundaries pushed up against each other so that no further annexations are possible. With industrial and transport development, the economic influence of one urban place may spill into and evade the territory of another.

Thus, in practice, metropolitan areas as a whole must be dealt with. Measures of urban concentration then will be strongly affected by the extent of clustering of cities. What does the theory in Chapters 2 to 4 have to say about that? Section 1 presents a model of clustering and metropolitan area formation and size. Section 2 investigates empirically the determinants of urban concentration.

1. Clustering of Economic Cities into Metropolitan Areas

Why do cities cluster together into metropolitan areas? One reason might be some type of urbanization economies or externality benefits of related industries, coupled with localization economies. To exploit localization economies, firms cluster together into one nucleus, and to exploit either urbanization economies or external scale benefits from related industries, a number of nuclei cluster together to form a metropolitan area. The problem with this explanation is that, as we saw, in Chapters 5 and 6, manufacturing industries generally did not appear to be influenced by either urbanization economies or external benefits of related industry scale. However, some type of urbanization economies may exist in the initial stages of product development for manufactured products. So the modern manufacturing concerns in the infancy stage in a developing country might cluster into a central metropolitan area of a country. Section 2 partially explores this hypothesis. Second, the econometric examinations in Chapter 5 only deal with manufacturing. It may be that the clustering and concentration of modern services in large metro areas (see Chapter 1) are explained by urbanization economies.

While urbanization economies as a partial basis for clustering cannot be ruled out completely, the central explanation is different and simpler. Different types of cities cluster together simply to reduce the transport costs of intercity trade among themselves. Considering only this and ignoring the environmental implications, all cities in an economy would cluster into one mammoth metro area. What prohibits this is the need for production centers to spatially disperse to utilize spatially dispersed raw material deposits and other natural resources.

To see the forces at work, we first consider formally the polar case, opposite to the case where cities are all monocentric. This is an economy composed only of metropolitan areas, where metropolitan areas are spatially clusters of monocentric cities. A simple model that generates different size metropolitan areas and intermetro area trade is as follows. Suppose some types of cities require the use of natural resources in production, while others do not. These resources include mineral deposits, fertile land, sea resources such as harbors, cheap hydroelectric power, clear skies, and so on. The natural resource locations are at various spots on the flat plain of the economy and unprocessed natural resources are very expensive to transport. Cities locate at resource sites to process these resources through, for example, the various stages of weight reduction on the way to final products. Different types of cities using different types of resources would generally be separate spatially and would trade with each other across space.

In addition to natural resource using cities, there are a variety of other types of cities that are footloose. To reduce the costs of intercity trade, these footloose cities cluster around the cities using site specific natural resources, to form multinucleated metropolitan areas composed of numerous different cities. Intermetropolitan trade involves only natural resource products, and metropolitan areas are self-sufficient in footloose products.

Specifically, assume the footloose type of cities are indexed by t and there are h types of them, or $t = 1, \ldots, h$. For a natural resource city labeled i, the characteristics of its metropolitan area are as follows. Within the metropolitan area the demand (see equation 2.22) for the good produced by the jth footloose type of cities is

$$\left(\frac{a_j}{f}\right)\left(\frac{f}{f + \gamma\beta b}\right)\left(w_i^* N_i^* + \sum_{t=1}^{h} w_t N_t m_t^*\right) q_j^{-1}$$

where m_t^* is the number of tth type footloose cities in the metropolitan area. This is the demand for X_j by residents of the base natural resource city, i, and all the clustered footloose cities (including X_j types), where there are m_t cities for each of the h types. The supply of the jth good (assuming no intrametropolitan area transport costs of trade) is $m_j^* X_j$. Substituting in equation 2.13 yields

$$m_j^* X_j = m_j^* \{ [f - b\beta(1 - \gamma)](f + \gamma\beta b)^{-1}(1 - \alpha_j)^{(1-\alpha_j)/\alpha_j} A_j^{1/\alpha_j} \}$$
$$\cdot N_j^{1-1/\alpha_j} q^{-1+1/\alpha_j} g_j(N_j)^{1/\alpha_j}$$

This is the supply in each city of type j multiplied by the number of cities of that type. Equating demand and supply for the h footloose goods, substituting in for w from (2.4) and then for q_i/q_j and q_t/q_j from equation 2.18, and rearranging, we end up with a set of h linear equations in h unknowns, m_t^*, which may be solved directly by applying Cramer's rule. The solutions take the form

$$m_j^* = \left(\frac{N_j}{N_j}\right)^{1+1/\psi} |J_j|/|J_0| \qquad (10.1)$$

where $|J_j|$ and $|J_0|$ are defined parametrically.[2] This defines the number of footloose cities of each type. It is, of course, desirable that the m_j^* be large enough numbers to avoid lumpiness problems in solution. This requires that $N_i >> N_j$ if $\alpha_j a_j/f$ is relatively small.

Metropolitan area population is the sum of populations around each center, or is $N_i + \sum_{t=1}^h m_t N_t$. From equation 10.1 this equals

$$N_{MA} = N_i + [N_i^{1+1/\psi}] \left[\sum_{t=1}^h \frac{|J_t| N_t^{-1/\psi}}{|J_0|} \right] \qquad (10.2)$$

Metropolitan area population is an increasing function (at an increasing rate) of the base natural resource city population (N_i).

What are the properties of the system of metropolitan areas, given equation 10.2? First, consider general sizes of metropolitan areas. If an economy produces relatively few footloose products and, say, fills its consumption gaps through international imports, then N_{MA} for all metropolitan area types is unambiguously smaller than in an economy producing more of its consumption of footloose products or even exporting them. For example, in equations 10.1 and 10.2 $|J_j|/|J_0|$ increases as the range of *produced* footloose goods rises. Thus, the numbers of existing type of footloose cities rise as well as the numbers of new types. For a second example, as demand for the jth footloose good is satisfied less and less by international imports, the numbers of j (and all) type cities will rise in the metropolitan area. In short, the need for and extent of clustering will increase. The second aspect of the system of metropolitan areas concerns the relative numbers of areas. Equation 10.2 requires a reanalysis of the size distribution of cities when cities are defined as metropolitan areas. As in equation 2.22 the numbers of each type of metropolitan area are defined by the numbers of each type of natural resource cities consistent with national demand for those products only.

The book has now modeled two polar cases, one where urban areas are implicitly all monocentric and the other where they are all multinucleated. We now will mix the two cases. Unfortunately, to do so immediately introduces city size lumpiness problems (Chapter 4), which makes formal analysis cumbersome. However, the basic ideas can be outlined. A critical assumption in the metro area analysis is that each core natural resource city of each cluster has sufficient population to support a number of each type of footloose city.[3] However, some resources cities may be so small that they cannot support any footloose cities or only one or two of the smallest types. Moreover, some footloose cities may be so large or their national demand sufficiently small that the whole economy can only support one or two of that type of city. Then only one or two metropolitan areas would have that type of footloose production.

These considerations suggest the following pattern of urban areas. Small independent monocentric cities (and farms) and small metropolitan areas would import almost all footloose products and all natural resource products except the ones in which they are specialized. They would export their own natural resource product to all other types of cities and metropolitan areas. Larger metropolitan areas would be self-sufficient in all except a few footloose products and each would be self-sufficient in only one natural resource product. They would export some footloose production to independent monocentric cities and smaller metropolitan areas. They would each import from all other types of resource cities (whether independent or contained in metropolitan areas) and import their missing footloose products from the very largest metropolitan areas. These few very largest areas would be self-sufficient in all footloose products and in only one natural resource product. They could export a whole range of footloose products to small metropolitan areas and independent monocentric cities, and also could export a few footloose products to medium-to-large size metropolitan areas.

2. Empirical Determinants of Urban Concentration

This section examines the empirical determinants of urban concentration, comparing a cross section of countries. One explanation of concentration will be the extent to which there is clustering of economic activity in an economy. Others will include economy size, geography, level of human or economic development, centralization of government, and so on. Missing from the list, however, are measures of national government "nonspatial" distortionary policies such as tariffs, minimum wages, and capital market restrictions that influence urban concentration and are the focus of Chapter 7. Indices of such distortions were not available for the time period of the sample (roughly 1975), although such indices exist now (see World Development Report 1985, World Bank). An updated analysis should include them, accounting for lags in response to changes in policies.

To do a cross section regression analysis of urban concentration requires a single measure of the size distribution of urban areas in a country. Three measures are commonly used—primacy as measured by the population of the largest urban area divided by the population of the next n largest areas, the estimated exponent of the Pareto distribution as applied to the size distribution of urban areas in each country, and a measure of urban concentration used by Wheaton and Shishido (1979) taken from the standard industrial concentration measure of sum of squared shares (Adelman, 1969). The primacy index is rejected as a measure representing the whole size distribution of cities in a country. The exponent of the Pareto distribution is rejected for two reasons. First, estimation of the parameters for the countries is currently only available as applied to cities defined by political boundaries (Rosen and Resnick, 1978), not metropolitan area concepts, which seems the relevant geographic unit. Second, it is unclear how the exponent will vary as urban concentration varies; Wheaton and Shishido (1979) point out that a large exponent could be estimated for a country composed of a very few large cities and many small ones while Rosen and Resnick (1978) point out that a large exponent is also consistent with any uniform distribution of population across cities whether the cities are large or small! Remaining is the Wheaton and Shishido urban concentration measures, which fortunately are available for cities defined by urban area concepts and which have desirable properties.

The measure of urban concentration for each country is

$$UC = \sum_{i=1}^{n} \left(\frac{N_i}{N}\right)^2 \qquad (10.3)$$

where N_i = population of urban area i
N = total urbanized population
n = number of urban areas

The empirical work uses the inverse of (10.3), which measures urban deconcentration (UD), or

$$UD = (UC)^{-1} = \left[\sum_{i=1}^{n} (N_i/N)^2\right]^{-1} \qquad (10.4)$$

UD has the following desirable properties.

If an economy grows by churning out new metro areas in each size category at the same rate, UD rises in proportion to the increase in the number of metro areas, indicating the *decline* in the *proportion* of the urban population residing in any one metro area or *set* of metro areas. In fact, if areas in a country are of equal size, UD equals the numbers of cities. Second, for a fixed total urbanized population, any shifts of population from a smaller town to a larger town results in UD declining and an opposite shift to a smaller town results in UD rising. That is, any increase in concentration of a fixed urbanized population is captured by the index, as is any movement toward greater uniformity in the size distribution. For example, increased clustering of potentially independent monocentric cities in an economy is reflected in a lower UD.

UD measures are taken from Wheaton and Shishido. Their calculations are based on metropolitan area population figures taken from the 1976 Rand-McNally, *Commercial and Marketing Atlas*. Because different countries use different definitions of minimum size urban areas, a cutoff point must be determined. Wheaton and Shishido base UD on the largest urban areas in each country that account for 70% of the urbanized population, which is consistent with the notions of proportionality inherent in the UD measure.

The hypotheses to be tested in this chapter are as follows.

1. As a country's urbanized population rises, *ceteris paribus, UD* rises. This hypothesis follows directly from a simple growth model such as in Chapter 3, where a country grows by churning out new metro areas under the assumption that it is inefficient only to accommodate the population growth in already existing cities.

2. Holding the urbanized population fixed, UD rises as the extent of agricultural activity rises, measured by either total farm land area under permanent cultivation (CROPLAND) or total employment in agriculture. Increased agricultural activity represents an increase in natural resource activity (fertile land utilization). It requires a spreading out of the footloose segment of the urbanized population to serve the agricultural population with urban services.

3. An increase in the ratio of manufacturing activity to service activity for a given urbanized population leads to an increase in UD. The estimation roughly classifies manufacturing as resource-oriented activity and services as footloose. Thus a relative increase in service production increases the number of footloose industry cities to cluster around fewer resource-bound industry cities.

There are two measures of the ratio of manufacturing to service activity. They both use employment data. The primary measure is percent of labor force in manufacturing over the percent in services, where the latter percent is a residual obtained by subtracting from 100 the percent in manufacturing, mining, and agriculture. Generally included in this residual are employment in wholesale and retail trade, transport, communications, finance, insurance, real estate, and utilities, as well as community, social and personal services. The second employment measure uses for services only this last category of community, social, and personal services that reflects employment in the "modern" service sector, including health care, education, research, recreation, repair services, and public administration, rather than the "traditional" commercial sector. The reason for this distinction is that the "traditional" sector may be less footloose, being part of the economic base of every city.

4. For a fixed urbanized population, countries with federalized systems of government will have higher UDs. A critical assumption in the determination of efficient city sizes is the existence of autonomous local governments competing for residents through optimal provision of urban infrastructure. In highly centralized countries, this competitive mechanism does not exist. These countries may favor (i.e., overinvest in) a few urban areas such as the national capital region at the expense of (i.e., underinvest in) other areas. This draws population into the favored areas away from other areas and hence increases urban concentration.

There are several reasons for the favoritism hypothesis. Centralization removes adequate representation of local tastes in the sense that the national government may not be able to assess local needs. There is no ballot box directly communicating an incorrect assessment of a locality's needs nor is there necessarily a strong incentive to do a correct assessment of local needs. As such, provision of public services may also be biased toward national capital regions and key metropolitan areas, ignoring the needs of other areas.

People working in a centralized system may be biased toward providing the best services in the city where they live and work, assuming that this will increase their quality of life per se. (Hence, they either may ignore or may be able to insulate themselves from the negative effects of the resulting induced in-migration, which may ultimately dissipate the quality of life advantages. Of course, as landowners, they will benefit from increased land values as city size increases.) In a federalized system, their ability to exploit this bias is limited since they cannot control local public services set elsewhere in the country.

In a centralized system there may also be differential extents of corruption. Corruption in the national capital in terms of public service provision may be subject to local censure (from both higher officials, newspapers, etc.). However, central government officials may more easily set up and maintain corrupt provision of local public services in other parts of the country. With inside information, for example, they can privately buy up land where public sector investments are slated in advance of public (re)purchase of this land. Or they can place relatives in key positions in production of local public services. All this activity diverts resources from the provision of actual services. In a federal system they have neither inside information nor appointment power in other localities. And in a federal system, local public officials and their practices are subject to the censure of the local ballot box.

Finally, notions of hierarchy can be exploited in a centralized system. For example, in Brazil (see Chapter 8) and in China (see Chapter 11), there are strong notions of hierarchy. The working hypothesis of central policymakers and formulators is that public investments of all kinds should be focused in key (coastal) metropolitan areas because that is economically efficient (not to mention that they live there). Benefits of such coastal concentration of resources are expected somehow to "trickle down" to the less sophisticated interior regions in a natural efficient process. Federalism limits the power of central bureaucrats to satisfy their provincial tastes and biases.

This federal versus central influence is measured by the use of a dummy variable representing a form of government categorized politically as being federal. The basic criterion is the existence of at least regional legislative bodies with autonomy in the provision of some local public services. Also experimented with successfully was a variable measuring the share of local governments in total government expenditures.

5. The level of technological development should also affect urban concentration, as noted in Chapter 3 and earlier in this chapter. As a country moves from the very low levels of technological development, for example, scale economies in new "modern" manufacturing concerns may be enhanced by these concerns clustering into a few metro areas. As a country moves into standardized production technology, agglomeration economies in urban production may decline as sophisticated communications technology reduces the importance of face-to-face interpersonal interactions and the need for spatially concentrated labor and retail markets. This may lead to urban decentralization and development of dispersed specialized urban manufacturing centers. The level of technological development is measured by the adult literacy rate (reflecting the ability of the population to utilize existing world technology), as well as GNP per capita.

Data. The data on employment are taken from the 1976 *Year Book of Labour Statistics* of the ILO. Apart from *UD*, the rest of the data are from the World Bank (Dillinger, 1979). In general, this cross-sectional data is drawn from the years 1974 to 1976, with some items in some countries going back to 1970. The sample size for the basic regressions in 34 countries. Means and standard deviations of variables are given in Table 10.1.

Results. Table 9.1 shows the empirical results. In the course of the empirical work it became apparent that the manufacturing/service activity variables are related to the measures of technological development, as would be expected from the product cycle theory. Thus once the ratio of manufacturing activity variables are included, the GNP per capita variables become unimportant and some experimentation with the literacy variable is required to yield positive results. Otherwise, the empirical work is as successful as could reasonably be expected. The adjusted R^2's are quite high, indicating that the formulation is basically successful in explaining variations in urban concentration. It should be noted that urban population and the federal variable together account for most of the explained variance (each accounting about equally at the margin).

A 1% increase in urban population generally leads to a 0.19% in *UD*, con-

Table 10.1. Regression Results

	(i) $\log_e(UD)$	(ii) $\log_e UD$	(iii) UD	(iv) UD
$\log_e$(Urban population)[a]	0.191 (1.73)	0.185 (1.67)		
Urban population			0.863×10^{-2} (0.76)	0.640×10^{-2} (0.54)
(Urban population)^2			-0.835×10^{-5} (0.82)	-0.638×10^{-5} (0.62)
Federal system[b] of government	0.541 (2.76)	0.534 (2.72)	7.435 (2.92)	7.390 (2.84)
Cropland[c]	0.495×10^{-5} (1.90)	0.463×10^{-5} (1.79)	0.224×10^{-3} (2.75)	0.208×10^{-5} (2.54)
Manufacturing employ-ment/service	0.345 (1.46)		6.756 (2.16)	
Manufacturing employ-ment/service (residual)		0.904 (1.38)		16.610 (1.86)
(Literacy)$^{-1}$	4.510 (1.09)	4.546 (1.09)	54.200 (1.03)	53.037 (0.99)
Constant	0.639	0.666	-2.940	-2.162
adjusted R^2	0.49	0.49	0.69	0.68

	Mean	Standard Deviation
Urban population	266.213	387.661
Federal	0.441	
Cropland	23417.114	46799.586
(Literacy)$^{-1}$	0.012	
Manufacturing/service employment	0.973	0.395
Manufacturing/service (residual) employment	0.383	0.143
$\log(UD)$	2.298	0.713
UD	13.049	11.737

[a]Urban population is measured in hundreds of thousands.

[b]We have used the following, perhaps arguable, division of countries in our sample. Federal countries are India, Netherlands, Yugoslavia, United States, South Africa, Brazil, Malaysia, Italy, Canada, Germany, Switzerland, Venezuela, Argentina, Australia, and Mexico. Nonfederal are Spain, Turkey, Japan, Sri Lanka, France, Britain, Morocco, Philippines, Iran, Finland, Denmark, Norway, Israel, Thailand, Austria, Greece, Sweden, Indonesia, and Colombia.

[c]Cropland is measured in thousands of hectares.

trolling for all other variables. This positive coefficient reflects an increase in the number of cities. However, the coefficient is low. (Without controlling for other variables, notably cropland, the coefficient is still only 0.38 but highly significant.) In a simple growth model where a country grows by simply replicating the existing distribution of cities the coefficient would be 1. In similar formulations when the dependent variable is simply the numbers of metro areas, the coefficient is about 0.6. Thus the results suggest that concentration in individual metro areas, or in the sizes of existing areas, grow as urban population grows and as the number of cities increases.

The manufacturing-to-service ratio (hereafter M/S) and cropland variables that are central to the hypotheses in Section 1 hold up rather well, considering that they are crude estimates of the ratio of natural resources to footloose production. For the first, increases in M/S lead to increases in UD, reflecting the spatial dispersion of footloose urban production that services resource-oriented production. Both employment measures yield similar effects. A 1% increase in either ratio from its mean leads to about a 0.34% increase in UD. Alternatively stated, a one standard deviation increase in either ratio leads to a 13% increase in UD. These are very strong quantitative effects. The variables are not always highly statistically significant, in light of the gross measurement problems (both in approximating the ratio of natural resource oriented to footloose production and in variations in cross-country definitions and the reliability of the measurement of industrial employment). However, the consistency of the two estimates and robustness of the results across formulations supports affirmation of the hypothesis.

Increased cropland leads to decreased concentration as expected, reflecting the need for the footloose urban population to diffuse spatially to serve the agricultural population. A 1000 hectare increase in cropland (1 hectare = 3.9 square miles) leads to approximately a $5\% \times 10^{-4}$ increase in UD; and a 10,000 square mile increase leads to a 1.38% increase in UD. If agricultural employment is used in place of cropland, the general results are similar.

The system of government in a country has an exceptionally strong impact on UD. Holding all other variables constant, comparing a federalized country (44% of the countries in the sample are federalized) with a nonfederalized country with an average UD, UD almost *doubles*; or $\log_e(UD)$ increases by more than 0.75 standard deviation. Clearly, centralized forms of government provide an environment for the centralization and concentration of urban population.

This result is insensitive to respecifications of functional form or variables used to measure country size, technology, industrial composition, or centralization. For example, if centralization is measured by the central government's share in total government expenditures, a one standard deviation increase in that share (mean and standard deviation of 57.2% and 21.3%, respectively) results in a 0.80 standard deviation decrease in $\log_e(UD)$.

Finally, the measure of ability to utilize existing technology or the literacy rate after some experimentation yields plausible results. Literacy effects are assumed to peter out at higher literacy levels. Given that, the results suggest that as literacy rises [(literacy)$^{-1}$ falls], UD decreases. This captures the notion that increases in usable technology from very low levels are associated with increases in agglomeration effects. This is the basic scale effect of the movement out of traditional production methods into modern methods with basic mechanization. Thus an increase in the literacy rate from 26% (the level for Morocco) to 50% (the level for Iran) leads to an 8% decrease in UD (or 0.12 standard deviation of log UD); or an increase from 36% (India) to 74% (Colombia) leads to a 6% decrease in UD. However, an increase from 74% (Colombia) to 94% only decreases UD by under 1.3%.

3. Conclusions

The primary empirical determinants of urban concentration are the size of country and the system of government. Increases in national urban population decrease concentration. Being a federal as opposed to a centralized country dramatically lowers urban concentration. This suggests that centralized systems tend to favor development of public services and government employment opportunities in one or two cities such as a national capital region, reflecting discrimination against outlying/interior regions.

Also strongly impacting urban concentration is the composition of national output. Increases in relative production of goods utilizing natural resources, such as fertile land or raw material deposits, leads to decreases in concentration, as the population spatially disperses to utilize directly and indirectly the spatially dispersed natural resources. Countries relatively favoring footloose production tend to have more multicentered metropolitan areas, representing clusters of "economic cities," or (sub)centers engaged in different production activities. The clustering reduces the transport costs of trade amongst these "cities," or centers.

NOTES

1. SMSAs have now been replaced by new political-geographic definitions still based on counties. These seek to distinguish between types of SMSAs, such as Metropolitan Statistical Areas (MSA's) for smaller SMSAs that stand alone (do not run into other metro areas), Consolidated Metropolitan Statistical Areas (CMSA) for urban behemoths (e.g., New York, Chicago), and Primary Metropolitan Statistical Areas (PMSA) for metropolitan components of the CMSAs.

2. $|J_0|$ is the determinant of a matrix with diagonal elements $[f - b\beta(1 - \gamma) - a_t\alpha_t]/(a_t\alpha_t)$ and off-diagonal elements all (-1). $|J_j|$ is that determinant when the jth column is replaced by a column with elements all equal to 1. The J_0 matrix is a dominant diagonal matrix and thus there is a unique solution with the $m_j^* > 0$ (MacKenzie (1960)).

3. Suppose the core city can support $n + 1/z$ type j footloose cities of *efficient* size where n is an integer and $z > 1$. If n is large, the $(1/z)N_j$ population can be split among the n cities without significantly altering factor payments; thus for illustrative purposes these fractions are ignored. However, if n is small (e.g., 1 or 2), splitting $(1/z)N_j$ among n cities will alter conditions significantly.

CHAPTER 11

Urban Issues in a Planned Economy: China

Analyzing the urban system of an authoritarian, centrally quasi-planned economy such as China is difficult. First, industrial census data of the type collected in the West do not exist, and any relevant industrial data for local areas are not collected centrally in disaggregated form and generally are not released at the local level. There are few random samples, and data organization and definitions are not based on neoclassical economic criteria. Second, the understanding of the economic system is limited. While in theory it can be analyzed in neoclassical terms, models have not been developed that deal with such phenomena as the equilibrating forces in markets in the face of persistent sources of excess demand or supply, interaction of sectors with different incentive systems, the politico-economic process of investment decisions and allocation of intermediate inputs. In short, any theoretical or empirical analysis of China is necessarily at the moment informal. So why is there a chapter on China?

First, it seems appropriate to have even an informal analysis of the urban system of a "planned economy" country, since it is an introduction to the understanding of the urban system of a large part of the world. Second, it gives an example of how informal analyses can be conducted—what clues one looks for in trying to grasp the nature of the system. Finally, it is an opportunity to give a picture of the Chinese urban system. Most of the data and information collected are based on the World Bank missions to China in the winter and spring of 1984, culminating in a seven volume report on the Chinese economy summarized in the Bank Report No. 5206-CHA entitled *China: Long Term Issues and Options,* May 1985.[1] Data on urbanization were collected both nationally and at the local level in the provinces of Gansu, Jiangsu, and Hubei, representing poor, rich, and middle income regions.

The current Chinese urban system can only partially be explained by "market" forces. Its evolution is also strongly based on the history of government planning and objectives since 1949, as well as its geography and the institutional economic setting. The objective in this chapter is, first, to show how the Chinese urban system is different from the urban systems examined so far in this book and,

Fig. 11.1 China

second, to explain why it is different based on the differences in economic systems. However, before doing that, it is essential to briefly review the geography, history of urban policy, and basics of the current Chinese economic system, so as to have a background for the discussion of the current urban system.

1. Geography, Urban Policy, and the Economic System

1.1. The Country

Figure 11.1 shows the People's Republic of China (PRC). Typically a number of geographic regions are differentiated. An excellent review of this is contained in *China: Socialist Economic Development,* World Bank Report No. 3391-CHA, 1981, the Main Report and Annex C, plus related maps. Briefly, China's vast population must rely on relatively little arable land and varying and uncertain climate. Most of China's population and economic activity is concentrated in the East. While more than half the land area is west of Chengdu, less than 10% of the population and even less of output occur there. The land west of Chengdu is at best generally suitable only for marginal farming or grazing. There are, however, rich mineral and oil deposits in the West.

In the east near 35° latitude there is a mountain range splitting the east into north and south. In general, the southern part has good reliable rainfall, an almost year-round growing season, rich coastal deltas, and dense rural population, although parts of the far south are unproductive mountainous tropical areas. The north outside of Manchuria contains, in the North China Plain, one of the mostly densely populated agricultural areas of the world, and is dry farm based. It features unreliable rain, vast erosion, and dust storms in the spring. While there is a water base from the Huang He (Yellow River), there is a problem of flooding and excessive silt and salt content in the water. Manchuria is much less densely populated and has a rich rural grain base. Industry is concentrated in the big coastal cities such as Tianjin and Beijing in the north and Shanghai in the south, and in Manchuria.

As an overview of economic development, China falls in the ranks of low income countries despite an educational and literacy attainment for its population consistent with middle income rank. Under the current economic reforms of the personal responsibility, or incentive, systems in agriculture, and to some extent in industry, its rate of real per capita income growth is very high (6–7%). There are widespread social services, so health and education services are utilized nationwide. However, the quality variation is enormous. Finally the degree of income inequality is very similar to other low income countries, with the poorest 40% controlling the same proportion of national disposable income as in India, for instance. Even the richest 10% arguably may control almost the same proportion of real incomes as in India. While incomes are fairly equal within and across urban areas and within rural areas, there are vast differences across rural areas and between rural and urban areas, creating the inequality.

1.2. Urban Policy

Prior to the formation of the PRC, only the coastal areas, Manchuria, and to some extent Sichuan were developed and had some type of industrial base. In the 1949–1957 period, the official policy was to neglect the former capitalist coastal cities, and focus on development of "key" industrial cities in the interior, partly to exploit the interior mineral resources and to act as "growth poles." In this period a number of large key cities were established on sites of small regional towns and survive today (e.g., Lanzhou and Xining). Some intra- and interregional migration occurred. However, starting with the Great Leap Forward (1958–1961), there were two major policy changes lasting to the post-Mao period. First, industry was supposed to be decentralized into smaller cities and rural areas. Second, population movements were generally prohibited. In 1958–1961 the commune system and the decentralization of small-scale industry and political power was established. In the period of readjustment (1961–1965) while power was recentralized, heavy industrial development in big cities was restricted and agricultural self-sufficiency ("ruralization") of big cities was stressed. The Cultural Revolution (1966–1976) was antiurban and stressed industrialization of the countryside and widespread rural and small town production of pig iron, chemical fertilizers, cement, electricity, agricultural machinery, and coal. During this last period the national planning system in large part broke down and provincial autonomy and self-sufficiency were critical factors. Good reviews of urbanization policies and de facto location policies are contained in Kwok (1982), Paine (1982) and Lyons (1980).

While this constitutes a brief summary of what are viewed as the key urban policies, their practical impact is limited, in part because direct economic control by the center is so limited in China, consisting only of vertical control. For example, one ministry controls one sector (e.g., energy) but provides little coordination with other sectors. Official policies from 1949 to 1976 supposedly deemphasized development of the formerly capitalist coastal cities; however, those cities remained the overwhelmingly key industrial cities, where concentrated industrial investment still took place. The key point cities of the interior often only had an extractive and gross processing role for raw materials, and dispersed small-scale industries often were unproductive.

The post-Mao period has seen a strong official reassertment of the role of coastal cities. Policy formulations contain strong notions of hierarchy where large coastal cities are given the role of leading smaller and interior cities and smaller cities the role of leading the countryside. Leading means that old technology and machines are exported down the hierarchy and the new technology and investment are restricted to large coastal cities. It also attempts to restrict contact with the West to coastal areas and to delegate parts and less sophisticated product production to smaller cities as suppliers to the larger cities. Finally, leading seeks to limit urban population growth to small and satellite cities.

1.3. The Economic System

The current Chinese economic system is a hybrid of quantity planning, price controls, restrictions on occupational choice, and extensive free market activity. In theory the whole system is guided by economic planning where the levers of control are either prices, quantities, or both. Planning is "twice up and twice down," referring to the way plans from the lowest planning units (the firm or workshop) are initially formulated and sent up through the planning hierarchy of municipal, provincial, and central levels, each with their different (un)coordinated branches and ministries. Plans are then sent back for revision, sent up again, and then returned to production units as directives. In practice, planning at the center involves general guidelines, with successive details filled in by the planning units at successive moves down the hierarchy. Exceptions are central "monopolies" in, for example, parts of the utilities, transportation, and minerals industries, where the respective ministries have vertical control of almost all levels of operations but are poorly coordinated horizontally at any level with other ministries and the general economic plan. Moreover, even the planning for general products at the lowest levels covers only part of almost any firm's production, with "free" markets of some sort operating for almost all commodities, subject to price controls, monopoly elements, and trading restrictions. This overview of the system is now illustrated by examining three different spheres of the economy—the agricultural sector, the state industrial and service sector, and the collective or private industrial sector. While a reference point is the economic system at 1976, the focus is on the current evolving system as reformed post-Mao.

The commune system in agriculture has devolved back to the family as the basic decision-making unit. In fact, communes per se no longer generally exist, and the existing local bureaucracies of communes have had their functions reduced drastically. For the family, while there is no private land in theory, the land rented from the commune (now township) is on long-term leases with promises of "indefinite" renewals. Subletting and accumulation of subletted land are to some extent permitted, and some hiring of outside labor is permitted. In terms of prices and outputs, there is a complex system of quota production for the state, above quota state procurements, and private sales all at different prices. In essence, some intramarginal prices and quantities are controlled, but for most farm products and in most agricultural regions marginal production decisions and prices within at least a band are market determined. The bulk of "basic" agricultural products (grains and oil) are still allocated to consumers outside the market by rations at fixed prices, although even that is changing. But consumption of basic products is supplemented in the extensive free market in fruits, vegetables, and animal protein. Income in any area is determined by fertility of the land rented by the family and intramarginal state prices on quota production and above quota procurements, as well as enterprises in market activities. Farm incomes vary radically by region, as population density and land fertility vary. Rural-to-rural migration to equalize rural incomes is prohibited.

State industry is quite different in that market forces have less impact. On the quantity side, market forces do exist. Only a handful of goods, if any, experience strict central control with complete materials balances and production quotas. As noted before, any strong control tends to be vertical, so there is little overriding horizontal control across ministries at the national or sometimes even the provincial level, thus ensuring that strict material balances for a product generally will be infeasible. State firms do have quota production and allocations of material supplies (not particularly in proportion to each other), but they normally have above-quota production and are responsible for procuring significant proportions of their required inputs. Thus in some sense there are markets for products and raw materials and intermediate inputs. These markets are constrained in at least four ways.

First, even marginal prices on some material and intermediate inputs and most final outputs are strictly fixed in theory. Some effective price variability may be obtained by barter or intra-"firm" or consortium trading at shadow prices, but price controls are quite effective. Similarly, because basic wages are de facto controlled, with little national variation, state industrial employees face the same basic wages in different cities.

Second, restrictions on market operations constrain labor mobility; moreover, the primary purchaser and supplier of "market" products generally is a monopolist—the state. Apart from commercial fairs, wholesaling is almost exclusively done by the state and retailing is dominated by the state.

Third, there are limited incentives in the state industrial and service sector. While in theory there are bonuses to workers, they tend, in effect, to be uniform, based on a standardized number of hours worked. There are now retained profits after corporate income taxation, but the basic tax rate is prohibitive (80%). Also while only 30% of investment is from state funds per se, project selection is controlled. However, some incentive is provided for good performance through potential reductions in marginal corporate tax rates on increased production. Some incentive against shoddy products also is provided by recent greater selectivity in purchasing by the state purchasing bureaus.

Finally, the operation of markets is constrained by limits on the extent of interprovincial trade in particular. Part of the limits derive from the difficulty of interprovincial trade in goods because there is little coordination of interprovincial trade through central planning, and provinces have only recently started to engage in widespread bilateral agreements. Another limit on trade occurs because of the truly anemic road transport network and overburdened rail network. A third example is the lack of a proper legal environment to enforce contracts governing exchange. Since almost no lawyers and arbitrators exist with power to enforce decisions beyond their locality, enforceability for some time to come must rely on reputational considerations.

The third sphere of interest is the small collective and private sector. Private producers, especially of services, seem to face the most unrestricted markets, with prices and quantities determined "freely" in the context of licensing and restricted availability of inputs and space (land). While on the industrial side collective producers in either commune enterprises or urban collectives still face price controls, they seem freer in their choice of products to be produced within a given range of goods and in their choice of suppliers and purchasers. They also seem to have greater de facto price flexibility and work incentives. However, their access to transport and energy sources is more strictly limited. For typically undercapitalized producers, they seem remarkably efficient and boast of meeting orders with "better quality products at lower prices in a shorter time period," than their state-owned competitors.

This completes a textbook review of the PRC. With these abbreviated background notes in mind, Section 2 gives an analysis of the Chinese urban system. The goal is to document the unusual features of this system and explain their evolution based on the unusual features of the economic system. The first focus is on industrial location and the second on population distribution and urbanization.

2. Industrial Location

This section discusses three aspects of the allocation and location of productive activities in China. These are: (1) the degree of local specialization and the degree of diffusion of economic activities, (2) the allocation between big and small cities of heavy and light industry, and (3) the role of rural industry.

2.1. Specialization and Diffusion

Chapter 1 shows that in market economies cities tend to specialize so as to enhance scale economies in one productive activity, and that spatial diffusion of production is very low. For example, for Brazil and the United States an examination of manufacturing activities shows that most cities have negligible or zero employment in any one activity and only a handful have significant employment (say, over 150 employees) in that activity. China does not appear to exhibit these patterns fully, although the detailed data necessary to rigorously analyze the patterns on a national level are not available. However, data for certain localities and provinces are available.

Relative specialization in China does appear to occur in varying degrees and is certainly stressed in current writings—the idea of exploiting scale economies through specialization appears to have wide acceptance as a guiding principle. Casual examination of prefecture level data for Jiangsu, Hubei, and Gansu is consistent with relative specialization across prefectures. Industrial products such as tractors, bicycles, watches, and sewing machines are widely traded across provincial boundaries, which is consistent with some degree of specialization (e.g., 54% of

Table 11.1. Diffusion of Production in China

Production Activity	No. of prefectures producing goods	
	Jiangsu (out of 14)	Hubei (out of 14)
Pig iron	9	3
Steel	13	8
Fertilizers	14	12
Cloth	14	14
Bicycles	12	6
Sewing machines	n.a.	8
Watches	11	n.a.

Source: China: Long-Term Issues and Options: The Main Report World Bank Report No. 5206-CHA, 1985.

state procurements for bicycles cross provincial boundaries). However, trade in these items involves mainly exports from nonspecialized metro areas such as Shanghai, Tianjin, and Beijing (for bicycles more than 60% of trade involves exports of Shanghai and Tianjin). The data available on a few cities also support the idea that there is some degree of specialization. Wuxi (urban population of 0.8 million) in Jiangsu province has 11% of its total labor force in textiles, silk and apparel (1981 Statistical Yearbook of China), the county town of Dingxi in Gansu has a high concentration (15–20%) in public administration and related government activities. Larger metropolitan areas such as Lanzhou (1.4 million urban population) and Nanjing (urban population of 2.2 million), while having as expected more diversified economies, do exhibit some tendency toward specialization—Lanzhou in textiles and primary metals and Nanjing in petroleum and chemicals. However, the suspicion is that in general the degree of specialization is somewhat less than might be efficient, because of the apparently unusually high degree of diffusion of industries.

It appears that most types of manufacturing activities are diffused throughout the economy and found in a very high proportion of cities. The high degree of diffusion existing in the 1970s and before is documented in Lyons (1983). For 1982, for Jiangsu and Hubei provinces, Table 11.1 shows the number of prefectures (a collection of municipalities) involved in different activities which are typically ones of specialization in Brazil or the United States. In Brazil and the United States items such as bicycles, sewing machines, and watches would be produced in only a tiny fraction of cities and cloth in less than 50% of cities. In Jiangsu and Hubei they are found in high proportions of cities. Many items are produced for local sale only at high cost, given the quality of the product. The reasons for the high degree of diffusion and survival of inefficient producers are many and reinforce each other.

As noted in Section 1, diffusion of industrial activities was inherent in the self-sufficiency drive at the provincial and lower levels, which arose following the Soviet withdrawal and continued through the Cultural Revolution. Apart from the rhetoric of self-sufficiency, the poor transport system and lack of horizontal integration in planning across provinces fostered self-sufficiency.

Today, the high degree of diffusion of activities and the tendencies towards partial self-sufficiency are perhaps inadvertently encouraged by a variety of policies and the economic system in general. Some key elements are as follows.

1. *Price system*. For the set of goods traded internationally, state prices for raw material inputs tend to be low in relation to prices for products manufactured by light industry when compared with world prices. This means that trade in materials across regions to some extent involves selling low-priced materials in return for high-priced final good imports. To some extent it then may be more profitable for a region to forgo some of the benefits of specialization and trade, hang onto its own raw materials, and produce a wider range of own final outputs.

2. *Materials allocation*. Given underpricing, there should be a general excess "demand" for materials. For primary metals and energy, there is a reasonably strong central allocation system, leaving a limited market for above quota production and trade across provinces, so that at the margin there may not always be established markets for materials. This is reinforced by the inadequate transport system. Basically, for many local entities, it is difficult to purchase as much materials as desired, given state prices. For many producers, sales of own materials at least through the state system are not profitable, so that firms who are given excessive allocations stock pile materials. The difficulty in acquiring materials for many firms results in scavenging, where a commune enterprise may employ large numbers of people just to search for gasoline supplies above the allotment to its workshops. It also results in small-scale unprofitable production particularly in pig iron and steel at many administrative levels locally, so as to enhance supplies for profitable local production of final products. For instance, it may pay a province to produce pig iron and steel ingots at a "loss" (e.g., Gansu) to ensure supplies for local industries, given the shadow price of steel ingots. All this may enhance diffused local production, reducing the degree of concentration in production.

3. *Transportation*. The transport system is undeveloped. As noted earlier, rails are overburdened and trucking is almost completely undeveloped. Access to rail transport is very difficult for collectives and also difficult for smaller state firms. Moreover, in general trucking is an essential element in encouraging an efficient degree of specialization and trade. Because of transport deficiencies, smaller cities cannot specialize to the degree that is efficient because they cannot ship goods to larger regional markets. They cannot efficiently interact and trade with the rural areas without a better trucking system. Poor transport links also require firms to stockpile inventories of inputs and outputs to ensure that they always have reliable supplies to use in production or to ship to buyers.

4. *The Industrial and Commercial Tax (ICT)*. This is a pervasive tax (at rates varying by commodity) that covers almost all production for sale by all firms. The ICT is essentially a turnover tax. It can be largely avoided by integrating operations and doing all stages of production within the firm, so the tax is only paid on the final stage of production. This encouragement of integration is a distortion that discourages firm specialization and concentration in parts production.

5. *Restricted output*. It appears to be the policy of some provincial and mu-

nicipal light industry bureaus to restrict output of efficient firms, so as to maintain a market for both the higher cost and lower quality output of less efficient firms. In essence there are production limits ("quotas") imposed as trade barriers. This was observed in Jiangsu where the efficient production of the durable Long March bicycles in Wuxi is strictly limited to one million per year (1984), so as to leave a market for the less desired output of other firms in the province. The policy is inexplicable on economic grounds. Much the same story applies to watch production, where the state shows a reluctance to close or alter the production mix of weak firms. This policy encourages a profusion of small scattered firms and discourages specialization and concentration.

6. *Local level planners*. Planners at the lower level pride themselves on the long list of products produced in the city. They encourage investments that continually broaden their industry bases. In terms of the five year plan being formulated in 1984, most large municipalities suggested in preliminary planning that they would radically increase outputs across the spectrum of light and heavy industries and that they would expand into the electronics industry.

7. *Comparison with international standards*. By international standards the service sector in China is anemic, as indicated in Table 11.2. The same data indicate a vacuum in the trade sector—commerce and marketing, which includes in U.S. terms retail and wholesale trade, finance, insurance, and other business services. This sector is vital since it is what makes it possible for regions to trade extensively with each other.

One might question whether the figures for China in Table 11.2 on the size of the service industry are comparable to other countries. For example, almost the entire "commune" economy in rural areas appears to be lumped into the agricultural sector, with only 2% of collective and individual workers in rural areas being categorized in the service section. In contrast, the comparable urban group (staff and workers in urban collective units and individual urban workers) has 29% of its workers categorized in services. This might raise a suspicion that there must be "agricultural" workers doing service activity in rural areas. However, the more detailed figures on commune employment for 1983 refute this notion. Moreover, the notion that the trade sector per se is undeveloped appears to hold up, independent of the question of proper industrial categorization of activity. For example, looking at the *occupational* categories for Wuxi City (the only figures available), only 4% of the labor force is engaged in what appear to be sales activities (purchasing and sales of commodities, financial business, commerce, supply and marketing of materials, and customs officials). In the United States what appear to be similar types of trade activities occupy 12% of the labor force nationally and more in major urban centers.

2.2. Industrial Concentration in Large Metropolitan Areas

In contrast to countries such as India, the United States, and the United Kingdom both currently and historically, China appears to have concentrated both its light and heavy manufacturing in its very largest cities—Shanghai, Beijing, and Tianjin. In Table 11.3, the share of industrial output relative to population shares are noted for groups of Chinese and U.S. cities as well as for individual cities and

Table 11.2. Service Sector

(a) Percentage of labor force in the service industry (1980–1981)

China	Other low income countries	Low middle income countries	High middle income countries	Yugoslavia	Hungary	Romania
15	38	43	51	45	34	27

(b) Percent of labor force in the detailed service sector

	U.S. 1970 Nationally	U.S. 1900 Overall labor force	U.S. 1900 Nonagri. labor force	China 1981 Overall labor force	China 1981 "Nonrural" labor force[a]
Overall trade (commerce marketing, service trade, etc.)	n.a.	14%	23%	4%	14%
Wholesale and retail trade	21%				
Finance, insurance, real estate, and business services	7%				

Sources: Historical Statistics of the U.S.A. (1970), *Statistical Yearbook of China,* 1981, and *World Development Report,* 1980.

[a] For "staff and workers" nationally plus individual urban laborers.

Table 11.3.   Industrial Concentration in Large Cities[a]

Ratios of:	Share in national industrial output/Share of metro areas in national population	Share in national industrial output/Share in national urban population
18 Chinese key cities (1981)	4.5	1.5
15 U.S. metropolitan districts (1914)	2.2	1.0
17 largest U.S. urban areas (1972)	1.1	0.8
Shanghai (1981)	9.8	3.8
Chicago (1914)	2.6	1.2
New York (1914)	2.1	0.9
Chicago (1977)	1.4	1.1
New York (1977)	0.8	0.6
Beijing (1981)	4.7	1.6
Washington (1977)	0.2	0.2

[a] For China, these are for 1981. For U.S., the production figures are from the 1914, 1972, and 1977 Census of Manufacturers and the population figures from the 1910 and 1970 Population Census and Census estimates for 1914.

historical comparisons. Shanghai is compared to the United States's most industrial city (Chicago) and its largest (New York). Beijing is compared with the U.S. capital. Table 11.4 provides more detail, especially for types of industries. Even for Chicago, industrial concentration is much less than in Shanghai or Tianjin, and the two other U.S. urban areas today have relatively little industry and almost no heavy industry. Even doing a comparison with the historical United States, Shanghai's 1981 share of national manufacturing output relative to its population shares is about *fourfold* greater than Chicago or New York in 1914.

The industrial concentration in China's large urban areas might be expected to continue as reflected by the (State Council) investment shares going to these cities in various categories in 1981 (Table 11.4). In particular, Shanghai appears to be the recipient of high concentrations of industrial investment. Industrial investment in Beijing does appear to be less, but not total state investments, as social investments are emphasized. The numbers for 1982 indicate the same pattern, with Shanghai's share of new state industrial investment rising to 13.2%. Provincial figures also support this pattern. For example, between 1975 and 1982 fixed assets of state-owned industries in the four coastal provinces of Jiangsu, Zhejiang, Anhuei, and Fujian rose by 104%, while in the three interior provinces of Shanxi, Gansu, and Qinghai they rose by 71%.

Chapter 8 of the book argues that it is inefficient to focus industrial development on large metropolitan areas, particularly for certain types of heavy industry and for production of standardized products. First, many of these industries only experience localization economies and hence are just as well off in terms of scale effects in smaller cities, where the opportunity costs of land and labor are lower. Second, it is generally more efficient to locate resource-using weight-reducing production processes (e.g., iron and steel) near resource deposits than near consumption centers. Finally, locating heavy industry in large metropolitan areas in-

Table 11.4. Industrial Concentration[a]

Metropolitan Area	Shanghai (1981)	Chicago (1971)	New York (1977)	Beijing (1981)	Washington (1977)
Percentage of national population	1.2%	3.4%	4.9%	0.9%	1.4%
Urban area percentage of urban population	3.1	4.6	6.7	2.7	1.7
Percentage of national industrial output	11.8	4.9	3.7	4.2	0.3
Percentage of light industry	13.1	—	—	3.8	—
Percentage of heavy industry	10.3			4.6	—
Percentage of primary metals (i.e., metalurgy for China)	15.8	5.1	0.1	4.8	0
Percentage of machinery	15.8	5.7	0.1	5.0	0.1
Percentage of state industrial staff and workers	5.8			3.1	
Percentage of new state industrial investment	10.3			2.7	
Percentage of new state investment in:					
Civil public utilities	8.7			16.1	
Culture, education, public health, and social welfare	3.8			8.2	
Research	4.2			29.0	

[a] See Table 11.3 footnote.

volves putting the heaviest industrial polluters in the midst of the greatest number of victims.

The basis for locating production of standardized products in large metropolitan areas would be urbanization economies arising from incubation effects. Incubation effects arise in an infant urban-industrial economy, where there is an absence of high skills and industrial experiences. In China, at this point, these incubation effects for basic heavy industries producing standardized products should not exist to any great extent—China has the largest urban population in the world and ranks high in a variety of industrial products. Of course, there is an ongoing process of adapting new technologies from the West for the production of certain products.

Given these comments, why do policymakers in China focus on industrial development of the three big cities even for standardized products? As noted in Chapter 8, on the surface productivity data might indicate to policymakers that locating industry in large metropolitan areas is extremely efficient. Consider Shanghai. Shanghai's industrial output per worker is 2.4 times the national average. Clearly there are problems in making comparisons since the composition of industrial output in Shanghai is different than that of the nation, and its capital stock may be of different vintage. For example, Shanghai's heavy industry tends to involve the later stages of metals production, compared with the earlier production stages found in smaller cities in the interior. State prices relative to shadow prices tend to be higher for products from later compared to earlier production stages. However, even a less pronounced higher shadow average product per worker could easily be interpreted to mean that industrial investment should be focused on large urban areas.

As noted in Chapter 8, for large urban areas to be as socially efficient as smaller urban areas, they must have much higher average products of labor. This must occur because the social costs of living in larger urban areas are much higher, including the opportunity costs of land and housing, commuting, food, and so on. To assess whether Shanghai's high output per worker indicates that it is a more socially efficient production site would require an assessment of what its opportunity costs of production are and to what extent firms face these costs. In calculating true unit costs of production, four basic adjustments are required. First, an opportunity cost must be assessed for land used in production. Land in production and used in housing for workers is available at a zero financial cost. Land opportunity costs in Shanghai could be 10 to 20 times land costs in nearby cities of size 0.5 to 1 million and 100 to 150 times prices in agriculture. Second, wage costs must be reassessed to account for the additional cost of housing and feeding workers in larger cities. Using numbers from Chapter 8 as a guideline, true labor costs in Shanghai would be 2.5 to 3 times costs in county towns of 10,000 to 15,000. Third, capital costs per unit of output should reflect an opportunity and depreciation cost of approximately 15% of stock value, rather than the 3 to 4% currently used. This would adversely reflect on high capital using cities such as Shanghai. Finally, costs of materials must be reassessed to allow for greater transport and distribution costs of bringing materials into Shanghai.

Thus, it could be possible to take most standardized production activity out of Shanghai, put it in a smaller city on the same scale of operation (hence, in a much more specialized city), and reduce the social unit costs of production. The response by some Chinese officials to this idea is that industrial management in smaller cities is inferior. However, that is merely a product of the state allocation of managers, where better managers are assigned to larger cities. For example,

there is the Shanghai Bicycle Factory, one of the major and visible bicycle manufacturers in the PRC. From its accounting figures it appears that if it had to pay
the full opportunity costs of its production, this would add Y10 to 20 to the unit
cost (about 20%) of each bicycle compared to a medium-size city (including doubling wage costs and pricing land use at Y120/square meter per year for its 180,000
square meters).[2] In other words, transferring the factory to a nearby medium-size
city would save Y10 to 20 bike in opportunity costs, provided that the same excellent management was retained.

There is little to indicate that the pattern of industrial concentration in major
metropolitan areas is changing. If anything, the concentration is increasing. Although from the population perspective officials recognize the social costs of locating people in larger cities (see Section 2.3), this recognition does not appear
to apply to assessing the unit costs of production. The major impetus would be
drastic price reform, which would include removing food and housing price subsidies, taxation of land to raise its price to opportuniy cost, and proper costing
of capital.

2.3. "Rural" Industrial Activity

China's patterns of rural nonfarm activity are markedly different from other developing countries. First, the percent of the rural labor force in nonfarm activity
and the percent of household income deriving from that activity are, respectively,
12% and 11% compared with 20 to 40% in other countries (Ho, 1984). Second,
while in most countries the majority of nonfarm workers engage in service activity, in China the percent is trivial. Finally, within nonservice activities, China has
a very high proportion of people in heavier industries, such as machinery building
and coal extraction activity, besides the expected textile and building materials
industries, and a relatively low proportion of workers in food processing, handi-
crafts, and wood products in contrast with other countries.

Two questions are examined here. First, why within nonfarm activity is there
so much heavy industry? Second, why is there so little nonfarm activity, particularly in the service, food processing, and handicraft sectors?

The heavy industry focus of China's nonservice nonfarm rural activity in part
results from definitional problems. Many of the former large brigade and commune headquarters where heavier industry is found would be counted in the urban
sector in other countries. For example, in Wuxi county, while the official urban
population in communes is 71,600, Wuxi officials considered the actual urban
population of communes to be either 182,000 or 224,000, based upon the populations in the large commune headquarters respectively, excluding or including
local "agricultural" households. Many of these headquarters are industrial towns
with 10,000 or more residents. This definitional problem will be further explored
in Section 3.1.

Apart from the definitional problems, the strong focus on heavier industry also
reflects the general diffusion of economic activity discussed earlier. It is part of
the history of central government policies from 1958 to 1976, emphasizing self-
sufficiency, and it continues under the current pricing and materials allocation
systems.

To understand why there is a lack of service, food processing, and handicraft
activities in rural areas, the functions of small towns in rural areas are examined.
As detailed by Fei (1983), the traditional linking roles of small towns between

farm communities and the industrialized urban sector were largely destroyed in China during the last 30 years. The traditional linking roles in a market economy, such as urban–rural transport, hierarchical commerce, food processing, and household handicraft industries, were drastically reduced by several factors. The state commerce sector with its rigid structure and relatively few rural outlets cut rural commercial activity to a miniscule level and eliminated the detailed functions of different towns in an interactive hierarchical system. The emphasis on grain production and self-sufficiency eliminated many forms of food processing, and much remaining food processing was regionally centralized. Finally, the role of the handicraft sector was sharply cut back in the economic system.

Under the current reforms, these lost economic activities are reviving, with the development of private and cooperative retailing and transport in rural areas. These sectors still are economically deprived because of a lack of fuel, a poor road system, and inadequate supplies of consumer durables to rural commercial outlets. Even the state stores in richer communes in Jiangsu have difficulties in getting supplies of high quality items, with the result that their potential customers often travel to nearby cities to buy the durables they need. The problem remains that the state monopolizes the formal wholesale sector and limits its rural participation. Strong wholesale and transport sectors in rural areas are critical to rural distribution of urban-produced goods. Moreover, as noted earlier, the lack of commodity distribution encourages small-scale inefficient rural production of potentially standardized consumer goods, so that rural areas can supply themselves.

3. Population Location

This section examines urban versus rural and coastal versus hinterland population location with many of the details of the section concerning urban location. We have just outlined basic population location policies in China. Before describing urbanization policies per se, we need to review aspects of the Chinese social system and the classification of people into rural versus urban residence in terms of defining what a city is and what a city's size is in China.

In China population movements are controlled and strictly limited. The mechanism of control is to assign everyone a permanent location, typically the place of birth. The location is either a commune (now township) or city; and housing or land plus other benefits (see below) are assigned by the bureaucracy of that location. Permission to relocate permanently (or even temporarily) can be extremely difficult to receive. Given the vast differences in urban–rural (see below) and rural–rural standards of living, the incentive to migrate, particularly into cities, is strong. The method of controlling population movements has one unfortunate side effect and also affects the definitions of what is urban.

3.1. Urban versus Rural Classification of People and Places

Classifications of people. As part of the control mechanism there has developed in China a type of both de facto and de jure class system. Initially the system was instituted as part of the food allocation system to the nonfarming population. Today it is a policy that protects the status of urban residents and regulates migration. Under the system all people are legally either urban people or peasants. People start life as urban people if and only if their *mother* is an urban person.

A peasant can only become an urban person by gaining regular employment in a state enterprise or becoming a cadre. Urban people get urban grain and oil rations at subsidized prices, rent subsidies, and medical care subsidies from their local bureaucracy. In 1981 it would appear that each urban *person* received on average a Y226 financial subsidy, roughly a quarter of worker income and maybe half of earned family income. Urban people get to vote at the state enterprise level and in urban neighborhood elections. Their children have access to state schools in urban areas. In short, being an urban (or "grain ration") person gives one certain entitlements generally not available to a peasant, even if the peasant has moved to the same city and works in the same firm.

While most urban people live in official urban areas, not all do. State employees and cadres in rural areas are urban people. Also, many people living in smaller official urban areas and de facto urban areas are peasants. These people can be agricultural workers, but most are now peasant–workers or "temporary" people. Peasant–workers in cities appear to work as contract workers in state enterprises, as self-employed or as workers in collectives. Temporary people include students and part-time workers.

It is useful to compare an urban family in an official urban area with a peasant family in a rural area. In particular, the household income of an urban family per capita was still roughly double that of a rural (peasant) family in 1982, although there may still be greater labor force participation in urban areas. Unlike market economies where such a difference in nominal incomes may mainly underlie a corresponding difference in cost of living between urban and rural areas, in China these are real income differences. In fact, given the enormous food subsidies in urban areas and the differences in quality of schooling and medical care, the nominal differences may understate the true differences. Not only is per person consumption of consumer durables much higher in urban areas (the multiples higher in 1982 are for sewing machines 3.1, watches 5.5, bicycles 4.1, radios 2.2, and TV sets 10.2), but so is the consumption of cloth. Even caloric intake, which is typically 20% higher in rural areas in developing countries given the differing physical work requirements, is higher in urban areas in China!

These large income differences generate pressure for peasants to migrate to cities and become grain ration people by obtaining regular employment in state enterprises. Such migration is generally prohibited and obtaining regular (as opposed to contract) employment in state enterprises is very difficult. However, especially in those parts of the country where rural conditions are poor, by moving to the city and obtaining either contract or temporary employment, peasants can gain materially even without the benefits of grain ration status. The difficulties are in finding housing, particularly if one has no grain ration relatives, in moving families, especially children who could be denied access to local schools and medical care, and, in general, maintaining residence without the necessary papers or by attempting to renew temporary permits continually. Some movements do occur nevertheless. To assess the extent of these, the classification of people by urban versus rural residence, as distinct from grain ration-peasant classification, must be examined.

Definitions of urban areas and populations. In China as of 1982, the official urban population was 21% of the total population. That is similar to other low income countries. However, it is very unclear how accurate the 21% figure is. While the 21% is supposed to include the population of all towns with 3000 or more permanent residents, at least 70% of whom are nonagriculture, in practice the actual count to get the 21% may deviate significantly from this definition. First, the definition appears to vary by province. In Jiangsu, for example, the official urban population appears to cover only and all people on urban grain rations (*irrespective* of where they live), while Gansu tries to count all urban residents (irrespective of grain ration status), but only in statutory towns and municipalities.

Second, "temporary" residents are excluded from official urban counts. This includes those officially estimated to be on temporary residence permits in the 1982 Census even if they have been there over one year and are in effect part of a "permanent" (and expanding) population base. Also among the de facto temporary residents are those officially in cities on temporary residence permits but who were reported in the 1982 Census by their families as living in their home villages (the Census does not involve house-to-house interviews or reporting in person). Finally, there are people such as domestics who live in urban areas without any type of registration there. Officials in individual cities cited figures indicating that 5% to 15% of their populations were these types of temporary residents.

A third factor is the long (perhaps on occasion indefinite) lag in upgrading of urban areas from one official category to another, which appears to exclude many small towns from the urban category. In economic terms, China has statutory municipalities (cheng shi) that are cities of more than 200,000 residents, county towns (xian cheng), and other statutory towns (cheng zhen) that are not the seat of a county. The application procedure to change from being a town to a municipality and, more critically, from a rural place to a statutory town seems very uncertain. In particular, township centers (xiang zheng fu), which are the former commune headquarters and administrative villages (xing zheng cun), seem unlikely or extremely slow to be upgraded to cheng zhen status, even if they become large market towns (zi zhen) of 10,000 people.

It is instructive to illustrate this problem with the example of Wuxi municipality in Jiangsu province, which consists of three counties. In the three counties there are one municipality, Wuxi, and two county towns, Yshing and Jiangying. In addition, there are nine statutory towns and 101 xiang. Since the municipality is in Jiangsu, its official urban population is the 0.95 million in the area receiving urban grain rations. If it followed the national criterion for urban populations, its urban population would probably rise to 1.1 million. This would add in the 0.16 million peasants living in Wuxi city and subtract out those receiving grain rations in the xiang.

However, the de facto urban population is considered to be much larger by local officials. First, there are 100,000 official (from the Census) "temporary" residents in Wuxi who have been there for over a year. Second, the county towns contain 30% more people than are officially counted as urban (i.e., have grain ration status). Third, officials would include as urban all residents of township centers that average 5000 to 6500 in population even though in Jiangsu their official urban populations are only one-third of this count and nationally officially they would be zero. The nine statutory towns and 101 township centers together contain roughly 0.62 million people as opposed to Jiangsu's official count of 0.21 million. These adjustments would raise the de facto urban population to 1.65 million, probably a number comparable to counts in other countries. But that is 70% higher than the official estimate.

A caveat is in order. First, based on the numbers for Wuxi city and the two counties in the municipality outside Wuxi county, 18% to 19% of this population is in agricultural or sideline activities, which is high by international standards and reflects the significant agricultural activity in China that occurs alongside factories and apartments in urban areas.

Second, this problem of official counts of urban populations as opposed to counts consistent with typical international definitions appears also in examining suburbs of metropolitan areas. By population density figures, the suburban populations of Shanghai, Beijing, and Tianjin would be counted mostly as urban in the United States. For example, the suburban population density (excluding farm land) in Shanghai is well over 2300/square kilometer. In the United States a population density of 400/square kilometer qualifies as an urban area and densities in the suburbs in New York, Los Angeles, Chicago, and San Francisco (excluding rural areas) are, respectively, 1526, 1906, 1394, and 1551. For Shanghai there appears to be a problem of not including as urban large suburban market towns or industrialized township centers.

Given official definitions, it is still useful to examine China's official size distribution of cities. According to Table 11.5a it is not an unusual distribution by international standards, compared with other large countries, except for its proportion of population in small cities. China seems to have a significantly lower proportion of its population in smaller cities (under 100,000) with only 32% compared to 42%, 41%, and 47% for Brazil, the U.S.S.R., and, India, respectively. This probably reflects in part the omission of large spatial concentrations of people at commune headquarters, which are not counted as urban in China. There may also be a relative true lack of smaller cities given the absence of an infrastructure of small cities performing urban functions (wholesale and retail trade, finance, repairs, and other services).

3.2. Urbanization Policies

Table 11.5b presents the numbers of cities by size and future projections by the Ministry of Urban and Rural Construction. Partially implicit in these figures are the official policies on future urbanization, allowing for only a 7% increase in the numbers of official cities during the next 20 year period of predicted rapid economic development. Thus the growth in numbers and also sizes of larger cities is to be strictly limited at least in official terms. In particular the growth in numbers of regular state enterprise employees and therefore grain ration people is to be strictly limited. Apart from rhetoric on big city evils, one practical reason is to limit state food subsidies to urban people, which already take up over 25% of the government budget. However, an economic rationale is apparent for *part* of the policy.

As documented in Section 3.1, the private advantages of moving from rural areas to cities are large and probably increase with city size in China. As noted in Section 2, however, the *net social* benefit of a worker moving to a large city may be negligible or even negative, given the high costs of feeding, transporting, and housing workers in large cities. Thus from a particular social point of view, it may be optimal to restrict entry to *existing* large cities.

While it may be desirable to restrict existing city sizes, this does not imply per se that the *number* of large cities should not increase. If the service and high tech

Table 11.5a.   Distribution of Urban Population by City Size

Brazil 1970[a]			China 1981[e]		
Over 250,000	49	} 57	1 million+	36	
100,000–250,000	8		0.5 to 1 million	15	} 69
			100,000 to 0.5 million	18	
20,000–100,000	15	} 42			
Under 20,000	27		Under 100,000	32	

U.S. 1970[d]			India 1971[c]		
1 million+	47		100,000+	52	
0.5 million to 1 million	10	} 75	50,000–100,000	12	} 47
100,000 to 0.5 million	18		under 50,000	35	
50,000–100,000	4	} 26			
Under 50,000	22				

U.S.S.R. 1977[b]		
Over 0.5 million	31	} 60
100,000 to 0.5 million	29	
150,000–100,000	10	} 41
Under 50,000	31	

[a] Based on urbanization definitions as described for SMSAs in the United States (*Source: Brazil Human Resources,* World Bank Special Report).
[b] These are for U.S.S.R. "settlements" (*Source:* James Bater, *The Soviet City*).
[c] These are for Indian "cities" (*Source:* A. Bose, 1977, "Urbanization in India," IUSSP Working Paper #3).
[d] These are for U.S. urbanized areas (see previous subsection) more than 50,000 plus urban places <50,000 people (*Sources:* Statistical Abstract, U.S.).
[e] These are for Chinese cities and towns.

sector in China were to rapidly expand relative to other (growing) sectors, this could indicate that many more larger cities would be beneficial. There is also the notion that China is focusing state investment on a few cities to spur industrial growth without labor force growth in those cities. It might be better to spread this investment among a greater number of large cities and thus allow labor force growth in more currently medium size cities so that they can grow into large size cities.

The migration pressure to move to large cities is becoming more difficult to restrain. As noted in Section 3.1 unofficial estimates for large cities already indicate that the number of official temporary workers and unofficial workers is 5%

Table 11.5b.   Number of Cities by Size in China

	1982	2000 A.D. projections
Urban areas over 0.5 million	48	59
200–500,000	71	73
Cities under 200,000	126	253
County and statutory towns	3107 (1983)	3200

to 15% depending on the city. Obviously price reform and elimination of the grain ration–peasant classification would be one way to restrain migration. However, it would imply a massive redistribution of income from the urban to rural sector. This reform would involve increases in agricultural prices, elimination of urban food and housing subsidies, and shadow pricing of land and hence of housing in cities. Naturally urban people oppose these types of reforms and prefer the status quo of prohibited migration. Particularly, the cadres who have experienced already a loss of power in the post-Mao period are entrenched against losses in their absolute standard of living.

The second aspect of urbanization policy in Table 11.5b is that while the number of small cities is projected to double, the number of county level towns will remain unchanged. The population of existing county towns is projected to double to 140 million. While given current tendencies there should be rapid growth in urban areas under 200,000, the miniscule increase in the number of county level towns implies that the growing industrialized township centers (commune headquarters) will not be permitted to become statutory towns.

What are the social implications of these plans? First, the current expansion in urban labor forces in small cities and towns is primarily through contract workers—that is, peasants who will not be granted urban, or grain ration status. This division within cities between those with urban entitlements and those without could produce social conflicts if left intact. Under current guidelines workers but not their families will be allowed to move to county level towns. This implies either that families will be split or that generally only single people will move. However, single people eventually want to marry, implying that they are likely to seek out other single peasant workers in the city or to bring rural spouses into the city by whatever means. While the new migrants may be happy to accept these restrictions in return for an increased living standard, their children could resent the classification imposed on them by birth that sets them apart from their de facto neighbors in terms of living standards, political rights, and access to urban schools and medical care.

Second, the continued separation of official urban and unofficial urban areas (largely township centers) could, as living standards rise, produce strong pressures to remove these arbitrary classifications. Within rural areas, as township centers continue to industrialize, there may become a social distinction between people who have high paying commune enterprise jobs and those who have lower paying agricultural jobs. Within townships, at least in parts of Jiangsu, some transfers of industrial profits to agricultural workers occur through subsidization of grain procurement prices. Also, industrial jobs tend to be spread around among township households. However, such equitable treatment may not prevail everywhere or last indefinitely. One already sees a distinction between the young who get industrial jobs and the old who are left on the farms, and between the better educated and the less educated. In a decade or so, these individual distinctions could easily turn into distinctions across entire families, where there will be high income "urbanized" rural families and low income "agricultural" rural families living within short disitances of each other. Again, this situation could nurture social tensions. Price reform would help this situation by raising agricultural prices and incomes relative to industrial prices and incomes, which would induce rather than force people to farm. But again, this implies massive income redistribution.

Finally, under the current system there is a hierarchical brain drain involved. Higher education is the key to moving up the system from agricultural to commune industry employment and from rural to state enterprise employment and urban status. The strong selection process for higher education starts early with the selection of students to attend key schools starting at the junior middle school level or even earlier. The best rural students will go through the higher education system and graduate into a state enterprise with urban status. The next best set of rural students will graduate from high school and get formal technical training locally and then a good paying job in a local industrial enterprise with, perhaps, a change from rural to urban status. There is only a very limited economic basis for this type of social hierarchy. Agriculture and rural industry also need bright, well-educated people. In fact, as noted in Chapter 6, in a developed country such as the United States, there is a zero correlation between city size and the ratio of well- to less-educated people.

3.3. Regional Issues

The other aspect to migration and population location concerns regional population issues of peasants especially. Under the current system, the policy basically permits no interregional movement of rural people and low skill workers, "free" movement of high skill workers from richer to poorer regions, and temporary (1–5 years) movement of high skill workers from richer to poorer regions under cooperative arrangements between provinces.

The most basic economic problem concerns the inability of agricultural workers to move. In some regions families are farming land year after year that is unable to support them; thus, they must subsist in part on grain transferred in by the state (e.g., Dingxi County in Gansu). There is no economic basis for people farming unproductive land when there are so many other productive opportunities in the economy. Moreover, as a basic equity issue, peasants in richer areas have incomes several times higher than in poorer areas. This income gap is not a difference based on skill and ability differentials per se or an effort—it is a gap based primarily on birthright and migration restrictions. However, elimination of the restrictions on migration could involve uncontrolled migration not just between rural areas but also to existing large cities. The latter would probably be socially inefficient.

This rural inequality in cases such as Gansu, is compounded by other considerations. Although suffering from poor agricultural conditions due to geography and lack of rainfall and water economically able to be tapped for irrigation, Gansu has a fairly rich mineral base. Gansu is paid no royalties on its minerals, and the entire nonferrous sector has been taken over by the Center. Moreover, the labor force recruited in the 1950s and 1960s for state enterprises involved in primary metals and related activities was largely brought in from outside the province (over 1 million workers, in a province with about 2.3 million grain ration people currently). Thus the employment opportunities in the state sector were largely closed to the indigenous residents. Minerals are priced far below world prices and shipped to coastal areas for processing into high-priced consumer goods, which are then exported back to Gansu for sale. In short the indigenous people of Gansu are constrained to farm largely unproductive land and remain very poor. They cannot migrate to richer agricultural areas, and they cannot derive benefits from their rich natural resource endowments.

4. Conclusions

This chapter examined the regularities and peculiarities of the Chinese urban system. The peculiarities were related to the nature of China's economic system. In terms of industrial location, there is broad diffusion of industry absent in Western economies. Each municipality has a wide industrial base, producing a wide range of products often inefficiently and often just for local consumption. This implied low level of intercity trade was encouraged previously by self-sufficiency drives; today it is supported by high costs of trade in terms of transport and wholesaling, restraints on trade, and the pricing system, as well as local government policies that encourage broadening of the local industrial base and continued survival of inefficient producers.

China is similar to Brazil in encouraging new industrial development in only the largest cities. The policy appears misguided and stems from an incomplete assessment of the costs of locating heavy and standardized production in large coastal cities. Land and labor are priced far below opportunity cost in large relative to small cities.

China prohibits rural to rural migration and restricts rural to urban migration and transformation. There are large income differences between urban and rural residents and between rural residents of different regions. Removing restrictions on migration would result in massive population movements. Such movements to large existing cities would probably be socially inefficient and, under the current pricing scheme, free migration would result in an irrational pattern of population location. Thus migration is restricted.

Part of the method of restricting migration is the classification by birth of people into urban versus peasant status. Generally, peasants can rent land only from their own commune-township and can get their grain allocations only from there. Similarly, urban residents require permits to get their subsidized rations and housing, and are generally restricted to live in the city of their birth unless officially transferred. Thus migration restrictions result in a status based upon birth, which confers enormous differentials in economic well-being. Of top status are urban people, followed by rural people in rich rural areas, and, below, by the poverty-stricken residents of poor rural areas. It is paradoxical that such a class system is maintained in a country that prides itself on its egalitarian approach to social services.

Eliminating the system and moving to a situation where migration is based on socially correct private incentives would involve opportunity pricing of urban land, reflection of transport costs in retail goods, opportunity cost pricing of urban labor, increases in prices of agricultural produce, opportunity cost pricing of capital, and so on. Apart from dismantling the price control system, such a solution and the resulting migration would imply massive redistribution of income from the current urban people to the peasants. Naturally this would be an unpopular solution among the urban and politically dominant elite.

NOTES

1. The author was part of the 1984 spring mission that visited Beijing and parts of Jiangsu and Gansu provinces. The information in the chapter is based on both published

sources and notes from the extensive meetings with officials in all places visited plus numerous site visits to factories and residents. I have not attempted here to reference the latter source of information partly because of disclosure problems. Many members of the mission were very experienced travelers in China and also were fluent in Chinese. I have no reason to believe that we were shown "Potemkin" villages and factories or were given misleading information, although data were often withheld. It seemed the Chinese intended to display both their prosperous areas (Jiangsu) and reveal without dissembling their abjectly poor areas (Gansu). The author's private visit to China in 1985 to some of its poorest regions, involving visits to unauthorized places and on-the-spot unofficial visits to factories, homes, and schools, only confirmed that what was seen the year before was authentic.

2. In 1984, at official exchange rates $ (U.S.) $\approx$ 2Y. By early 1986 officially $ (U.S.) $\approx$ 3Y. Black market rates coverting $ U.S. directly into RMB ("People's" currency) ranged from 3.5Y to 5Y although that may reflect simply the demand for currency ($ U.S. or FEC) by consumers wishing to purchase special products unavailable in RMB (or available only after an extensive queue if paid in RMB). The official exchange rate may be a reasonable number for the international (as opposed to Chinese domestic) currency prices.

CHAPTER 12

Conclusions

The Introduction discussed the two broad themes of this book. The Conclusions summarize the key findings that support these themes. Related points from different chapters are pulled together and to some extent the findings of the individual chapters are reevaluated for consistency and a fresh overall interpretation.

The first theme is that the system of cities in an economy and the processes and pains of urban growth and development are orderly phenomena explained by simple economic models and verifiable by basic econometric work. In particular, the Introduction stated

> For example, in developing countries, the processes of massive rural-urban migration, population explosion of large metro areas with their overcrowed industrial neighborhoods and squatter settlements, deconcentration of industries from large metro areas into specialized smaller cities, switches in production patterns of cities, draining of skilled workers from small towns, and individual city limits on growth and entry are all natural outcomes of market forces operating in particular institutional environments.

The second theme is that many government policies have unintended spatial impacts distorting the spatial allocation of resources and in general unnecessarily increasing the degree of urban concentration. While increasing the degree of urban concentration may sound innocuous, in practice it involves massive flows of people from traditional towns into large metro areas, eroding the country's traditional social fabric, and requiring massive reinvestment in urban infrastructure in these large metro areas with the accompanying financial and administrative burdens. The government policies inducing these changes may be politically necessary, desired given particular (noneconomic) national objectives, or mistaken. For desired policies the spatial reallocations are necessary and the economist can simply point out the economic costs of the programs. For other policies, one can try to point out ways to ameliorate their effects. The conclusions reevaluate typical government policies that distort the degree of urban concentration, note their impacts, and discuss the ways governments try to affect population location, sometimes with the intent of ameliorating the spatial impacts of other policies.

1. The Economics of Systems of Cities

1.1. The System at a Point in Time

About half the urban areas in a large free market economy such as the United States or Brazil are specialized in traded good output having anywhere from 10 to 40% of their employment in, typically, just one three-digit manufacturing or service activity. Thus it is possible to classify many urban areas into types, such as steel, auto, or textile cities, or college and state government cities. Cities smaller than urban areas or SMSAs (under 50,000 in the United States and 20,000 in Brazil) are also known to be highly specialized according to the hierarchy literature. Complementing this relative specialization in production is the fact that production of the manufacturing goods in which cities specialize is not diffused. Most cities have zero employment in these industries, some have small to medium employment, and a few, the specialized ones, have high concentrations of employment. Different types of cities generally appear to have different equilibrium sizes, although it is difficult to find samples sufficiently large to be precise about this. However, it appears that among urban areas the smallest types are traditional resource processing centers such as food processing and pulp and paper, followed by traditional manufacturing such as apparel and textiles, then modern processing or heavy machinery such as steel and autos, then sophisticated and diversified machinery, and finally, in the largest metro areas, high tech and modern services such as finance, insurance, entertainment, and advertising.

A basic reason why specialization occurs might be that economies of scale in manufacturing production tend only to depend on own industry size, not on the general scale of economic activity. That is, economies of scale are ones of localization and not urbanization. Also, for any city size with its associated rent gradient and cost of living, economies of scale are best exploited by concentrating traded good employment in one industry, rather than by dissipating the exploitation in any one industry through diffusion of employment. Econometrically, in Brazil, the United States and to some extent Japan, most heavy and many light industries display only localization economies, not urbanization economies. In particular, the industries that cities tend to specialize in display localization economies, whereas ubiquitous types of industries such as nonmetallic minerals, furniture, and printing and publishing display no localization economies.

In general in manufacturing, localization economies start off high at low levels of local own industry employment (500 in Brazil, 2000 in the United States), where a 10% increase in industry employment generates a 1 to 2% increase in firm output for the same firm inputs. However, scale economies appear to generally peter out as local own industry employment reaches high levels, one factor limiting (the benefits of) urban agglomeration. These economies of scale are Hicks' neutral in terms of capital vs. labor employment, but tend to be high skill relative to low skill using. Finally, not only do most manufacturing industries not display urbanization economies, but their economies of scale also appear to be unaffected by employment in related industries. Thus when related industries locate together, it is not for internal manufacturing efficiency per se but generally to conserve on transport costs of interindustry trade in intermediate products.

When we view any individual city, heuristically speaking, we see that equilibrium size is achieved by trading off the marginal benefits of further scale economy exploitation against the rising marginal costs of providing housing and commuting services as city size increases. Cities specialized in traded goods with greater degrees of scale economies have larger sizes because the marginal benefits of increasing city size have shifted out so as to intersect the marginal costs at a larger size. Because the magnitude of scale economies varies across industries, equilibrium (and efficient) city sizes vary by city type. Each of these different sizes by city type are in net as efficient as each other, so that small types of cities can pay the same utility and capital rental rates as large types of cities. In a simple model, although wages payable rise with city size, urban costs of living rise by the same percent to maintain the same "real" wage. Econometric results suggest in the United States each 1% increase in city population is accompanied by a 0.50% rise in wages, while in Brazil the wage rise is 0.63%, both controlling for skill composition and holding amenities fixed. In practice, some endogenous amenities may improve with city size so that actual compensating wage differentials are less. For example, in Southern Brazil, there is a threefold compensating differential for low skill steel workers between Grande São Paulo (more than 10 million people) and small steel towns of 10,000 to 20,000, a magnitude supported by studies on cost-of-living differentials.

The equal net efficiency of different size cities and the implications of that appear to be overlooked by planners in some state capitalist societies (Brazil) and some planned economies (PRC). Compare steel production in a smaller city (100,000 population) with that in a larger (1 million) city. To pay the competitive wages that are perhaps twice as high in the larger city, the average product of labor in the larger city in steel production must be approximately double that of the smaller city. This has two implications. If a policymaker notices that an average product of labor in steel in the larger city is 1.5 times (rather than twice) that in the smaller city, that means in net that steel production is *less* efficient in the larger city, not the reverse. Usually the deduction is the opposite. Second, in general, steel cannot competitively achieve the higher marginal products and pay the higher wages in metro areas because there are either no or insufficient scale benefits from locating there. For steel producers to locate in larger metro areas and hire labor, they must, for example, have very high capital-labor ratios induced by subsidized capital (Brazil) or underpriced labor (PRC).

Given different types of cities have different equilibrium sizes, in theory there is a correspondence between the industrial composition of national output, the numbers of cities of each type, and the size distribution of cities. For example, as the composition of national output shifts from traditional to modern manufacturing industries, the degree of urban concentration, or the ratio of larger to smaller cities will rise. Thus any government policies that impact the composition of national output potentially affect the degree of urban concentration.

In application, this relationship between the composition of national output and the size distribution of cities and index of urban concentration is an imprecise one at best. First, the relationship between city type and city size itself is a noisy one. For most types of cities the standard deviation of average size is very large. The size of a particular city depends on natural site amenities (climate, access to national markets, coastal or noncoastal location) and on historical and "accidental" factors (age and appropriateness of urban infrastructure and efficiency of the public sector in providing flows of urban services). Cities on better sites have shifted up utility schedules they can offer. These cities then expand in size. With free entry, expansion occurs until the benefits of better site quality in terms of realized utility levels are dissipated through increases in city sizes and associated costs of living. The beneficiaries of the dissipation are landowners. The relationship between city size and type is also a noisy one empirically, because empirically typing is done at a two- or three-digit industry level, whereas it often may occur at four- or five-digit level.

The imprecision of the relationship between national composition and the size distribution of cities also occurs because of failure to type about half of the urban areas. Many cities are highly diversified in certain types of manufacturing or interactive service activity, and others may be only somewhat specialized or specialized in fairly unique activities. Typically these are larger urban areas. In typing, there is also another problem, this one conceptually more difficult.

The theoretical notion of a city of limited size is a monocentric city, where each expansion in size entails increasing commuting and congestion costs. However, metro areas are typically multicentered and could be interpreted as clusters of potentially monocentric cities that are spatially separate. These cities cluster together to form a multinucleated metro area to conserve on the transport costs of intercenter trade. For the overall economy, production is bound to specific geographic locations, through transport cost considerations, because of the need to process (in weight-reducing fashion) deposits of raw materials or semiprocessed materials. Centers of footloose production then cluster around these resource bound centers for the purposes of trade in both outputs and intermediate inputs. Large resource bound centers with critically sized consumer markets attract many footloose centers while the smallest resource bound centers attract none and stand as monocentric cities. As the ratio of footloose to resource bound production in an economy rises, the extent of clustering or the sizes of metro area and, hence, the measures of urban concentration should rise, ceteris paribus. Indeed in cross-country comparisons this relationship holds. However, again it is an imprecise relationship. There are difficulties in classifying activities into resources bound or not, especially since that classification varies across economies with the level of economy development. Also the specification, for example, of the congestion costs of increased clustering or increases in individual large metro area sizes is problematical.

1.2. The System in Motion: Economic Growth and Development

In a simple model of a system of cities, given the efficient sizes for each type of city, steady-state economic growth simply involves replication. As national population grows, all types of cities in a large economy grow at the rate of national population growth. Individual city sizes are unchanged; so if the economy doubles in population, the system of cities replicates itself with the number of cities of each type doubling. Empirically in cross-country comparisons controlling for the level of economic development and land area, doubling the size of the economy almost doubles the number of cities. Individual city sizes also increase.

There are several possible explanations of the cross-section relationship. Two involve Ricardian influences. Each country has an endowment of urban sites of differing natural amenities and hence qualities. Through competition the best sites are occupied first and, with population growth, successively lower and lower quality sites are occupied. As lower quality sites are occupied, the comparative advantage of cities on higher quality sites rises relative to the quality of the lowest occupied site. As national population expands and the quality of the last occupied site declines, then the sizes of existing cities increase with their increased comparative advantage. Thus, if we control for national land area (a proxy for the availability of different quality urban sites), with population growth, existing cities will grow and new cities will form.

The second Ricardian influence involves raw material endowments. Within a country there is a spectrum of resource deposits of differing availability. Expanding extraction involves exploiting high cost/lower quality sites. Thus in controlling for land area, as a country's population grows, the ratio of nonresource using production to raw material dependent production may increase as expanding resource dependent production becomes relatively more costly. Also raw or semi-raw material import shares may rise. In that case with population growth, the ratio of footloose to resource-bound production may rise, increasing the extent of clustering of production centers and the observed populations of metropolitan areas. Thus, if we compare different countries, controlling for land area, the level of economic development, and only partially for the ratio of footloose to resource-bound production, population growth could be accommodated through both the growth of numbers of cities and the sizes of existing urban areas.

It is more complicated to observe how growth in a country over time is accommodated. With growth over time comes technological change and changes in the composition of output worldwide. Technological improvements, especially in transportation and commuting, lead to increases in efficient city sizes. In fact, the increase in urban concentration in the United States over the last hundred years can be correlated roughly with commuting technology improvements. Thus population growth and technological improvements may have opposing effects on urban concentration.

As technological improvements increase efficient city sizes at a point in time, the number of currently required cities falls. First, if urban infrastructure capital is immobile and nonmalleable, there may be some abandoned towns and infrastructure. Second, across the types of cities, producers in formerly smaller types of cities may shift their location to original larger types of cities because of their desired increases in size and required infrastructure and because of the declines in required numbers of original larger type cities. Thus there may be considerable shifts in production patterns, given the immobility and nonmalleability of urban infrastructure.

The process of economic development, of course, is a form of economic growth. We typically think of it involving a switch from traditional goods (textiles) and technologies to successively more modern goods (steel and machines) and technologies, where the switch may be driven by forced increased saving (and investment in capital goods), by exogenous technological changes, by changes in social institutions, by changes in educational attainments and possibilities for effective technologies, and so on. Regardless of what drives the process, the switch from "traditional" to "modern" goods and processes appears to universally involve a switch from traditional small towns and cities into large types of cities. The switch is effected by rural-urban migration, small town to large city migration, growth of some existing towns (suitable as sites for modern production), and decline of other existing towns.

In terms of urban phenomena, notions of the product cycle will be relevant for a developing country. A developing country goes through processes of adapting existing technologies from abroad. Much like the process of refining entirely new technologies, adapting existing technology involves extensive experimentation and refinement to discover exactly what processes best meet consumer needs and best match the existing quality of factors and relative endowments at that stage of economic development. Such experimentation may be best carried out in large metro areas with their ready consumer markets for experimenting, their easy information flows, their available specialized and skilled laborers, and their large institutional and perhaps national governmental sector. Once production processes become standardized and adapted to the social and economic environment of the country, then production can deconcentrate to smaller cities with their lower labor and land costs. Such scenarios have been used to explain the increases in urban concentration experienced in some developing countries, which are then followed by a stage of deconcentration.

For some smaller countries, the explanation of the concentration-deconcentration sequence could simply lie in the development of institutions for properly functioning land and capital markets, which may accompany the development process. One of the key assumptions of a model where the timing of the formation of new cities is efficient is that there are active entrepreneurial land developers who have access to developed capital markets and who operate in an environment where land markets function properly with clearly defined and transferable property rights. Appropriately timed formation of new cities is not based on atomistic moves of consumers, but rather involves mass movement and inhabitation of new cities in relatively short spaces of time. Such moves will only occur if there is an institutional and market environment where entrepreneurs coordinated with local governments can facilitate mass movements by providing appropriate infrastructure for housing and industrial development and advertising of opportunities.

For example, the typical development of new large cities probably involves rapid development of an existing small town into a large city. That involves manufacturers and land developers coordinating with local governments to provide necessary roads, utilities, industrial parks, and residential developments, along with the necessary financing. If the institutions for financing and massive land development do not exist in a country, the development of new large cities outside, say, the national capital region, will be inhibited until such institutions or their substitutes develop. For some countries there may be an ongoing problem of overconcentration of resources in one or two metro areas because of the lack of an institutional environment for the development of small towns. If such institutions develop, then deconcentration may quickly follow.

1.3. Details of a System of Cities

Apart from the examination of a system of cities at a point in time and evolving over time, several basic considerations remain. First, how and why does the population composition of cities in terms of high skill versus low skill labor vary across cities? Second, although the production patterns of cities in general has been discussed, there is the question of how to start predicting what an individual city will produce, or more generally, in what locations production of various goods is likely to occur.

Skill composition of cities is determined by the interaction of the demand for different skill groups on the part of a city's industries and the supply of different skill groups to a city. On the demand side, there is the issue of whether skill intensities vary across industries and whether skill groups are readily substitutable, so that cities find it relatively easy to absorb and substitute different skill groups. Econometric work for Brazil and the United States indicated that, for manufacturing, different skill groups tend to be complements or weak substitutes so that skill ratios in production are quite inflexible. This means that if a city is specialized in a manufactured traded good product in general, the composition of its labor force (at least in traded good production) does not respond much to changes in supply conditions and the prices of one skill group versus another. Second, the intensity of high to low skill usage according to type of manufactured good and corresponding type of city, tends to rise with sizes of different types of cities, suggesting the use of high skill to low skill labor will also rise with city size.

It should be observed that this relationship may not apply to larger metro areas since they tend not to be specialized in manufactured products. It is also weakened because the bulk of city employment is in nontraded good production common to all cities, where skill usages may not vary widely across cities. Third, while skill ratios and city sizes are positively correlated in Brazil, they are not in the United States, suggesting that in nonmanufacturing cities either skill usages do not rise with city size or there are forces on the supply side offsetting the impacts of the industrial demand for labor.

On the supply side, two basic considerations are at work. First, different cities have different endowments of natural amenities, such as climate and access to outdoor recreation alternatives. If different skill groups value these amenities differently (defined by percentage of wages they are willing to forgo), then a site with one particular combination of amenities will attract the skill groups that relatively value such an amenity the most. This type of statement can be extended to manmade amenities that are inflexible given historical or institutional factors. Such amenities include urban infrastructure investments and state set characteristics of the schooling system. In general from econometric work, measures of amenities often receive approximately the same value by different skill groups or are valued by none. In terms of the latter it appears that for many amenities their variation within cities is of more importance than across cities. Examples may be pollution levels, burglary rates, and efficiency of provision of city services. In terms of differences in evaluation, only better climate in the United States and better schooling characteristics in Brazil seemed to be substantially and significantly valued more highly by high skill people.

The second consideration on the supply side is that city population and city population composition in themselves either may be amenities or may be the prime determinants of consumer variables such as the cost of living, the availability of specialized and sophisticated consumer products and services, and the quality of local public services (peer group effects in schooling), and the effectiveness of the local government. In terms of population amenities high skill people appear to have a lesser aversion than low skill people to larger cities, while low skill people appear to have a strong preference for locations with a greater high skill to low skill population composition. This heuristically suggests a (potentially stable) pattern where high skill people agglomerate in large cities and low skill people to some extent follow them there, helping to populate large cities.

2. Government and the System of Cities

The book covers both normative and some positive aspects of government operating in an urban system. The normative analysis provides a benchmark of what the relevant role of government is in population allocation and as such is worth reviewing. Unfortunately, the actual impact of government upon population allocation is both so profound and far from the benchmark that, in practical terms, first best welfare analysis at least may have little relevance. The real focus must be on national government policies and institutions that impact perhaps unintentionally on population allocation across the system of cities. We need to identify the impacts of these national government policies and analyze when it is appropriate to attempt to ameliorate their impacts.

2.1. The Welfare Economics of Population Location

In terms of first or second best welfare economics, there are many population externalities present in a system of cities, such as scale (dis)economies in production, population congestion, and fiscal externalities created by financing in the public sector. In terms of analyzing the impacts of these externalities, there are three cases. The first is a large economy with "many" cities of each type. In that case externalities are internalized. Equilibrium city sizes are achieved when markets set city sizes to maximize utility levels, holding capital rental returns fixed, so that equilibrium sizes are Pareto-efficient. Even if other unpriced nonpopulation externalities such as pollution are present, no second best population policies are implied. Equilibrium sizes, accounting for these other unpriced externalities, are achieved so as again to maximize utility for any given return on capital.

The second case is a small economy where for existing types of cities there are a small number of each type. Lumpiness, or discreteness problems in solving for city size, is present and sizes are not set to maximize potential utility on utility paths. In general for all cities, the marginal benefits of adding population either exceed or fall short of the marginal costs. An optimal population policy calls for city sizes to be set so that the *gap* between marginal benefits and costs is equalized across all types of cities. In general, this will require a set of taxes/subsidies on residence in the different types of cities, which could only be imposed by a national government. However, no actual national government population policies are based on these notions.

The third case is a mixture of the first two. For at least one type of city in the economy, there is a large number of that type—this could even be farm communities. Then sizes of that type have no lumpiness problems and will be set so that the social marginal benefits and costs of adding population are equalized, or the gap between the two is zero. However, there are some types of cities that are limited in number, meaning that lumpiness problems persist. These types of cities will tend to be overpopulated compared with those types whose numbers are many. However, national government policies to correct this are not necessarily required.

There is an incentive for landowners in a city (who could be some group of original residents) to restrict city sizes by imposing some type of entry fee. Profits from entry fees are maximized by setting city sizes at Pareto-efficient levels where the marginal utility benefits of adding population equal opportunity costs (the going utility rate in the economy), so that the gap between social marginal costs and benefits is zero. This is in contrast to equilibrium levels where city sizes expand until average utility benefits equal opportunity costs. Note the intended analogy with unpriced common property resources (a city) where the appropriate policy is to restrict labor employment so that the marginal product rather than the average product of labor equals opportunity costs.

Entry fees in reality typically are not direct, although original residents could restrict entry through zoning regulations, and collect entry fees imposed as a lot size surcharge by land developers who must transfer the surcharges to original residents in return for development rights. However, fees may be indirectly collected and entry restricted through discriminatory provision of public services and land allocation and discriminatory tax-assessment policies. So original residences may live in neighborhoods with the best public services, later residents in legal neighborhoods with minimum quality public services, and the last residents in unstable squatter settlements with no public services.

To the extent this last scenario is generally the case, national government population policies to correct population externalities are probably not required generally. Moreover, the information requirements for calculating correct national population location taxes and subsidies are prohibitive, and the impacts on city sizes of mistakes very large. Thus, if there is a base type of city in an economy (e.g., farm communities) where the numbers of cities are very large, and if local landowners (or their representatives such as a local government) have the tools (zoning, discriminatory provision of public services) to restrict entry in other types of cities, it seems most reasonable to assume entry will be internally restricted to potentially overpopulated cities. That is, national government population externality policies may not improve things. This could be one reason why no such articulated policies really exist in any countries.

Population location policies that do exist have two bases. First, certain federal countries, especially multilingual and multicultural ones such as Canada and India, have constitutionally stated objectives to maintain a mosaic. That is, a noneconomic objective (or argument in the country's "social welfare function") is to retain regional identities. Retention of regional identities requires limiting mixing and interregional population movements, which may in turn require interregional transfers to maintain approximate equalization of interregional standards of living, as comparative advantages among regions change over time.

Second, rather recent population location policies involve attempts to deconcentrate or limit the concentration of population in certain large metro areas, typically national capital regions. These are intended as nth best policies, correcting for adverse impacts of other national government policies. To evaluate the appropriateness of deconcentration policies, the other government policies that are creating the hypothesized problem must be examined. This brings us to a general examination of the "unintended" spatial impacts of nonspatial national government policies.

2.2. The Spatial Impacts of Nonspatial National Government Policies

This summary distinguishes between three types of national government policies. The first type are policies designed to deliberately alter the composition of national output. The second type are pricing policies with particular equity or political objectives. The third type concern the national institutional and constitutional environment for providing local public services. Not only do the three types have different spatial impacts but the desirability of offsetting population location remedies differs.

The first type includes tariff protection policies, national forced savings policies that raise the rate of capital accumulation and production of capital goods, and capital market subsidies available to producers of designated products. In general, all these policies favor the national expansion of certain goods at the expense of others. In developing countries the favored goods tend to be modern capital goods such as steel and nonferrous metals, machines, and transport equipment, which are promoted at the expense of traditional products such as food processing and textiles. In general, this shift in national output composition also involves a shift from production in smaller types of cities to production in larger types of cities, given the typical differences in average sizes between cities specialized in production of "modern" versus traditional goods. This is enhanced if, particularly for state-owned firms, heavy industry is forced into large metro areas.

One of the costs of such policies is the required shift or migration in population from villages and towns to larger cities, which erodes the traditional social fabric/ "capital" of the country and which, from an economist's point of view, involves massive reinvestment in urban infrastructure, as immobile, nonmalleable infrastructure is abandoned in some villages and towns and new infrastructure is required in the cities experiencing immigration. However, if one accepts that the national objectives, such as certain (perhaps misguided) development objectives or certain national defense objectives underlying these policies, deliberately change national output composition, no offsetting population location policies are called for. The shift in population allocation is a necessary (and desirable) feature of the desired output composition shift. The economist can simply point out the economic welfare costs of attaining the perhaps noneconomic objectives underlying the shift in national output composition.

Note that these general tax-subsidy policies altering the composition of national output are to be distinguished from policies aimed at just a few firms. Some firms may receive special concessions or may be forced to locate in certain cities (state-owned firms). In general, their impact on national output and location patterns will be minimal, because these are policies that involve intramarginal production-location decisions. As such their primary impact may be distributive, rather than allocative.

The second type of policies are pricing policies. Included in these are minimum wage policies, price controls, and transport cost structure rates. Minimum wage policies tend to increase urban concentration, raising the equilibrium sizes of typically low wage–small size types of cities. The impact of price controls depends on what prices are raised versus lowered below their "shadow" levels. In China and perhaps elsewhere price controls may tend to raise the prices of final outputs relative to raw materials. This may reduce the volume of trade and degree of specialization as regions horde their raw materials and produce a wide range of final outputs, to avoid selling low-priced raw materials in return for high-priced final products. Similarly the volume of intercity or interregional trade is reduced by high transport costs and tariffs, such as the octroi tax in India. The impact of these types of policies is to reduce in an inefficient manner the degree of urban specialization and encourage unnecessary local diversification. The impact on urban concentration is usually ambiguous. A good example is uniform pricing policies in India that require both the received factory and consumed retail prices to be spatially invariant (independent of where the factory output is sold). That is, transport charges are the same per unit shipped, regardless of distance shipped. This favors population location in remote areas, since they implicitly get subsidized consumer products. It also favors centralized production since there is no incentive to disperse spatially to locate near consumers. All this seems to be at the expense of producers and consumers in spatially intermediate locations. The overall impact on urban concentration, however, is ambiguous.

If the policies just outlined are political window dressing with no other clear national objectives, then population location policies that offset the spatial impacts of these policies may have an nth best justification (assuming the desired window dressing is maintained). Alternatively viewed, such policies may be the misguided design of one ministry of the national government. Another ministry, for instance the urban and rural construction and works ministry, then sets about to design policies to ameliorate some of the negative impacts of the errant policies of the first ministry. An example from the above paragraph would be policies subsidizing urban infrastructure in cities in intermediate locations.

The final type of policies involve political centralization that leads to economic centralization and concentration. There are two main examples. First, in countries with a central as opposed to a federal type of governmental structure, the degree of urban concentration is empirically much higher ceteris paribus. The reason appears to be that in providing public services, either for reasons of personal gain or through unconscious or "justified" discrimination, smaller cities and cities in remote areas from the national capital are discriminated against. Given underprovision of public services in remote areas or small cities, migrants overconcentrate in larger central cities favored by the central government. In countries with a federal system such favoritism is limited because constitutionally many local public services fall under the domain of the local and state governments, as opposed to the central government.

Second, is that many countries favor their national capital regions with special infrastructure investments financed out of national rather than local taxes. Arguably, pride in one's national capital is an argument in some people's utility functions or an attractive national capital may be helpful in attracting foreign investments and aid. While such investments may be so justified, the problem is that they attract migrants from other cities not favored with special investments. With free entry, migrants would enter at least until the benefits to them are dissipated through cost-of-living increases or when the quality of life declines, to that obtainable by the benefits available in unfavored cities.

It is possible, of course, to limit entry. For a national capital, if it is managed by the national government, the usual entry restrictions imposed by landowner-voters may not be feasible. In particular, discriminatory provision of public services and land development resulting in massive squatter settlements in some sense defeats the objective of pride in national capital. A dilemma then exists. If the national capital region is to be made a special place to live, that will attract migrants who will dissipate the benefits of the region's specialness. An extreme solution to this problem is Brasilia, where entry is controlled by careful restrictions on possible jobs as well as residential locations. However, most countries appear to follow a deconcentration policy of trying to deflect migrants and recent arrivals (in squatter settlements) from the national capital to nearby satellite towns. However, that presents a further problem. Improvement of the living condititons of migrants encourages more migrants to settle, presenting a potential situation in which the national capital and nearby satellite towns spread out to form one massive megopolis of inordinate and unnecessary size and dubious quality of life. In a society with unrestricted population mobility, an attempt to sustain the national capital as a special place to live appears to be a difficult if not impossible long-term objective. Perhaps it is better to spread the public infrastructure investments to other parts of the country as well.

References

Adelman, M. (1969), "Comment on 'H' Concentration Measures," *Review of Economics and Statistics*, 51, 99–101.

Alexandersson, G. (1959), *The Industrial Structure of American Cities*, Lincoln: The University of Nebraska Press.

Arnott, R. (1979), "Optimum City Size in a Spatial Economy," *Journal of Urban Economics*, 6, 65–89.

Baer, W. (1969), *The Development of the Brazilian Steel Industry*, Nashville: Vanderbilt University Press.

Beckmann, M. J. (1958), "City Hierarchies and Distribution of City Size," *Economic Development and Cultural Change*, VI, 243–248.

Beckmann, M. J. (1968), *Location Theory*, New York: Random House.

Berglas, E. (1976), "The Distribution of Tastes and Skills and the Provision of Local Public Goods," *Journal of Public Economics*, 6, 409–423.

Bergsman, J., P. Greenston, and R. Healy (1972), "The Agglomeration Process in Urban Growth," *Urban Studies*.

Bergsman, J., P. Greenston, and R. Healy (1975), "A Classification of Economic Activities Based on Location Patterns," *Journal of Urban Economics*, 2, 1–28.

Berry, B. (1968), *Geography of Market Centers and Retail Distribution*, Englewood Cliffs, NJ: Prentice-Hall.

Brooks, D. (1987), "Industrial Location and Decentralization Policies in Developing Counties," Brown University unpublished Ph.D. dissertation.

Brown, C. and J. Medoff (1978), "Trade Unions in the Production Process," *Journal of Political Economy*, 86, 355–378.

Buchanan, J. and K. Wagner (1972), "An Efficiency Basis for Federal Fiscal Equalization" in J. Margolis (ed.), *The Analysis of Public Output*, New York: Columbia University Press.

Burmeister, E. and R. Dobell (1970), *Mathematical Theories of Economic Growth*, New York: Macmillan.

Chipman, J. S. (1970), "External Diseconomies of Scale and Competitive Equilibrium," *Quarterly Journal of Economics*, 84, 347–385.

Christaller, W. (1966), *The Central Places of Southern Germany*, Englewood Cliffs, NJ: Prentice-Hall.

Clawson, M. (1969), "Open Space as a New Urban Resources" in *The Quality of the Urban Environment*, H. S. Perloff (ed.), Johns Hopkins Press: Baltimore.

Datta, A. (1981), "Municipal Finances in India," IBRD, UDD Report No. 18.

David, O. and A. Whinston (1967), "Piecemeal Policy in the Theory of Second Best," *Review of Economic Studies*, 84, 323–331.

Denny, M., J. D. May, and C. Pinto (1978), "The Demand for Energy in Canadian Manufacturing," *Canadian Journal of Economics*, 11, 300–313.

Diewert, E. (1973), "Functional Forms for Profit and Transformation Functions," *Journal of Economic Theory*, 6, 284–316.

Dillinger, W. (1979), "A National Urban Pattern Data File for 114 Countries," IBRD, Urban and Regional Report No. 79-5.

Dixit, A. (1973), "The Optimum Factory Town," *Bell Journal of Economics and Management Science*, 4, 637–654.

Dornbusch, R., S. Fischer, and P. Samuelson (1977), "Comparative Advantage, Trade, and Payments in a Ricardian Model With a Continuum of Goods," *American Economic Review*, 67, 823–839.

Evenson, R. and Y. Kister (1975), *Agricultural Research and Productivity*, New Haven: Yale University Press.

Fei, Xianto (1983), "Small Towns, Big Issues," transcription of speech delivered to "Jiangsu Small Town Study Seminar," Nanjing PRC, 9-21-83.

Flatters, F., V. Henderson, and P. Mieszkowski (1974), "Public Goods, Efficiency, and Regional Fiscal Equalization," *Journal of Public Economics*, 3, 99–112.

Fuss, M. and D. McFadden (1978), *Production Economies: A Dual Approach to Theory and Applications*, 2 vols., Amsterdam: North-Holland.

Getz, M. and Y. Huang (1978), "Consumer Revealed Preference for Environmental Goods," *Review of Economics and Statistics*, 449–458.

Hamer, A. (1983), "Decentralized Urban Development and Industrial Location Behavior in Sao Paulo Brazil," World Bank working paper.

Hansen, E. R. (1983), "Why do Firms Locate Where They Do," IBRD No. UDD 25.

Harberger, A. (1971), "Three Basic Postulates for Applied Welfare Economics: An Interpretive Essay" *Journal of Economic Literature*, 9, 785–797.

Hausman, J. A. (1978), "Specification Tests in Econometrics," *Econometrica*, 46, 1251–1271.

Heckman, J. (1979), "Sample Selection Bias as Specification Error," *Econometrica*, 14, 153–161.

Hekman, J. (1982), "Branch Plant Location and the Product Cycle in Computer Manufacturing," North Carolina working paper.

Henderson, J. V. (1972), "The Sizes and Types of Cities: A General Equilibrium Model," unpublished Ph.D. dissertation, University of Chicago.

———— (1974), "The Sizes and Types of Cities," *American Economic Review*, 64, 640–656.

———— (1977a), "Externalities in a Spatial Context: The Case of Air Pollution," *Journal of Public Economics*, 7, 89–110.

———— (1977b), *Economic Theory and the Cities*, New York: Academic Press.

———— (1978), "Economic Growth and Technological Change in a System of Cities," mimeo., Brown University.

———— (1980), "A Framework for International Comparisons of Systems of Cities," IBRD, Urban and Regional Report No. 80-3.

———— (1982a), "The Impact of Government Policies on Urban Concentration," *Journal of Urban Economics*, 12, 280–303.

———— (1982b), "Systems of Cities in Closed and Open Economies," *Regional Science and Urban Economics*, 12, 325–350.

———— (1982c), "Evaluating Consumer Amenities and Interregional Welfare Differences," *Journal of Urban Economics*, 11, 32–59.

———— (1983), "Industrial Bases and City Size," *American Economic Review*, 73, 164–168.

———— (1985), "Population Composition of Cities: Restructuring the Tiebout Model," *Journal of Public Economics*, 27, 131–156.

———— (1986a), "Efficiency of Resource Usage and City Size," *Journal of Urban Economics*, 19, 47–70.

———— (1986b), "Urbanization in a Developing Country: City Size and Population Composition," *Journal of Development Economics*, 22, 264–293.

———— (1986c), "The Timing of Regional Development," *Journal of Development Economics*, 23, 275–292.

—————— (1987a), "Aspects of Urban Concentration in Brazil," in *The Economics of Urbanization*, G. Tolley and V. Thomas (eds.), Baltimore: Johns Hopkins Press.

—————— (1987b), "Industrial Location and Decentralization," Brown University Working Paper.

Henderson, J. V. and Y. Ioannides (1981), "Aspects of Growth in a System of Cities," *Journal of Urban Economics*, 10, 117–139.

Hochman, O. (1977), "A Two Factor Three Sector Model of an Economy with Cities: A Contribution to Urban Economics and International Trade Theories," mimeo.

—————— (1981), "Land Rents, Optimal Taxation, and Local Fiscal Independence in an Economy with Local Public Goods," *Journal of Public Economics*, 59–85.

Jones, R. W. (1968), "Variable Returns to Scale in General Equilibrium," *International Economic Review*, 10, 261–272.

Kanemoto, Y. (1978), "Optimal Growth of Cities," Discussion Paper 78-02, University of British Columbia, mimeo.

—————— (1980), *Theories of Urban Externalities*, Amsterdam: North-Holland.

Kelly, K. C. (1977), "Urban Disamenities and the Measurement of Economic Welfare," *Journal of Urban Economics*, 4, 379–388.

Krueger, A. (1974), "The Political Economy of the Rent Seeking Society," *American Economic Review*, 64, 291–303.

Kwok, Y. W. (1982), "The Role of Small Cities in Chinese Urban Development," *International Journal of Urban and Regional Research*, 6, 549–564.

Kwon, W. Y. (1981), "A Study of the Economic Impact of Industrial Relocation: The Case of Seoul," *Urban Studies*, 18, 73–90.

Lau, L. (1976), "A Characterization of the Normalized Restricted Profit Function," *Journal of Economic Theory*, 12, 131–163.

Lee, K. S. (1982a), "A Model of Intra-Urban Location," *Journal of Urban Economics*, 12, 263–279.

—————— (1982b), "Changing Location Patterns of Manufacturing Employment in the Seoul Region: A Summary Report," mimeo.

Little, I. et al. (1970), *Industry and Trade in Some Developing Countries*, Oxford: Oxford University Press.

Lösch, A. (1954), *The Economics of Location*, New Haven: Yale University Press.

Lipsey, R. G. and K. Lancaster (1956), "The General Theory of Second Best," *Review of Economic Studies*, 24, 11–32.

Lyons, T. (1983), "Economic Integration and Development in China 1957–79," unpublished Ph.D. Dissertation, Cornell University.

McKenzie, L. W. (1960), "Matrices with Dominant Diagonals and Economy Theory," *Proceedings of a Symposium on Mathematical Methods in the Social Sciences*, Palo Alto: Stanford University Press.

Mera, K. (1975), *Income Distribution and Regional Development*, Tokyo: University of Tokyo Press.

Mills,, E. S. (1967), "An Aggregative Model of Resource Allocation in a Metropolitan Area," *American Economic Review*, 57, 197–210.

—————— (1972), *Urban Economics*, Glenview: 1st ed., Scott Foresman.

Mills, E. S. and C. Becker (1986), *Studies in Indian Urban Development*, Oxford: Oxford University Press.

Mirrlees, J. A. (1972), "The Optimum Town," *Swedish Journal of Economics*, 74, 114–135.

Mitra, A., S. Mukheiji, R. Bose, and R. Lobenath (1981), *Functional Classification of India's Urban Areas by Factor Cluster Method 1961–1971*, New Delhi: Abhinav Publications.

Moomaw, R. L. (1981), "Productivity and City Size: A Critique of the Evidence," *Quarterly Journal of Economics*, 96, 675–88.

Murray, M. D. (1983), "An Illustration of Analytical Tools and Their Transferability to Other Cities," mimeo.

Nakamura, R. (1985), "Agglomeration Economies in Urban Manufacturing Industries: A Case of Japanese Cities," *Journal of Urban Economics*, 17, 108–124.

Neary, J. P. (1978), "Dynamic Stability and the Theory of Factor-Market Distortions," *American Economic Review*, 68, 671–682.

Paine, S. (1981), "Spatial Aspects of Chinese Development: Issues Outcomes and Policies 1949–79," *Journal of Development Studies,* 17, 132–195.

Purdy, J. F., Jr. (1981), "The Evolution of the Brazilian Urban System Between 1950 and 1980," IBRD, Urban and Regional Economics, mimeo.

Renaud, B. (1979), "National Urbanization Policies in Developing Countries," World Bank Staff Working Paper No. 347.

Richardson, H. W. (1977), "City Size and National Spatial Strategies in Developing Countries," World Bank Staff Working Paper No. 252.

Rosen, K., and M. Resnick (1978), "The Size Distribution of Cities, the Pareto Law, and Primate Cities," Princeton University, mimeo.

Sato, K. (1966), "On the Adjustment Time in Neo-Classical Growth Models," *Review of Economic Studies,* 33, 263–268.

Schaeffer, G. P. (1977), "The Urban Hierarchy and Urban Area Production Function," *Urban Studies,* 14, 315–326.

Scott, A. D. (1950), "A Note on Grants in Federal Countries," *Economica,* 17, 416–22.

Segal, D. (1976), "Are There Returns of Scale in City Size," *Review of Economics and Statistics,* 58, 339–50.

Sekhar, U. (1983), "Industrial Location Policy: The Indian Experience," World Bank Staff Working Paper No. 620.

Smith, R. A. (1978), "Measuring the Value of Urban Amenities," *Journal of Urban Economics,* 5, 370–387.

Song, B. N. and S. C. Choe (1981), "Review of Urban Trends in Korea," IBRD, UDD Working Paper.

——— (1982), "An Evaluation of Industrial Location Policies for Urban Deconcentration in Seoul Region," IBRD, UDD Working Paper.

Stiglitz, J. E. (1977), "The Theory of Local Public Goods," in *The Economics of Public Services,* M. S. Feldstein and R. P. Inman (eds.), New York: Macmillan.

Sveikauskas, L. (1975), "The Productivity of Cities," *Quarterly Journal of Economics,* 89, 393–413.

——— (1978), "The Productivity of Cities," mimeo., I-94.

Thomas, V. (1978), "The Measurement of Spatial Differences in Poverty: The Case of Peru," World Bank Staff Working Paper No. 273.

Tobin, J. and W. Nordhaus (1972), "Economic Growth," NBER Fiftieth Anniversary Colloquium, Vol. V, New York: Columbia University Press.

Tolley, G. et al. (1979), *Urban Growth Policy in a Market Economy,* New York: Academic Press.

Townroe, P. (1981), "Location Factors for Industrial Decentralization from Metropolitan Sao Paulo," World Bank working paper.

Upton, C. (1981), "An Equilibrium Model of City Sizes," *Journal of Urban Economics,* 10, 15–36.

Vernon, R. (1966), "International Investment and International Trade in the Product Cycle," *Quarterly Journal of Economics,* 80, 190–207.

Weiss, L. W. (1972), "The Geographic Size of Markets in Manufacturing," *Review of Economics and Statistics,* 245–58.

Wheaton, W. (1974), "A Comparative Static Analysis of Urban Spatial Structure," *Journal of Economic Theory,* 9, 223–237.

Wheaton, W. and H. Shishido (1979), "Urban Concentration, Agglomeration Economies, and the Level of Economic Development," *Economic Development and Cultural Change.*

Williamson, J. G. (1977), "Unbalanced Growth, Inequality and Regional Development: Some Lessons from American History," mimeo.

Yap, L. (1977), "The Attraction of Cities: A Review of the Migration Literature," *Journal of Development Economics,* 4, 239–264.

INDEX